Business Management I

Solomon | Tyler | Taylor

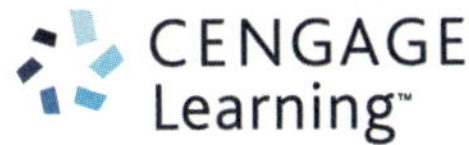

CENGAGE
Learning™

Australia • Brazil • Japan • Korea • Mexico • Singapore • Spain • United Kingdom • United States

Business Management I

Executive Editors:
Maureen Staudt
Michael Stranz

Senior Project Development Manager:
Linda deStefano

Marketing Specialist:
Courtney Sheldon

Senior Production/Manufacturing
Manager:
Donna M. Brown

PreMedia Manager:
Joel Brennecke

Sr. Rights Acquisition Account Manager:
Todd Osborne

Cover Image:
Getty Images*

*Unless otherwise noted, all cover images used by
Custom Solutions, a part of Cengage Learning,
have been supplied courtesy of Getty Images with
the exception of the Earthview cover image, which
has been supplied by the National Aeronautics and
Space Administration (NASA).

For product information and technology assistance, contact us at
Cengage Learning Customer & Sales Support, 1-800-354-9706

For permission to use material from this text or product,
submit all requests online at **cengage.com/permissions**
Further permissions questions can be emailed to
permissionrequest@cengage.com

This book contains select works from existing Cengage Learning resources and
was produced by Cengage Learning Custom Solutions for collegiate use. As such,
those adopting and/or contributing to this work are responsible for editorial
content accuracy, continuity and completeness.

Compilation © 2011 Cengage Learning

ISBN-13: 978-1-111-95376-8

ISBN-10: 1111-95376-7

Cengage Learning
5191 Natorp Boulevard
Mason, Ohio 45040
USA

Cengage Learning is a leading provider of customized learning solutions with
office locations around the globe, including Singapore, the United Kingdom,
Australia, Mexico, Brazil, and Japan. Locate your local office at:
international.cengage.com/region.

Cengage Learning products are represented in Canada by Nelson Education, Ltd.
For your lifelong learning solutions, visit **www.cengage.com /custom.**
Visit our corporate website at **www.cengage.com.**

Table of Contents

CHAPTER OUTLINE

Setting Goals for Your Professional Pursuit

Know Yourself

Gaining Experience: The Overview

The Internship

1 Assessing and Developing Skills for the Workplace

LEARNING OBJECTIVES

By the end of this chapter, you will achieve the following objectives:

- Define *technical skills* and *transferable skills*.
- Define *internship*.
- Explain the importance that goals can have on success.
- Discuss goals that can be established while in school.
- Describe the different types of self-assessment tools.
- Discuss the various types of career-building activities that students can utilize to gain experience in their profession.
- Explain the purpose and goals of an internship.
- Discuss various methods one can use to locate an internship.
- Discuss tips on being successful in an internship.
- Demonstrate the ability to research possible internship sites.

TOPIC SCENARIO

In her last year of college, Alanna Phillips began to develop her resume. During the process, Alanna analyzed her strengths and identified areas to develop. She discovered the following:

- Her college degree had given her a good start on developing the skills necessary for an entry-level job in her field.
- Development of some technical skills was still needed.
- Soft skills such as communication were effective but still could use some work.
- She had learned skills such as negotiating, delegating, and marketing but had no experience in utilizing these skills that could be documented on the resume.

After reaching these conclusions, Alanna decided that gaining further experience using her skills was critical to obtaining the job she wanted after graduation. Alanna began to explore options for obtaining an internship. Based on this short description of Alanna's situation, answer the following questions:

- How can Alanna be sure that she has correctly identified her strengths and weaknesses?
- How can Alanna be sure that the skills learned in college are transferable to the workplace?
- What might Alanna do to identify more clearly what employers in her field are looking for when hiring entry-level employees?
- Would an internship help Alanna build on her skills? If so, how might she find out which internship would best benefit her needs and goals?
- What type of internship do you think would best serve Alanna's needs?
- How can an internship be helpful in promoting oneself to a prospective employer?

SETTING GOALS FOR YOUR PROFESSIONAL PURSUIT

It is important to begin planning and preparing for your professional career while still in school. Being successful and competitive in your profession requires having well-defined goals. In addition to developing your skills and graduating, there are other goals that are important for students to achieve while attending college. These goals should be developed with an appreciation of the influence that both academic and co-curricular experiences can have on overall professional success. Actions that can contribute to goal achievement include the following (Bruce, 2005):

▶ **Make a good impression while in school.** Faculty members, advisors, and other students may be the individuals who recommend you for a job.

▶ **Take leadership roles in and outside of school.** Develop and demonstrate your abilities to work with a variety of individuals. For example, being involved in school activities, community activities, or volunteer work demonstrates leadership and the ability to work with diverse individuals. If you are working in addition to attending school, taking leadership roles on the job also demonstrates this skill.

▶ **Find a mentor who can help guide and promote you and your professional pursuits.** A mentor is an individual who will guide and challenge you to develop both professional and personal skills. This individual may be a faculty member, graduate, or industry professional.

▶ **Be clear on your career objectives.** Develop an awareness of your professional direction and goals. Explore methods for establishing your niche in your profession. Develop career objectives based on where you want to be in your career.

▶ **Understand your strengths and weaknesses.** Explore how your strengths can contribute to your professional growth. Set goals for improving weaker areas. Use feedback from instructors, mentors, academic advisors, and employers to gain insight into your abilities and to set professional goals.

▶ **Gain professional experience while in school.** Participate in volunteer opportunities, co-op work, or an internship to gain experience in your field. Establish and demonstrate a strong work ethic during these opportunities.

> ### REFLECTION QUESTION
>
> • What goals do you need to establish that would help in your academic and professional success?

> ### ? CRITICAL THINKING QUESTION
>
> 1–1. What is your reaction to the following statement? "Goals are important, but because goals change so much, writing them down is unnecessary." Provide a rationale for your response.

success steps

ACTIONS FOR GOAL ACHIEVEMENT

1. Make a good impression while in school.
2. Take leadership roles in and outside of school.

continued

> *continued*
>
> **3.** Find a mentor who can help guide and promote you and your professional pursuits.
>
> **4.** Be clear on your career objectives.
>
> **5.** Understand your strengths and weaknesses.
>
> **6.** Gain professional experience while in school.

KNOW YOURSELF

Identifying and being aware of your existing knowledge, skills, experiences, and character traits is a necessary step toward being able to market yourself successfully. In school, students have the opportunity to use instructors' feedback to develop an understanding of their strengths and weaknesses in both technical and transferable skill areas.

Technical skills are generally thought of as those skills that are necessary to perform specific job tasks. The University of Manitoba Career and Employment Services office (n.d., p. 2) identifies the following *transferable skills,* which are those abilities that can be easily transferred to a variety of work settings. Interpersonal and communication skills are examples of transferable skills.

- analytical/problem-solving skills
- flexibility/versatility
- interpersonal skills
- oral and written communication skills
- organization/planning skills
- motivation
- leadership skills
- self-starter/initiative
- ability to work as part of a team

For future professional success, it is important to evaluate your strengths and weaknesses both in interpersonal skills ("soft skills") and technical abilities and to improve areas as needed during the college years.

SELF-ASSESSMENT TOOLS

Conducting a self-assessment can be both challenging and rewarding. Various assessment tools help students to match their interests, skills, and personality type with their school and career goals. Depending on the outcome of the

Knowing your unique and individual traits will help you to market yourself effectively.

various self-assessment tests, individuals may at times find the need to re-evaluate professional goals. Becoming more self-aware may prompt some students to consider other professions that better fit with their strengths, abilities, and personality type. If this is a consideration, students should seek out further guidance from individuals trained in career counseling.

A variety of self-assessment tools are available, often found online. The student services or academic advising department on your campus may also be able to provide resources for these tools. Assessment tools can include the following (University of California at Berkeley Career Center, n.d.):

- **Interest inventories.** Interest inventories include the Strong Interest Inventory, the Self-Directed Search (SDS), the Campbell Interest and Skill Survey (CISS), and the Career Key (Dikel, 2002). The Strong Interest Inventory assesses your interests and matches them to careers. The inventory tells you where you might enjoy working, based on the interests you have in common with other individuals in a given profession. The Strong Interest Inventory does not measure ability or aptitude.

- **Personality tests.** Myers-Briggs Type Indicator® (MBTI), Keirsey Temperament Sorter, and TypeFocus are examples of available personality assessment tests. These tests can provide information on how you communicate, gather information, and make decisions. They can also help you determine if your personality fits the job that you are considering (Dikel, 2002). TypeFocus helps answers questions such as, "What are my personal strengths?", "What careers will I find satisfying?", and "How do I use my strengths in a successful job search?"

- **Skills inventories.** The Skills and Attributes Inventory (SAI) and the SkillScan assessment can help in defining your skills and abilities. SkillScan helps you identify your skills and how they apply to various careers. In addition, it provides the opportunity to identify careers in which your skills are most applicable. The tool also assists you in strategizing to develop your career and in writing your resume to support your goals.

apply it

Self-Assessment Activity

GOAL: To develop a clearer appreciation for and understanding of your strengths and weaknesses.

STEP 1: From the various self-assessment tools mentioned in this chapter, select one.

continued

! **RESOURCE BOX**

SELF-ASSESSMENT TOOLS
- interest inventories
- personality tests
- skills inventories

▶ **REFLECTION QUESTION**

- What self-assessment tool interests you the most and why?

? **CRITICAL THINKING QUESTION**

1–2. What is your reaction to the following statement? "Other than the fact that self-assessment tests are fun to take, there is no validity to them and they are a waste of time." Provide a rationale for your response.

continued

STEP 2: Conduct further research regarding this tool and take the test.

STEP 3: Write a brief report regarding your findings and what you discovered about yourself.

STEP 4: Consider placing your self-assessment test in your Learning Portfolio.

GAINING EXPERIENCE: THE OVERVIEW

REFLECTION QUESTIONS

- What career-building activity most interests you?
- What steps do you need to take to begin your search for a career-building activity?

CRITICAL THINKING QUESTION

1–3. How can you determine the activities that are best suited to building your career?

Gaining employment after graduation is a typical goal of many college students. Seeking opportunities in and out of class to develop abilities and skills can significantly increase your employment opportunities. Having experience prior to beginning the job search can significantly increase your credibility and demonstrates commitment to your career choice. Career-building activities can include volunteer work, job shadowing, a part-time job, consulting work, or an internship. Through these activities, students can gain experience in utilizing both their technical and transferable skills.

Gaining experience in your field increases your marketability in the workplace as well as demonstrates your interest in and commitment to your field.

THE INTERNSHIP

In some professions, internships are commonly completed as part of the educational process as an option or, in some cases, as a requirement. Other names for internships include externship, on-site experience, or practicum. All refer to practical experience in the work setting. Loyola Marymount University Career Development Services (n.d., p. 1) defines an internship as "an educational experience whereby students learn to take on meaningful responsibilities within an organization and to adopt roles as contributing employees." Internships can take place at any time during the academic experience or as a capstone experience to classroom learning at the conclusion of academic preparation.

PURPOSE OF AN INTERNSHIP

According to McGill University Career and Placement Service (n.d., "Goals That Internships May Satisfy"), the purposes of an internship may include:

- learning more about a specific industry/field
- gaining practical experience while applying theoretical knowledge
- becoming more knowledgeable about specific work functions and learning career-related skills
- gaining experience working with others and seeing how decisions are made
- developing a relationship with a mentor and cultivating a network of contacts in your field
- increasing your marketability
- performing positive community service
- gaining experience in job-seeking skills, interviewing, and resume and cover letter preparation
- getting to know yourself better

Making the most of an internship is the responsibility of the student. Maximizing learning from the internship experience requires involvement in the process of choosing the best internship possible for personal growth and development. Each student should be directly involved in the internship selection process, regardless of whether the internship is or is not a requirement of the academic program. By being directly involved, the student can effectively meet individual goals. To determine individual internship goals, consider the following elements:

- **Your career interests.** Determine the areas of your field that are most interesting to you. Seek an internship that will provide you the opportunity to explore areas of interest. If you are unsure of your preference, an internship can help you define it by exposing you to various professional situations. Even if the internship is an academic requirement, do not consider it simply as another thing you have to do to graduate. Approach the experience with openness to learning as much as possible.

▶ **The internship environment.** Consider the environment in which you would like to complete your internship. Recall factors such as your goals, personality style, values, and the surroundings and atmosphere in which you like to work. Consider the size, philosophy, and other aspects of the potential internship site. Make sure the organization is a match with your internship goals and who you are as a person. Often success in an internship depends on the right fit. Internships can contribute significantly to the process of professional socialization.

▶ **Your current priorities.** Completing an internship requires the same level of commitment expected for a job. It is important to seek an internship experience that allows you to meet other life obligations. Consider the following aspects:

▶ **Location.** Whether you stay in your locale or travel across the country for an internship will depend largely on your other commitments. For example, an individual who has family responsibilities may choose to not accept an internship one thousand miles away, even though the internship site supports his interests and is a good fit. Conversely, another individual might make the opposite decision in the interest of gaining the experience. Making these types of decisions is frequently a part of selecting an internship site.

▶ **Finances.** Internships can be costly when they are full time (thus limiting available hours for paid employment) and when they have no stipend or other benefits. Benefits vary depending on the internship site. For example, a site might offer the intern a meal at the company cafeteria during her assigned shift. Other sites offer fully paid internships; still others offer a modest stipend. Be aware that paid internships of any kind are becoming less common. Some sites may be able to offer a part-time internship commitment to allow additional paid work hours. It is important to consider your financial priorities as part of internship selection.

▶ **Current employment.** If you intend to keep a paid job during your internship, it is important to negotiate a mutually acceptable plan with your employer. Taking a leave of absence or modifying your hours are examples of solutions to balancing your paid work with an internship. Some employers may be able to consider you for a different position in your field upon completion of the internship.

LOCATING THE BEST INTERNSHIP

Once the goals of the internship have been established, the task of locating the best internship to meet those goals begins. If completion of an internship prior to graduation is a goal, then the search should begin as early in the academic process as possible, as an early search maximizes the chances that you will find the best internship to meet your needs. Some students may choose to do a different internship each year during their academic training, depending on the length of the academic program. The following are resources for locating an internship (Hansen, n.d.):

- **Career services office.** Nearly all career services offices have a list of their school's internship programs, important application dates, and other sources of internship information. The wide range of resources available in this office makes it an effective place to start your search. Some offices have an internship coordinator dedicated to locating internship sites.

- **Major/minor department.** Major-specific internship programs are frequently maintained by the department office. One or more faculty members may specifically handle internships.

- **Networking sources.** Tell everyone you know that you are looking for a specific type of internship. Just as with job hunting, networking can be one of your best sources for internships, especially for competitive internships.

- **Internship and career fairs.** Most colleges offer at least one career fair during the academic year. Even if you are looking for an internship in a different geographic location, attend the fairs and network with the recruiters. Many organizations have multiple offices, and you may find an opportunity in your area of choice.

- **Alumni office.** Many colleges now ask alumni if they would be willing to sponsor current college students as interns. These alums can be a source for internships as well as for networking opportunities.

- **Company Web sites.** If you have already identified a specific set of companies where you would like to intern, consider researching them yourself by visiting the career section of each company's Web site.

- **Internship Web sites.** There are a few general internship Web sites, as well as a number of industry-specific Web sites. Conduct a search using the term "internships" or "internship (+ your field)" and explore your results.

- **Print resources.** Trade magazines, industry journals, and newspapers have advertisements from numerous organizations and companies. Reviewing journals can expose you to new organizations and aspects of your field.

- **Cold contact.** If other sources have not yielded results, then cold calling is an option. This process can involve calling contacts by phone or sending them an introduction letter to request further information. The phone book may be a source of companies for cold calling.

! RESOURCE BOX

EXAMPLES OF RESOURCES FOR ARRANGING INTERNSHIPS
- career services office
- major/minor department
- networking sources
- internship and career fairs
- alumni office
- company Web sites
- internship Web sites
- books and periodicals
- cold contact

▶ REFLECTION QUESTIONS

- What resources do you think you would find the most useful in locating an internship?
- What resource do you not feel comfortable using but believe could be worthwhile? How can you become more comfortable using this resource?
- How do you think you can document your search efforts for an internship? How might this documentation be helpful to you now and in your future job search activities?

apply it

Locating Internship Sites

GOAL: To demonstrate the ability to locate a variety of internship sites.

STEP 1: Utilizing the resources suggested in this chapter, conduct research to locate at least three different possible internship sites. (Before doing this, check the protocol in your field. In some professions, internships are arranged strictly between academic staff and site supervisors. If you are in this category, involve your internship coordinator in this activity.)

STEP 2: After locating an internship, call or write to the company to inquire if an internship in is available and what the company's requirements are. Ask for guidance during this process as needed.

STEP 3: Put together a brief report of findings to present to the instructor.

STEP 4: Consider placing the information from locating internship sites in your Learning Portfolio.

Once a number of possible internship sites have been identified, it is important to remain diligent in following through with the necessary calls and letters. Being persistent is important and can make a difference in whether or not you obtain the desired internship. Be sensitive to the employer's time and contact employers only when absolutely necessary during this process.

Preparing well-written resumes, cover letters, and thank-you letters for the internship search is also important.

INTERNSHIP SUCCESS

Success of an internship is up to the employer and the student. If academic credit is to be received for the internship, then the college can also be instrumental in helping to ensure that the internship experience is a success. School personnel can facilitate communication between the site supervisor and the student by initiating requests for necessary documents such as internship time sheets and site supervisor evaluation reports. Ultimately, it is the student's responsibility to follow up and ensure that required tasks and forms are completed and to make his or her internship a beneficial experience.

Certain actions and attitudes on your part will contribute to your learning and success. Maximize the benefits you gain from your internship experience by implementing the following recommendations:

▶ **Be informed.** Knowing what is expected of you by both the school and the internship site is critical to your success. Prior to arriving at the internship site, learn as much as you can about dress codes, schedules, policies, and other relevant aspects of the job. An introductory meeting or telephone call to the internship supervisor or coordinator offers an opportunity for you to introduce yourself as well as ask questions and get relevant information. You are also likely to have an orientation session upon your arrival at the site.

  If your internship is part of your academic requirements, there will be standards set by your school or program that you will need to meet. Examples are deadlines for submitting paperwork (which can have a direct influence on your grade or ability to graduate on time) and performance requirements for grades. The internship coordinator on your campus will be able to provide you with relevant information. Be sure to ask questions if anything is unclear.

▶ **Prepare.** Learning as much as possible about the site prior to your arrival will facilitate your transition to the site. For example, learn about the expectations of your role and the types of clients with whom you will work. Learn about the organization and its history. Being prepared will increase your comfort level as you begin your internship as well as demonstrate your initiative and interest.

▶ **Treat the internship as you would a new job.** The internship is where you make your debut into the professional world. Demonstrate the same commitment and investment that you would if you were starting a new job. The internship is similar to a first job and is the ideal place to develop positive professional habits. In addition,

1–4. How would you adjust your research tactics if you were trying to locate part-time work, consulting work, or a shadowing experience?

It is the student's responsibility to communicate effectively with the internship supervisor and to demonstrate the same professional skills that will be expected on the job.

internships are frequently listed on the resume as work experience, and you may be using your internship supervisor as a professional reference. Many interns are hired by the internship site either at the conclusion of the internship or later in their careers.

▶ **Be inquisitive and open to learning.** Demonstrate an interest in your work, the organization's activities, and other events related to the internship site. Be open to learning about new ideas and trying new things. Ask questions. Your interest demonstrates dedication to your work and the organization and a willingness to grow professionally.

▶ **Take responsibility.** The step beyond being inquisitive is to actively seek opportunities for learning. Find organizational and professional activities of interest and become involved rather than waiting to be asked. Be accountable for your actions.

▶ **Use supervision to your benefit.** You will probably have regular meetings with your supervisor to discuss your progress and to discuss any issues that might arise. Use supervision to ask questions, clarify information, and explore areas of interest. Pressing issues should be addressed immediately, but supervision is the appropriate venue for discussion and fostering professional development. Use positive feedback to develop your strengths; accept constructive criticism to set goals for growth and improvement.

▶ **Use your critical thinking skills.** Think through problems and issues objectively and thoroughly. Avoid personal bias and emotional responses that cloud professional judgment. Analyze data and base decisions on rational and verifiable information. Act on ethical principles and in the best interest of clients and the organization.

▶ **Respect professional boundaries and limits in a positive way.** All professionals—including seasoned ones—have limits to their knowledge and expertise. All professionals have room for growth and development. Recognizing what you *don't* know is as important as recognizing your strengths. If there is something you don't know or understand, ask for clarification or assistance, and in doing so, be sure that your attitude reflects your desire to learn. Do not use not knowing or understanding as an excuse for not doing a task. Likewise, professional roles have boundaries. For example, a health aide cannot administer medications, even though she might know how. Medication is administered by a nurse, for regulatory and safety reasons. These types of professional boundaries are in place for liability and management reasons. Understand your professional boundaries, recognize why they exist, and respect them.

▶ REFLECTION QUESTIONS

- What is your response to positive feedback? How can you use it to develop your professional strengths and skills?
- What is your typical response to constructive criticism? How can you use it to set goals and improve areas needing development?

❓ CRITICAL THINKING QUESTION

1–5. How would you respond if you were asked to do something that was clearly outside of your professional boundaries?

▶ **Pay attention to professional behaviors and standards.** Recall and know the importance of professional ethics and standards. It is your responsibility to know and apply these guidelines to your internship responsibilities. Maintain your awareness of these standards and consciously apply them to your decisions and actions. For example, if you are unsure about the "right" way to approach a problem that arises in your work, consider your professional code of ethics in addition to technical solutions. Consider whether your technical solution is acceptable from an ethical perspective.

▶ **Respect and fit into the organization's culture.** Be a team player. Participate in activities that contribute to a positive environment and work relationships. You might choose one or two activities that are suited to your interests and comfort level. It is important to be visible in your organization in a positive way.

▶ REFLECTION QUESTION

- What will you do to ensure success in your internship experience?

success steps

STRATEGIES FOR INTERNSHIP SUCCESS

1. Be informed.
2. Prepare.
3. Treat the internship as you would a new job.
4. Be inquisitive and open to learning.
5. Take responsibility.
6. Use supervision to your benefit.
7. Use your critical thinking skills.
8. Respect professional boundaries and limits in a positive way.
9. Pay attention to professional behaviors and standards.
10. Respect and fit into the organization's culture.

apply it

Internship Site Visit Report

GOAL: To gain a better understanding of the requirements of an internship site.

STEP 1: Groups of four or five students should each be given information for a prearranged internship site visit. The site should be different for each group.

continued

continued

STEP 2: When visiting the site, students should document what is learned about the site, how interns function at that site, and the site's requirements for interns. Students should also inquire into what makes a good intern versus a poor intern.

STEP 3: After the visit, group members should compile their information and prepare a brief report to present to the class.

STEP 4: Consider putting this report in your Learning Portfolio.

CHAPTER SUMMARY

This chapter emphasized the importance of recognizing your strengths and areas needing development and setting goals for professional development in preparation for the job search. You were encouraged to begin this process as early as possible by assuming leadership roles on and off campus, researching and becoming involved in your profession, and networking with individuals in your field. Completing an internship was discussed as a significant means to enter your field and gain experience in the workplace. You reviewed important phases of the internship, including selecting, preparing for, and completing the internship, and you were provided with guidelines for the successful completion of each of the three phases.

POINTS TO KEEP IN MIND

In this chapter, several main points were discussed in detail:

- To be successful and competitive within your profession requires having well-defined goals.
- Technical skills are those that are necessary to perform specific job tasks.
- Interpersonal skills are also known as soft skills and are the type of skills that can be easily transferred to another job or work setting.
- Self-assessment inventories can provide individuals with insight into their interests, skills, and personality type.
- Self-assessment tools include the Strong Interest Inventory, MBTI, TypeFocus, and the SAI.

▌ Gaining experience can provide more credibility and demonstrates commitment to one's career choice. This experience can come through obtaining a part-time job, performing volunteer work, engaging in job shadowing, doing consulting work, or completing an internship.

▌ Being directly involved in the internship selection process can help to ensure your goals are met.

▌ There are a variety of resources available to obtain an internship. These sources include Web sites, books, periodicals, and school officials.

▌ It is up to you, the student, to make the internship experience benefit your future professional success.

LEARNING OBJECTIVES REVISITED

Review the learning objectives for this chapter and rate your level of achievement for each objection using the rating scale provided. For each objective on which you do not rate yourself as a 3, outline a plan of action that you will take to fully achieve the objective. Include a time frame for this plan.

1 = did not successfully achieve objective

2 = understand what is needed, but need more study or practice

3 = achieved learning objective thoroughly

	1	2	3
Define *technical skills* and *generic skills*.	☐	☐	☐
Define *internship*.	☐	☐	☐
Explain the importance that goals can have on one's success.	☐	☐	☐
Discuss various goals one should establish while in school.	☐	☐	☐
Describe the different types of self-assessment tools.	☐	☐	☐
Discuss the various types of career-building activities that students can utilize to gain experience in their profession.	☐	☐	☐
Explain the purpose and goals of an internship.	☐	☐	☐
Discuss various methods one can use to locate an internship.	☐	☐	☐
Discuss tips on being successful in an internship.	☐	☐	☐
Demonstrate the ability to research possible internship sites.	☐	☐	☐

Steps to Achieve Unmet Objectives

Steps   Due Date

1. _______________________________________   _________

2. _______________________________________   _________

3. _______________________________________   _________

4. _______________________________________   _________

SUGGESTED ITEMS FOR LEARNING PORTFOLIO

▶ Reflection Questions: Include your written responses to these questions. Use them to review your development over time.

▶ Self-Assessment Test: Keep a record of what you discovered about yourself.

▶ Locating Internship Sites: Find and research potential internship sites.

▶ Internship Site Visit Report: Prepare a report on internship requirements at a particular site.

REFERENCES

Bruce, C. (2005). Career advice for engineering & other technical majors. The Black Collegian Online. Retrieved March 8, 2005, from http://www.black-collegian.com/career/engineer.shtml

Dikel, M. R. (2002). A guide to choosing tests that are right for you [Electronic version]. Retrieved March 9, 2005, from the Dow Jones Career Journal Web site: http://www.careerjournal.com/jobhunting/usingnet/20030429-dikel2.html

Hansen, R. S. (n.d.). How to find your ideal internship. DeLand, FL: Quintessential Careers. Retrieved March 8, 2005, from http://www.quintcareers.com/finding_ideal_internship.html

Loyola Marymount University, Career Development Services. (n.d.). Internship guide for students. Retrieved March 9, 2005, from http://www.lmu.edu/careers/Internships/internshipguide.pdf

McGill University, Career and Placement Service. (n.d.). Internships: Finding one that's right for you. Retrieved March 9, 2005, from http://www.caps.mcgill.ca/tools/internships/

University of California at Berkeley, Career Center. (n.d.). Evaluate yourself. Retrieved March 8, 2005, from http://career.berkeley.edu/Plan/Evaluate.stm

University of Manitoba, Career and Employment Services. (n.d.). Getting started. Retrieved March 9, 2005, from http://www.umanitoba.ca/student/employment/resources/search/started.php

CHAPTER OUTLINE

Elements of Time Management

Becoming Organized

Effective Scheduling

Overcoming Procrastination

Delegating Effectively

Reducing E-Mail Overload

Time Management: Some Final Tips

2 Time Management

LEARNING OBJECTIVES

By the end of this chapter, you will achieve the following objectives:

- Identify the steps for effective scheduling.
- Appreciate the importance of developing effective time management skills.
- Explain how to set effective goals.
- Describe several methods for becoming more organized.
- Discuss various types of planning aids and scheduling tools that can be used in the workplace.
- Explain how to break the habit of procrastination.
- Describe the steps for effective delegation.
- Discuss how to use e-mail effectively.
- Analyze your use of time and draw conclusions from this analysis.
- Demonstrate the ability to create a "to do" list and prioritize its tasks.

2

Success at school and in the workplace is dependent upon effective time management skills.

TOPIC SCENARIO

As a recent college graduate, Jane has just started her first job in her new profession, and today is her first day. Jane just left her boss's office after having met with her to discuss Jane's work. In this meeting, Jane was informed that she will be in charge of four projects, three of which need to be completed in the next two months. Jane is already worrying about meeting the deadlines and requirements of these assignments.

Based on this short description of Jane's situation, answer the following questions:

- What can Jane do to alleviate some of her concerns?
- What should Jane, as a new employee, learn about her working environment?
- Should Jane voice her concerns to her boss? If so, should she wait to do this or do it now? Explain your answer.
- What time management tools might be important for Jane to implement?

ELEMENTS OF TIME MANAGEMENT

As students, you know that academic success is dependent on applying effective time management strategies, because balancing the demands of school, home, and work is challenging. The skills you use to manage your time in school can help you succeed in your professional life. This chapter focuses on how to effectively manage time at work by further adapting to the workplace skills you probably already use, such as organizing, planning, prioritizing, scheduling, and delegating.

The concept of time management is really that of life management (Janssen, n.d.). If you learn and practice strong time management skills, the benefits can carry over into all aspects of life by generally increasing your level of organization and productivity. Author and business consultant Daniel Janssen tells us, "The most valuable things human beings have is time. You can always get more money, but once you spend time it's gone forever." Appreciating this fact can help you to see the value of time and the importance of developing effective time management skills.

Being proactive about time management and planning ahead requires making conscious decisions regarding how your time is spent. This, in turn, requires the ability to prioritize, set goals, and select activities that achieve both goals. Conscious planning allows you to be in control of your time rather than feeling overwhelmed by having too much to do in too little time (Tufts College, 2002).

PRIORITIZING

The first step in managing time is knowing what merits a time commitment. For example, professional, family, and personal activities are common priorities for many people. Knowing which of these areas (or others) are most important to you allows you to set goals that support these priorities. Be aware that priorities can change and that your goals will change accordingly.

GOAL SETTING

Establishing goals guides you toward success in all areas of your life, including your career. Without having goals to direct you, you may randomly choose activities that take up your time without producing clear or desired results—goal setting provides a foundation for selecting relevant activities. On a day-to-day basis, goals contribute to successful time management by defining tasks that need to be accomplished. Tasks that are clearly defined and that have a deadline for completion allow you to map out each task on the calendar. Following your plan contributes to effective time management, which, in turn, diminishes stress, because directing and organizing your tasks can help to alleviate the feeling of being overwhelmed and disorganized.

The following are suggestions on how to set effective goals (Mind Tools, 1995–2006):

- **State your goals positively.** State goals in terms of what you will do versus what you will not do. For example, "I will eat fruit for my daily afternoon snack" is a positively stated goal, while "I will not eat candy for my daily afternoon snack" is a negatively stated goal. Goals that are stated positively provide a clearer definition of what you need to accomplish.

- **Define an observable behavior.** Clearly define the action you will take to achieve your goal. Observable action is something that can be seen by you and those around you. Using the above example, stating that you will eat fruit is observable. (Eating is observable and most people agree on what fruit is.) An example of a goal that is not observable is, "I will engage in healthy habits." The difference is that the latter goal is not concrete and is open to numerous definitions.

- **Put a time limit on your goal.** Having a time limit for goal completion serves two purposes: A time limit holds you accountable, and it allows you to break goal-related tasks into manageable chunks. For example, if you have a goal to write a proposal for your business and you set a deadline two weeks in the future, you can break the proposal-writing task into daily segments over the two-week period. This makes the task manageable and is also one of the more critical components of time management. Your time limit lets you know how much time you will commit to the task and how much time you will have for other activities.

▶ **Make goals measurable.** A goal that is measurable lets you know when it is completed. For example, if you have to write a 10-page term paper, you know that when 10 pages have been completed, your goal is achieved. Having a measurable goal, like setting a time limit, also lets you know how much you need to complete each day to stay within your time budget.

▶ **Make your goals challenging, yet realistic.** Strive for the "just-right challenge." Goals should hold your interest and require you to try new things and learn new material, but they should also be within your abilities and resources. Goals that do not meet these criteria are less likely to be pursued and more likely to result in an unproductive use of time, thus affecting time management.

---

success steps

SETTING GOALS FOR EFFECTIVE TIME MANAGEMENT

1. State your goals positively.
2. Define an observable behavior.
3. Put a time limit on your goal.
4. Make goals measurable.
5. Make your goals challenging, yet realistic.

PLANNING

Once your goals have been defined, you must create and implement a plan for carrying them out. A "to do" list states the general tasks that you need to accomplish. An action plan focuses on a single task or objective and includes the specific actions you will take, the resources you will use, and how each step will be carried out (Mind Tools, 1995–2005b). An action plan may be written for a single task or for parts of a task. Action plans can be on a daily, weekly, or monthly basis, depending on the goal.

After you have created an action plan, a variety of planning aids are available to help you implement it. These include pocket-size planning books, electronic planners, computer programs, simple to do lists, and wall charts. It is important to select an aid that is suitable to you and that you will use. For example, if you have difficulty maintaining paper systems in an organized fashion, an electronic organizer might be your best choice. Figure 2–1 is an example of a to do list, while Figure 2–2 shows an example of an action plan, which is more detailed.

Use the following space to create a to do list of all the tasks you want to accomplish tomorrow. After you've listed them, assign each task a priority number from 1 to 4. Remember that #1 represents tasks that must be done without delay (highest priority); #2 represents tasks that should be done soon (important); #3 represents tasks that can be done next week (less important); #4 represents tasks that can be delayed for more than a week (least important). As you complete your tasks, cross them off your to do list.

TO DO LIST

1. ____

2. ____

3. ____

4. ____

5. ____

6. ____

7. ____

8. ____

9. ____

10. ____

FIGURE 2–1. A to do list allows you to prioritize tasks and organize your time based on that prioritization.

apply it

Create a To Do List and Action Plan

GOAL: To develop a to do list and prioritize each task.

STEP 1: Utilize the example of the list in Figure 2–1 to create your own to do list.

STEP 2: Divide the class into groups and have each group member share his or her list with classmates. Then, work in teams to help each other prioritize each task. Figure 2–1 can be a guide for this step.

STEP 3: Select a task from the to do list and create an action plan for it using Figure 2–2. Work in pairs to help each other develop an efficient plan.

STEP 4: Consider placing your to do list, action plan, and prioritized task list, as well as a report on creating a to do list and prioritizing tasks, in your Learning Portfolio.

REFLECTION QUESTIONS

- Does creating a to do list help you? If so, how? If not, why?
- Does creating an action plan help you? If so, how? If not, why?

The purpose of the action plan is to identify the steps and resources needed to complete a specific objective related to a goal. Use this form to identify your objective (what is to be accomplished) and complete the table to define key steps in reaching your objective.

Task Component (What needs to be done?)	Person Responsible (Who will do it?)	Resources (What is needed and where can I get it?)	Due Date	Progress Indicators (How will I know I am making progress?)	Completion Indicators (How will I know I have completed the step?)

FIGURE 2–2.   An action plan helps you determine which activities will accomplish a task effectively and efficiently.

An efficient way to prioritize tasks is to plan to complete the most important ones first according to the goals you have set. Using a form, such as the sample one presented in Figure 2–3, may help you prioritize tasks.

ANALYZING HOW YOUR TIME IS SPENT

Regardless of how much goal setting and planning you have done, if you do not use your time wisely, you will not meet deadlines and you will fall behind in completing tasks. As a result, you run the risk of being seen as nonproductive, which creates anxiety and frustration for both you and your employer.

Analyzing how you spend your time on the job can be very enlightening. An activity log is a useful tool for enabling you to discover how you are really spending time on the job. Create an activity log by documenting every activity as each is performed, and the time spent on it. Record all work-related activities in the log, including work on specific projects, reading and writing

LIST OF TASKS FOR THE WEEK

Week of: _______________________

1. The tasks that must be done immediately are:

____

____

____

____

2. The tasks that are important to do soon are:

____

____

____

____

3. The tasks that can be delayed for a few days are:

____

____

____

____

4. The tasks that can be delayed for a week, a month, or longer are:

____

____

____

____

FIGURE 2–3.   Use a sorting tool, such as that pictured here, to prioritize your tasks.

e-mail, and time spent socializing with coworkers. It is also helpful to note times when you feel peak energy versus times when you feel less energetic (Mind Tools, 1995–2005d). By keeping an activity log for a week or so, you can more clearly analyze where time is wisely used, where time is wasted, and the time of day when you are at your peak performance. An example of an activity log is found in Figure 2–4. Using the information documented in your activity log, use Figure 2–5 to assist you in analyzing your use of time.

2

Time Log

Time	Monday	Tuesday	Wednesday
7:00 a.m.			
8:00 a.m.			
9:00 a.m.			
10:00 a.m.			
11:00 a.m.			
12:00 noon			
1:00 p.m.			
2:00 p.m.			
3:00 p.m.			
4:00 p.m.			
5:00 p.m.			
6:00 p.m.			
7:00 p.m.			
8:00 p.m.			
9:00 p.m.			
10:00 p.m.			
11:00 p.m.			
12:00 midnight			
1:00 a.m.			
2:00 a.m.			
3:00 a.m.			
4:00 a.m.			
5:00 a.m.			
6:00 a.m.			

FIGURE 2–4.   Use a document such as a time log to track your activities and develop a better understanding of how your time is spent. Note time that could be used more constructively, as well as the times of day when you are most productive.

Week of _______________

Thursday	Friday	Saturday	Sunday

HOW WELL I USE MY TIME

Purpose: To identify how well you use your time.

Review the time log you kept for one week and then complete the following:

1. The total number of hours I spent on these activities:

   Sleeping: ____

   Eating: ____

   Working: ____

   Attending Classes: ____

   Commuting: ____

   Studying: ____

   Chores: ____

   Exercising/Recreation: ____

   Socializing: ____

   Watching TV: ____

   Goofing Off: ____

   Other: ____

   Total should be 168 hours.

2. The total number of hours I spent on worthwhile activities:

   ____

3. The total number of hours I spent on meaningless or trivial activities:

   ____

4. The activities I wish I had spent more time on are:

   ____

   ____

   ____

   ____

   ____

   ____

5. The activities I wish I had spent less time on are:

____

____

____

____

____

____

6. The activities that I wanted to do but didn't get around to doing during the week are:

____

____

____

____

____

____

FIGURE 2–5. Illustration of a method for determining where you spend your time and how you might allocate your time more effectively.

apply it

Analyzing Time

GOAL: To increase your understanding of how you utilize time.

STEP 1: Using the form provided in Figure 2–4, document for a week how you spend your time.

STEP 2: At the end of the week, conduct an analysis of how your time was spent, using the form provided in Figure 2–5. Write a brief report regarding what you discovered and how changes may be implemented to utilize your time more wisely.

STEP 3: Consider placing the forms and your report on analyzing time in your Learning Portfolio.

 BECOMING ORGANIZED

The people who manage time most successfully are those who have learned how to be organized. For some individuals, organization is a skill that comes naturally due to their upbringing and their innate tendencies. For others, this skill can be quite challenging. For those of you who struggle with organizational skills, it is important to realize that the more organized you become, the more effective you will be at using time (Idaho State University, n.d.). Being disorganized in your personal life can greatly impact your professional success. For instance, both at home and at work, you can waste a significant amount of time trying to locate items amid clutter. Likewise, continually having to "reinvent the wheel" by re-creating files that you have already made but cannot find wastes valuable time. Becoming organized includes reducing clutter at home and work and putting systems and routines in place.

Becoming organized begins with developing skills at setting goals, planning, and analyzing your use of time. If you are disorganized, then establish a goal to address the disorganization and write a plan to improve your organizational skills. Consider the following suggestions for getting organized.

▶ **Break down getting organized into manageable sections.** Set a goal to complete one aspect of organization per day, such as organizing one drawer or shelf. If you are consistent with this process, your area will become organized.

▶ **Decide what you can throw or give away.** A common guideline to use when reducing clutter is that if you have not used something in a year, discard it. If items are unusable or worn, throw them away. If they are in good condition, donate them to a charitable organization. Sort the items into labeled boxes according to what is to be kept, thrown away, and donated to charity.

▶ **Identify which areas need organization.** What areas need attention? For example, if you are continually looking for pieces of clothing, then you should devise a closet organization system. If you spend too much time looking through piles of papers on your desk, then you need a filing system.

▶ **Select an organizational system.** Once you have identified the areas that need organization, devise a system. For example, if disorganized desk drawers are an issue, get a compartmentalized drawer tray. If piles of paper are your main source of clutter, sort them by project or topic into a filing system or binders. If you need suggestions for organization systems, consider one of the many books written on the subject or conduct an Internet search using "organizational skills" or "organizational systems" as your search term.

▶ **Stay organized.** Staying organized takes less time than getting organized. Once you have a system in place, get in the habit of using it consistently. For example, when you are finished with a document, return it to its file or binder. A popular guideline to help you stay organized is to touch a piece of paper one time: Look at it, determine its value, and either recycle it or file it in its proper place. The goal is to not let paper accumulate in a pile that you plan to "look at later." Return desk items to their proper places. Discipline yourself to discard items you are not using.

> *success steps*
>
> **GETTING ORGANIZED**
>
> 1. Break down getting organized into manageable sections.
> 2. Decide what you can throw or give away.
> 3. Identify the areas needing organization.
> 4. Select an organizational system.
> 5. Stay organized.

REFLECTION QUESTION

- What areas in your life do you find the most difficult to organize? How might you become more proficient at organizing this area in your life?

EFFECTIVE SCHEDULING

There are many elements in the work place to be scheduled, such as tasks, meetings, and staff assignments. Learning how to schedule effectively directly impacts your time management. "Scheduling is the process by which you look at the time available to you, and plan how you will use it to achieve the goals you have identified" (Mind Tools, 1995–2005d, p. 1). Those who schedule their time wisely accomplish their tasks in a timely manner with less stress. Study the following steps for effective scheduling (Mind Tools, 1995–2005d):

▶ **Identify your available time.** Block off the time you devote to professional tasks. For example, in your dayplanner or on your calendar, color code the specific times dedicated to work-related activities.

▶ **Block in essential tasks.** Identify and note tasks that are an integral part of your job and that must be completed. For example, teachers must be in class to teach at designated times. Nurses must be available to patients during specific clinic hours. These nonnegotiable commitments must be prioritized on your schedule.

> **Categorize other tasks.** After you have scheduled nonnegotiable commitments, sort other tasks into high, medium, and low priority. For example, tasks related to upcoming deadlines will be high priority, while research for a project coming up in the next few months will be low priority. Required "housekeeping" tasks, such as reports and correspondence, must also be categorized according to priority. For example, weekly reports and recurring tasks, such as payroll activities, must be scheduled to be completed in a timely manner.

> **Schedule tasks according to priority.** Schedule high-priority tasks first, medium-priority tasks second, and low-priority tasks last. You may find that low-priority tasks can be postponed and may become a higher priority later. For example, the research for the upcoming project mentioned previously will become a higher-priority task as the project deadline draws near. Incorporate the concepts of the to do list discussed earlier in this chapter to track upcoming projects.

> **Leave room for the unexpected.** Factor in contingency time to handle unpredictable interruptions and emergencies. If you find that this time becomes "extra" time, use it to get ahead on other tasks.

Select scheduling tools suited to your needs.

---

success steps

SCHEDULING EFFECTIVELY

1. Identify your available time.
2. Block in essential tasks.
3. Categorize other tasks according to their priority.
4. Schedule tasks according to their priority.
5. Leave room for the unexpected.

Many electronic and paper-based scheduling tools are available to help you plan your activities. These tools include traditional calendars, paper-based organizers in loose-leaf and bound styles, electronic personal data assistants (PDAs), and software applications such as Microsoft Outlook™. Select the format that is best suited to your needs and that you will use. For example, if you find paper systems cumbersome and inefficient, consider a PDA. A key factor in effective time management is *using* your scheduling tool. If you select a tool that is incompatible with your preferences and style, you are less likely to use it and will have greater difficulty managing your schedule. An example of a simple weekly planner is provided in Figure 2–6.

Personnel scheduling is another task performed by some employees. A variety of personnel scheduling software is available, each with various features to meet specific scheduling needs. If personnel scheduling is one of your job requirements, you will be trained in the specific scheduling process used by your organization.

apply it

Research and Presentation

GOAL: To increase your understanding of the various types of planning or scheduling tools available.

STEP 1: Research planning or scheduling tools.

STEP 2: Research these tools using the articles presented in this chapter (see the References section at the end of the chapter) and other resources available on the Internet and/or at the library.

STEP 3: Write a brief report on what you learned from this activity. Be prepared to make a presentation to the class.

STEP 4: Consider placing this report in your Learning Portfolio.

 OVERCOMING PROCRASTINATION

Goal setting, planning, and scheduling are virtually useless if you procrastinate. Procrastination over the long term usually results in failure. People procrastinate for many reasons, including fear of failure, uncertainty about task requirements, and lack of interest. The first step to overcoming procrastination is understanding its cause; the second step is breaking the habitual cycle.

Study the following suggestions for breaking the habit of procrastination, which are based on the work of Duncan (2005a), Pavlina (2001), and Quek (2002):

- **Understand why you procrastinate.** Determining the reasons for your procrastination allows you to seek an effective solution. Establish why you procrastinate and address the causes accordingly. Common reasons for procrastination are listed above; you may identify additional reasons.

- **Seek the skills you need.** If you are faced with a task for which you may lack the skills, communicate this concern to your supervisor

Weekly Planner

Time	Monday	Tuesday	Wednesday
7:00 a.m.			
8:00 a.m.			
9:00 a.m.			
10:00 a.m.			
11:00 a.m.			
12:00 noon			
1:00 p.m.			
2:00 p.m.			
3:00 p.m.			
4:00 p.m.			
5:00 p.m.			
6:00 p.m.			
7:00 p.m.			
8:00 p.m.			
9:00 p.m.			
10:00 p.m.			
11:00 p.m.			
12:00 midnight			
1:00 a.m.			
2:00 a.m.			
3:00 a.m.			
4:00 a.m.			
5:00 a.m.			
6:00 a.m.			

FIGURE 2–6.   Use a planner, such as that pictured here, to map out your schedule. Many versions of planners are available in print and electronic formats.

Week of ________________

Thursday	Friday	Saturday	Sunday

and find out whether delegating the work to a more qualified employee is an option. If it is not, then work closely with someone, such as your supervisor or a colleague, who can encourage you and offer helpful suggestions for completing the task.

- **Break down large tasks.** If the task's size is overwhelming, break it down into smaller projects. Then, write down how each smaller task will be completed and note a deadline for each task. Use the to do list and action plan concepts and your scheduling tools to accomplish this.

- **Prioritize deadlines.** Make meeting deadlines a priority by planning how tasks will get done. Write down the goals of the project and create a well-thought-out schedule that you can meet. Discipline yourself to complete each task in the time you have allotted for it. Meeting deadlines will make you a highly valued employee with advancement potential.

- **Stay focused.** Avoid anything that distracts you from the task that must be completed. Review your schedule daily to remind yourself which tasks must be done that day.

- **Use technology.** Technology simplifies and expedites many tasks that previously required significant amounts of time to finish. Determine whether and how technology can help you complete your work more efficiently.

- **Use your scheduling tools.** Use a schedule to plan the work steps for tasks. Stick to the schedule, even if it means accomplishing something you do not enjoy. Once you have completed the "dreaded" task, congratulate yourself on a job well done. Celebrate and reward yourself for large accomplishments.

- **Stay organized.** Disorganization leads to procrastination. Consciously or unconsciously, people are likely to avoid disorganized and chaotic situations.

- **Make it fun.** Break up the monotony of working on a large project by completing tasks as creatively as possible. Of course, keep your creativity within professional boundaries and use it to produce work of high quality.

- **Avoid perfectionism.** Put forth your best effort. Strive for quality by giving your best performance, but recognize that it is acceptable to be imperfect.

- **Look for professional development opportunities.** Avoid thinking of the project as a chore but think of it as an opportunity and a challenge. Consider how you can grow professionally from the experience.

❯ **Seek assistance when necessary.** Ask for help when you need it rather than struggle on your own to figure out something that confuses you or that you lack the skills to understand or complete. Ask for clarification of anything you are unclear about.

---

success steps

BREAKING THE PROCRASTINATION HABIT

1. Understand why you procrastinate.
2. Seek the skills you need.
3. Break down large tasks.
4. Prioritize deadlines.
5. Stay focused.
6. Use technology.
7. Use your scheduling tools.
8. Stay organized.
9. Make it fun.
10. Avoid perfectionism.
11. Look for professional development opportunities.
12. Seek assistance when necessary.

❯ **REFLECTION QUESTION**

- If you are a procrastinator, how will you eliminate this habit?

DELEGATING EFFECTIVELY

Depending on the task that needs to be accomplished, you may need to delegate certain responsibilities to efficiently complete a project. When a task is issued to an individual, it is that person's responsibility to determine whether completing the task requires assistance from others and, if so, to communicate this. Delegating is typically the responsibility of department managers or project managers. If delegating is done correctly, it can be a major factor in good time management.

Study these steps to effective delegating, which are based on work by Morgan (2000; updated 2004) and McNamara (1999):

Step 1. Recognize when delegation is appropriate.

Step 2. Believe in and trust the abilities of others. Recognize that although their work may be different from yours, their work can still be satisfactory.

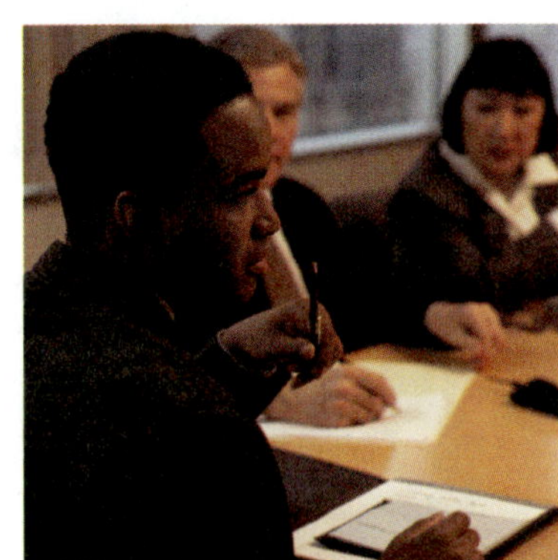

Effective delegation can be a major factor in good time management.

Step 3. Make sure you completely understand what the task entails prior to delegating it. If you are clear on what must be accomplished, then you can more clearly relay that information to others.

Step 4. Write down what must be accomplished to complete the task and your expectations for completion. Make sure directions are clearly stated. Have someone read them over and provide you with feedback to ensure that the steps are clearly stated and correctly ordered. Provide this written material when delegating the work.

Step 5. Select project team members based on their skills, abilities, and time availability.

Step 6. When you head a project team, create an open environment for informal communication and inform team members that questions are welcome. Schedule periodic meetings to ensure effective communication among team members.

Step 7. Depending on how long a project will take to complete, schedule formal methods of reporting progress and submitting work at regular intervals. Review and evaluate work as it comes in. Provide ongoing feedback to team members.

Step 8. Be flexible and make adjustments as needed regarding individual responsibilities.

REDUCING E-MAIL OVERLOAD

Distractions take up valuable time in the workplace. Distractions come in various forms, including telephone calls, visits with coworkers, and e-mails. Conducting an evaluation of your use of time through an activity log is the first step in determining whether distractions are a problem.

The Internet and e-mail enhance and improve communication, but using them can become a significant distraction that greatly affects your productivity. However, you can take steps to ensure that these technologies remain tools and do not become distractions.

Study the following tips on utilizing e-mail effectively (Duncan, 2005b, c):

▶ **Organize your e-mail.** Organize your e-mails into subject categories. Create separate files for subject categories. As e-mails are received, save them as needed in the appropriate file for future reference. This method helps to alleviate overload in your inbox, allowing it to contain only the most recently received messages.

Utilizing this method means that you take spend less time checking your inbox throughout the day. Think of the inbox as a temporary rather than a permanent storage area. If you have to scroll through your inbox, then you are either not checking your e-mail frequently enough or you need to further organize your inbox for more effective use.

▶ **Reserve specific times to check e-mail.** When scheduling your work, reserve certain times throughout the day to check and respond to e-mails. Responding to e-mails as they arrive can become a distraction and affect your productivity. When you do respond to e-mails, do so promptly, as procrastination creates disorganization and a backlog of messages to be dealt with.

▶ **Be selective about printing e-mails.** Avoid printing every e-mail; doing so wastes time and creates paper clutter. Save e-mails as documentation in their appropriate folder and print only those for which you actually need a hard copy.

▶ **Keep e-mails professional.** Sending and receiving e-mails of jokes and pictures is not appropriate in the workplace. Spending time sending and reading junk mail is unproductive, can reduce your credibility, and uses a significant amount of time.

▶ **Use technology to your advantage.** Use other software applications, such as Microsoft Outlook^{TM}, to address e-mail management issues.

▶ **Use e-mail filters.** Similarly, take advantage of software that blocks "spam." (Most organizations incorporate these types of filters into their systems.) Eliminating spam increases productivity because it eliminates the need for employees to spend time sorting through junk mail and reduces the risk of harmful programs being introduced into companies' computer systems.

success steps

1. Organize your e-mail.

2. Reserve specific times to check e-mail.

3. Be selective about printing e-mails.

4. Keep e-mails professional.

5. Use technology to your advantage.

6. Use e-mail filters.

2–2. What is your reaction to the following statement: "As long as I get the job done on time, issues regarding time management don't really concern me"?

TIME MANAGEMENT: SOME FINAL TIPS

The goal of effective time management is to be productive in both your personal and professional lives. You can accomplish a great deal by establishing wise time-use skills. There is no one solution to good time management, however: "Time management is a highly personalized skill, and whatever method works for you is the right one" (Idaho State University, n.d., p. 1). It is up to each of us to determine which time management tools work best for us.

CHAPTER SUMMARY

This chapter addressed major concepts related to time management. You were introduced to a process that includes determining goals and then using those goals to create a to do list of related tasks, as well as an action plan to complete each task and its objective. Next, you were introduced to scheduling steps that can help you prioritize tasks so that each can be completed in a timely manner. You learned that lower-priority tasks can be delayed and are likely to become higher priority as their deadlines draw near. Organizational strategies were emphasized as a means of using time wisely. Finally, you learned methods for addressing procrastination and concepts of delegating to maximize your time management efforts.

POINTS TO REMEMBER

In this chapter, several main points were discussed in detail:

- Learning strong time management skills can positively affect all aspects of your life.
- Using effective time management skills can make work more enjoyable and life in general more rewarding.
- Establishing goals that guide one in a successful career and help to balance all areas of one's life contributes to success.
- Set goals in a variety of areas in your life.
- Writing an action plan defines tasks more effectively and allows progress to be more easily monitored.
- Using planning aids, such as planning books, electronic planners, computer software programs, and to do lists, helps you organize your time.

▶ Using time unwisely results in uncompleted tasks and unmet deadlines, regardless of how much goal setting and planning is done.

▶ Keeping an activity log for a week or so can help you analyze where your time is wisely used, where it is wasted, and when you are at peak performance.

▶ Being disorganized in your personal life can greatly impact your professional success.

▶ Scheduling your time wisely enables you to accomplish tasks in a timely manner with less stress.

▶ Overcoming procrastination requires that you understand why you procrastinate and then learn how to break the habitual cycle.

▶ Delegating tasks when necessary is a key to good time management if the delegating is done correctly.

▶ Using e-mail enhances and improves communication, but if misused, it wastes valuable time.

LEARNING OBJECTIVES REVISITED

Review the learning objectives for this chapter and rate your level of achievement for each objective using the rating scale provided. For each objective on which you do not rate yourself as a 3, outline a plan of action that you will take to fully achieve the objective. Include a time frame for this plan.

1 = did not successfully achieve objective

2 = understand what is needed, but need more study or practice

3 = achieved learning objective thoroughly

	1	2	3
Identify steps to scheduling.	☐	☐	☐
Appreciate the importance of developing effective time management skills.	☐	☐	☐
Explain how to set effective goals.	☐	☐	☐
Describe methods to become more organized.	☐	☐	☐
Discuss various types of planning aids and scheduling tools that can be utilized in the workplace.	☐	☐	☐
Explain how to break the habit of procrastination.	☐	☐	☐
Describe the steps to effective delegation.	☐	☐	☐
Discuss how to utilize e-mail effectively.	☐	☐	☐

	1	2	3
Analyze your use of time and draw conclusions from this analysis.	☐	☐	☐
Demonstrate the ability to create a to do list and prioritize each task.	☐	☐	☐

Steps to Achieve Unmet Objectives

Steps   Due Date

1. ____   __________
2. ____   __________
3. ____   __________
4. ____   __________

SUGGESTED ITEMS FOR LEARNING PORTFOLIO

Refer to the "Developing Portfolios" section at the front of this textbook for more information on learning portfolios.

- Analyzing Time: This activity will give you insight into how you use your time.
- Create a To Do List and Action Plan: This activity will provide you with experience in prioritizing your tasks.
- Research and Presentation: The goal of this activity is to familiarize you with types of time management tools.

REFERENCES

Duncan, P. (2005a). Sweating right up to the last minute: Battling procrastination [electronic version]. Retrieved April 21, 2005, from http://stress.about.com/cs/timemanagement/a/aa112002.htm

Duncan, P. (2005b). Reducing e-mail overload and the stress that comes with it [electronic version]. Retrieved April 21, 2005, from http://stress.about.com/od/timemanagement/a/emailstress.htm

Duncan, P. (2005c). Three guaranteed ways to reduce e-mail overload and the stress it causes [electronic version]. Retrieved April 21, 2005, from http://stress.about.com/od/timemanagement/a/emailstress_2.htm

Idaho State University. (n.d.). Effective time management [electronic version]. *Lead to Succeed Leadership Education and Training Resource Information Series.* Retrieved April 21, 2005, from http://www.isu.edu/stdorg/lead/resource/time.html

Janssen, D. A. (n.d.). The ultimate self-challenge: Time management [electronic version]. Welcome to danieljanssen.com, A division of Practical Planning Publishing. Retrieved April 21, 2005, from http://www.danieljanssen.com/ArchiveArticles/timemanagement.shtml

McNamara, C. (1999). Basics of delegating [electronic version]. Retrieved April 21, 2005, from http://www.mapnp.org/library/guiding/delegating/basics.htm

Mind Tools. (1995–2006). Personal goal setting: Find direction—live life your way. Retrieved July 21, 2006 from http://www.mindtools.com/page6.html

Mind Tools (1995–2005a). To-Do lists—remembering to do all essential tasks in the right order [electronic version]. Retrieved April 21, 2005, from http://www.mindtools.com/pages/article/newHTE_05.htm

Mind Tools. (1995–2005b). Action plans—small scale planning [electronic version]. Retrieved April 21, 2005, from http://www.mindtools.com/pages/article/newHTE_04.htm

Mind Tools. (1995–2005c). Activity logs—finding out how you really spend your time [electronic version]. Retrieved April 21, 2005, from http://www.mindtools.com/pages/article/newHTE_03.htm

Mind Tools. (1995–2005d). Effective scheduling—planning to make the best use of your time [electronic version]. Retrieved April 21, 2005, from http://www.mindtools.com/pages/article/newHTE_07.htm

Morgan, R. L. (2000) (Updated 2004). 12 tips for delegating effectively [electronic version]. Retrieved April 21, 2005, from http://www.ivillage.co.uk/workcareer/survive/prodskills/articles/0,156890,00.html

Pavlina, S. (2001). Overcoming procrastination [electronic version]. Retrieved April 21, 2005, from http://www.dexterity.com/articles/overcoming-procrastination.htm

Quek, T. (2002). The problem of procrastination [electronic version]. Retrieved April 21, 2005, from http://webhome.idirect.com/~readon/procrat.html

Tufts College. (2002). Organizational development and training tip sheet . . . time management [electronic version]. Tufts University. Retrieved April 21, 2005, from http://www.tufts.edu/hr/tips/time.html

CHAPTER OUTLINE

Legal and Ethical Issues in the Workplace: An Overview

Legal and Ethical Issues

Leaving a Job

3 Legal Issues in the Workplace

LEARNING OBJECTIVES

By the end of this chapter, you will achieve the following objectives:

▶ Understand what constitutes discrimination and harassment in the workplace and provide examples of sexual and racial harassment.

▶ List and explain various laws that protect individuals from discrimination and harassment.

▶ Discuss how an employee can determine if he or she has been discriminated against.

▶ Explain methods for reporting discrimination and harassment incidences in the workplace.

▶ Explain the importance of employees understanding their legal rights and obligations in the workplace.

▶ Discuss methods that employers use to minimize employee misuse of office computers.

▶ Describe the various types of monitoring systems available to employers to track employees' computer activities and general productivity.

▶ Explain employees' rights to privacy and laws that affect the right to privacy.

▶ Discuss the purpose of the law of employment-at-will and explain its advantages and disadvantages.

▶ Explain the benefits that employers are required and not required to offer employees.

TOPIC SCENARIO

Over the last five years, Darlene has been an employee at the local hospital. About two months ago, a new manager took over the department where Darlene works. Recently, Darlene has been feeling uncomfortable about some of the behavior directed at her by her boss. For example, once when he was looking over her shoulder, he leaned in and put his hands on her shoulders. He has also occasionally sent sexually suggestive jokes to Darlene via e-mail.

Based on this scenario, answer the following questions:

- Is Darlene justified in feeling uncomfortable?
- What does the law say about Darlene's predicament?
- What should Darlene do?
- Have you ever been confronted with this type of situation? If so, what did you do? Would you do anything differently if confronted with the same situation again?

LEGAL AND ETHICAL ISSUES IN THE WORKPLACE: AN OVERVIEW

Employers and employees face a variety of legal and ethical issues in the workplace. It is the employer's duty to understand his or her responsibilities to employees, and, in turn, employees must be fully aware of their rights and obligations. This chapter is meant to give an introduction to some of the various legal and ethical issues that employees may face. Due to the breadth of information on these topics and the variability in laws among states, individuals are encouraged become familiar with how these issues relate to specific circumstances. The information provided here is of a general nature, and specific issues of personal concern should be addressed with a legal professional. The information in this chapter is not intended to be legal advice.

LEGAL AND ETHICAL ISSUES

The issues discussed in this chapter concern the legal rights and ethical behavior of employers and employees. It is the responsibility of each individual to understand his or her rights as an employee. Employees who do not understand their rights and obligations may not only be forfeiting rights guaranteed by law, but at the same time may be putting themselves in situations

REFLECTION QUESTIONS

- With what legal and/or ethical workplace issues are you familiar?
- What legal and/or ethical issue(s) in the workplace concerns you? How might you address your concerns?

CRITICAL THINKING QUESTION

3–1. If an employee's rights have been violated, what steps should the individual take to address the situation?

that may have serious legal consequences. Ignorance is not bliss when it comes to protecting yourself from potential problems with legal and ethical issues in the workplace. Arming yourself with knowledge is the way to begin protecting yourself legally and ensure that your rights have been honored. Be aware, however, that laws and rights vary according to state laws and the size of the company.

PRIVACY ISSUES IN THE WORKPLACE

Technology and the advanced use of the Internet have created a variety of both legal and ethical issues in the workplace. One of the most significant issues that employers have faced is the right of the employer versus the employee regarding the use of the Internet. Business lawyer Mark Grossman (1998–2006) highlights some of the issues that employers face regarding the use of the Internet in the workplace and affecting the need for Internet use policies. Grossman's findings include the following:

Using workplace technology for reasons other than work-related tasks is an ethical choice that employees must make. Many organizations have had to implement policies to ensure the appropriate use of company computers.

- The Internet gives employees access to sites and activities not related to business. Personal use of the Internet on company time costs the business.

- Cookies that are placed on a hard drive, such as those from adult Web sites, can be used against employers in certain lawsuits.

- E-mails can also be used as evidence against employers.

- Unauthorized use of copyright material (such as a graphic on a screensaver) may be considered copyright infringement for which a company can be held liable.

Grossman (2001) points out that the cost to business of employees surfing the Web during work hours exceeds one billion dollars annually. Although choosing not to abuse the Internet can be an ethical decision made by individual employees, many employees use the Internet for nonbusiness reasons during work nonetheless, and employers have had to take action in order to diminish the high cost of this misuse.

Many employers implement a published policy regarding use of office computers to try to curtail unauthorized use of the Internet in the workplace. Such policies stipulate that employees will use office computers only for company business. In order to enforce this type of policy, employers can employ a variety of monitoring options. The prevalence of these monitoring systems continues to be on the rise, according to a study performed by the American Management Association. Approximately 80% of employers use some type of monitoring system to track employees' use of the Internet and e-mail. Other systems include recording telephone conversations and videotaping (Towns, 2002).

An employer can more easily track an employee's computer activity and general productivity through the use of monitoring systems. The following list provides examples of monitoring systems currently utilized in business. These systems are examples of the types of information employers are capable of scrutinizing (Towns, 2002; Weil, 2000).

- A software product by WinWhatWhere Corporation is capable of tracking everything an individual does on a computer, such as opening windows, sending e-mail, and posting responses on discussion boards. The software sends a report to the individual responsible for tracking the activity. The software is undetectable to the employee.

- A monitoring program created by SpectorSoft Corporation takes randomly timed pictures of the employee's computer screen The employer can review the records at a later time.

- Software produced by Content Technologies called Pornsweeper is capable of reviewing images and tags anything that appears to be pornographic.

- Technology called "keystroke monitoring" allows an employer to determine what an employee types by tracking each keystroke. The technology tracks both saved and unsaved work.

apply it

Monitoring Systems

GOAL: *To gain understanding regarding monitoring systems.*

STEP 1: Schedule an appointment with an employer that uses a monitoring system.

STEP 2: Interview the employer and ask questions such as: What is the purpose of the monitoring system? Why was this particular type of system selected? Has the system been effective? What problems, if any, have occurred as a result of using the system? Write a short report regarding your findings and be prepared to share it with the class.

STEP 3: Consider placing your report on monitoring systems in your Learning Portfolio.

The increased use of monitoring equipment by employers has raised the issue of employees' rights to privacy. In general, the law has favored the employer as long as the employer clearly informs the employee of the existence of any monitoring systems and has published behavior expectations for office computer use and general conduct. Office policies regarding the Internet usually address the use of e-mail in the work setting. A standard policy commonly states that because the computer is owned by the employer, the employer has the right to know how it is being used and that employees should not expect privacy (Weil, 2000). As an employee, it is your responsibility to know your employer's policy. If one is not offered at the time of hiring, ask about it.

It is important to know your company's policy regarding personal phone calls. Court rulings have determined that employers have the right to monitor phone conversations if monitoring is done in the interest of business-related matters.

Privacy related to phone monitoring or recording has also received attention. The courts have stated that the employer may monitor employee telephone conversations if it is done to "evaluate business-related matters such as efficiency, productivity, and client service" (Towns, 2002, p. 5). It is illegal for an employer to monitor an employee's phone calls "if the employer knows that the call is a private call and is made with the expectation of privacy" (*Workplace Fairness,* 2005a, p. 1). Be aware that if your employer has published a policy that prohibits personal calls, the employer has a right to terminate the employee for violation of the rules (*Workplace Fairness,* 2005a).

As an employee, it is important to recognize that the issue of right to privacy extends beyond the workplace. Courts have determined that an employer has the right to know employees' personal information that affects the employee's ability to perform work-related responsibilities (Canter,

2005). For example, employers can complete credit checks on potential employees to determine their fiscal responsibility. Certain fields, such as those related to child care and the health professions, may require criminal background checks. It is critical to realize that what you do in your personal life can ultimately affect you as an employee.

EMPLOYMENT-AT-WILL

Private sector employees fall under the law of employment-at-will. The employment-at-will law provides flexibility to employers and employees to terminate employment. This law enables employers to release employees from employment at any time without providing any explanation or notice as long as the reason is not illegal (*Workplace Fairness*, 2005b). Employees have the same right to terminate their employment at any time. The disadvantage of this law is that as long as the action is based on legal reasons, employees do not have much protection from unfair treatment or being released from employment. For instance, according to employment-at-will, an employer can legally fire you simply because he does not like you, because he wants to hire a friend in your place, or because he has expectations that are impossible to meet. These reasons are ethically questionable, but they are not illegal. Currently, only individuals who work in Montana, Puerto Rico, and the Virgin Islands are protected from being terminated for unjust treatment. Union employees, government employees, independent contractors, and temporary employees are not affected by the employment-at-will law (*Workplace Fairness,* 2005b).

A physical exam may be required for some jobs.

EMPLOYEE PHYSICAL AND DRUG TESTING

Depending on the type of work an individual will be performing, a physical exam may be required prior to employment. This is particularly true for health care workers or for those who will be performing demanding physical tasks. Documentation of immunizations or other health-related issues also may be required.

Other legal requirements of employment may include taking a drug test. This is particularly true for federal government employees. Drug tests may be performed on a random basis following initial employment. Employees must be notified in writing at the time of employment that these random and unannounced tests may be performed.

Pre-employment drug tests screen for numerous substances including, but not limited to, THC (marijuana), alcohol, cocaine, barbiturates, amphetamines, and steroids. Drugs remain stored in the body for varying periods following their ingestion. For example, THC can remain in the body for up to a month following its use. The amount of time that a drug remains detectable in the body depends on numerous factors, such as the drug's half-life, your metabolism, your body size, the method of ingestion, and the duration of use (CollegeGrad.com, 2005).

It is important to realize that certain prescription and over-the-counter medications can cause falsely positive results on drug tests. Usually, test-givers ask whether you are taking any medications. To be safe, you should list all medications that you have taken during the preceding month. If a false-positive result does occur, discuss the issue with the employer, explaining why you believe the result to be false, and request that a second test be completed. If your request for a second test is declined, you may wish to seek legal advice.

EMPLOYMENT BENEFITS

A variety of benefits may be offered to employees as part of an employment package. State laws and a company's size define which benefits a company is required to provide to employees. Benefits that are generally not required by law include vacation pay and meal and rest breaks. Benefits that are typically required by law include those pertaining to pregnancy and sick leave.

Although some benefits are not required by law, employers must consider what is ethically right in addition to what is legally required. Most employers want to treat their employees with respect and fairness, but offering appropriate benefits that are not legally determined is an ethical choice rather than a legal obligation.

The following is a short list of benefits that employers may or may not be legally required to offer their employees (*Workplace Fairness,* 2005c; *Workplace Fairness,* 2005d; *Workplace Fairness,* 2005e).

▶ **Vacation pay.** Employers are not required to give vacation time, although most employers choose to offer vacation time in order to keep productivity high. Companies have found that if employees do not take some time off, the rate of "burnout" is high and morale is low. To receive vacation time, employees often must be with the company for a certain period. For example, vacation time is often accrued each month and then can be used after six months to a year of employment. Most companies try to schedule employee vacations so that productivity is not affected. Senior employees typically have first choice of vacation calendar days. Some employers also have a "use it or lose it" policy, meaning that employees must use their vacation days within a certain time frame (commonly, the calendar year) and cannot carry over accrued days to the next year. Although employers are not obligated to allow an employee to take his or her vacation days before losing them, most employers try to be as

There are numerous federal laws that prohibit discrimination the basis of race, religion, gender, and disability.

accommodating as possible. Depending on state requirements, accrued unused vacation must be paid back to employees who quit prior to the end of the year.

▶ **Meal and rest breaks.** Employers are not required by law to provide meal or rest breaks unless the workplace is unionized or state labor regulations stipulate otherwise. The Fair Labor Standards Act (FLSA) requires that employers pay their employees for hours worked and distinguishes between rest breaks and meal breaks. Rest periods typically are paid time, while meal breaks generally are not (*Workplace Fairness*, 2005d). The length of a rest or meal break is at the discretion of the employer. Employers are required to provide bathroom breaks, which are a health obligation rather than a privilege.

▶ **Leave.** Although sick leave is generally not a legal requirement, many employers offer this benefit either on a paid or unpaid basis. Various types of leaves may be requested, including leave for the birth or adoption of a child and caring for a seriously ill child, parent, or spouse. Employer requirements for granting leave are set forth by the Family and Medical Leave Act and the American with Disabilities Act.

WORKPLACE DISCRIMINATION

Various types of discrimination can occur in the workplace, and many laws exist to minimize the chances that discrimination will occur. The federal antidiscrimination laws protect employees who fall into various categories of "protected class" (*Workplace Fairness*, 2005f). Employees can be discriminated against for a variety of reasons, including age, disability, immigration status, language, marital status, sexual orientation, national origin, pregnancy, race, religion, and gender.

Various laws protect individuals from discrimination. Individuals are encouraged to become familiar with the federal and state laws that provide them with discrimination protection. The following is a list of some of the federal laws (*Workplace Fairness*, 2005g; *Workplace Fairness*, 2005h; *Workplace Fairness*, 2005i; *Workplace Fairness*, 2005j):

▶ Americans with Disabilities Act of 1990

▶ Title VII of the Civil Rights Act of 1964

▶ Pregnancy Discrimination Act of 1978

▶ Family and Medical Leave Act of 1993

▶ Age Discrimination in Employment Act

▶ Older Workers Benefit Protection Act of 1990

apply it

Discrimination Laws

GOAL: *To gain an understanding of the various discrimination laws.*

STEP 1: Divide the class into small groups.

STEP 2: Assign each group to study one or two laws that directly deal with discrimination. Each group should gain as much knowledge as possible regarding those laws and then present a brief report to the class.

STEP 3: Exchange copies of each group's work. File the information in your Learning Portfolio for future reference.

Proving discrimination requires that the employee fall into a protected class status and can show either direct or circumstantial evidence of the discrimination (*Workplace Fairness,* 2005f). The following are questions that may be asked to assist an employee in substantiating circumstantial evidence of the apparent discrimination (*Workplace Fairness,* 2005f, p. 2):

1. "Were you treated differently than a similarly situated person who is not in your protected class?"

2. "Did managers or supervisors regularly make rude or derogatory comments directed at your protected class status or at all members of your class and related to work?"

3. "Are the circumstances of your treatment so unusual, egregious, unjust, or severe as to suggest discrimination?"

4. "Does your employer have a history of showing bias toward persons in your protected class?"

5. "Are there noticeably few employees of your protected class at your workplace?"

6. "Have you noticed that other employees of your protected class seem to be singled out for adverse treatment or are put in dead-end jobs?"

7. "Have you heard other employees in your protected class complain about discrimination, particularly by the supervisor or manager who took the adverse action against you?"

8. "Are there statistics that show favoritism toward or bias against any group?"

9. "Did your employer violate well-established company policy in the way it treated you?"

10. "Did your employer retain less qualified, nonprotected employees in the same job?"

If an employee believes that discrimination has occurred, it is imperative to report the perceived discrimination to the appropriate authorities. Documenting the occurrence(s) is critical, so keep as complete a record of the incident(s) as possible, including time, date, and the names of any witnesses. For further advice, contact your state's Equal Employment Opportunity Commission. If the issue is related to family and medical leave discrimination, call the Department of Labor (*Workplace Fairness,* 2005h).

HARASSMENT IN THE WORKPLACE

Harassment at work can come in a variety of forms. The two most common forms are sexual and racial harassment. Any form of harassment is illegal and should not be tolerated in the workplace.

Sexual Harassment

As an employee, it is important to know when you may be experiencing sexual harassment on the job. Sexual harassment can be experienced by men and women, and it can occur between opposite-sex or same-sex individuals. State laws and Title VII of the Civil Rights Act of 1964 make it illegal for an individual to be sexually harassed in the workplace. The following are some examples of sexual harassment conduct (*Workplace Fairness,* 2005k, p. 3):

- **Verbal or written conduct.** Comments about clothing, personal behavior, or your body; sexual or sex-based jokes; requesting sexual favors or repeatedly asking you out; making sexual innuendoes, spreading rumors about your personal or sexual life; or threatening you

- **Physical conduct.** Rape or assault, impeding or blocking your movement, inappropriate touching of your body or clothing, kissing, hugging, patting, stroking

- **Nonverbal conduct.** Looking up and down your body, making derogatory gestures or facial expressions of a sexual nature, following or stalking you

- **Visual displays.** Posters, drawings, pictures, screensavers, or e-mails of a sexual nature

If an employee believes that he or she is experiencing sexual harassment, it is important to address the situation by taking the following steps (*Workplace Fairness,* 2005k):

Step 1. Inform the harasser that you are not interested. For future legal actions, it is important that you establish from the very beginning that the behavior is not welcome. Be as direct as possible in saying "no."

Step 2. Document the incident(s). It will be helpful for you to be able to provide documentation at a later time. Record all the event(s), including both parties' behavior, the time, the date, and the names of any witness(es).

Step 3. If the harasser is not your direct supervisor, alert your supervisor, administrator, or personnel director of the situation. If the harasser is your direct supervisor, alerting the personnel director might be your best alternative. Provide the documentation as required. If the harasser is your supervisor and no other individual is available, report the problem to legal counsel.

Step 4. Communicate with other coworkers, family members, and friends about the incident(s). This is important not only to gain support, but it may be necessary later as evidence regarding the problem.

Step 5. If the sexual harassment continues, even after the employer's involvement, seek legal advice from an attorney or the Equal Employment Opportunity Commission.

---

success steps

STEPS FOR ADDRESSING HARASSMENT IN THE WORKPLACE

1. Inform the harasser that you are not interested.

2. Documents the incident(s).

3. If the harasser is not your direct supervisor, alert your supervisor, administrator, or personnel director of the situation. If the harasser is your direct supervisor, alerting the personnel director might be your best alternative.

4. Communicate to others regarding the incident.

5. If the harassment continues after the employer's involvement, legal counsel may be appropriate.

Racial Harassment

"Racial harassment is unwelcome behavior that happens to you because of your race, such as verbal or physical conduct of a racial nature" (*Workplace Fairness,* 2005l, p. 1). Although no specific federal and state laws make race-based harassment illegal, racial harassment is considered to be a form of race discrimination and, as such, is covered under Title VII of the Civil Rights Act of 1964 (*Workplace Fairness,* 2005l). Forms of racial harassment are very similar to those described earlier for sexual harassment. The difference is that the individual is experiencing harassment based on their race versus gender

©Digital Vision

Leaving your job for new employment opportunities requires obtaining references from and closure with your current employer.

or sexuality. As with sexual harassment, reporting race harassment is important. To report racial harassment, follow the same steps as for reporting sexual harassment.

LEAVING A JOB

Exiting a job occurs either voluntarily or involuntarily. If you are leaving voluntarily and on good terms, it is appropriate to give your employer at least a two-week notice. Most employers either have the employee stay for the final two weeks or let the employee leave immediately with pay for the two weeks. Complete the following tasks prior to leaving a job (*Workplace Fairness,* 2005m):

▶ Obtain letters of references.

▶ Negotiate a severance package if the situation warrants one.

▶ Establish that the company is willing to rehire you at a later date.

▶ Be aware of signed contracts with possible industry noncompete clauses. If you do not have a copy of your contract, obtain one prior to leaving the company. In the event any questions arise, for instance, regarding an issue such as a noncompete clause, having a copy of your contract will help you determine the legitimacy of the employer's claim.

Although no one wants to experience being fired, it does happen. If it does, it is important that you obtain in writing the reason you were terminated. Depending on the state in which you live, the employer might be legally obligated to provide such a written explanation. If your employer is not required by law to provide one, and you are unable to obtain one, get a verbal statement from your employer. Record the reason and the date, time, and place that the statement was made. Note the names of any witnesses. Read it back to your supervisor/employer, request confirmation, and note the date (*Workplace Fairness,* 2005m). If the termination is involuntary and the employee is in good standing, then the employee likely is eligible for unemployment compensation.

Regardless of whether termination is voluntary or involuntary, it is the employer's responsibility to deliver the employee's last paycheck within a reasonable time, usually within 30 days or on the next payday (*Workplace Fairness,* 2005n, p. 1).

It is important to be aware that after you have left a place of employment and begun the search for a new job, your previous employer has the legal right to comment on your abilities, performance, or attitude. The courts have determined that employers have a right to know information about an individual that is relevant to that individual's employment

▶ REFLECTION QUESTION

- What other legal and ethical workplace issues do you think are important for you to be familiar with?

? CRITICAL THINKING QUESTION

3–2. How would you respond to the following statement: "Laws change so much that it is impossible to stay current with all the laws that affect employment"?

(Spolter, 2005). This is why it is important to leave an employer on good terms to as great an extent as possible.

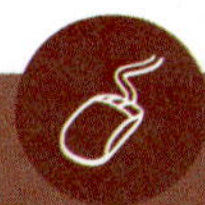

apply it

Internet Research

GOAL: To develop a better understanding regarding topics discussed in this chapter.

STEP 1: Conduct Internet research on one or more topics covered in this chapter that you want to understand more clearly.

STEP 2: Write a brief report regarding your findings. Be prepared to present your report to the class.

STEP 3: Consider placing your report in your Learning Portfolio.

CHAPTER SUMMARY

This chapter explored the rights and responsibilities of employers and employees in the workplace, as well as your rights to privacy and employers' rights to monitor employees' behavior. You were introduced to the laws that affect your rights as an employee and learned steps to take in the event you experience harassment or discrimination. You learned what benefits employers are legally required to provide and the factors that determine those benefits. Finally, you learned appropriate considerations for leaving a job and how to do so while maintaining positive professional relationships.

POINTS TO KEEP IN MIND

In this chapter, several main points were discussed in detail:

- It is the responsibility of both the employer and employee to understand their rights and obligations in the workplace.
- Many employers use monitoring systems to track employees' computer activities and general productivity.
- Laws regarding privacy favor the employer as long as the employer clearly informs the employee of the existence of monitoring systems and the expectations for office computer use.
- The purpose of the employment-at-will law is to allow employers and employees the flexibility of deciding when to terminate employment.
- The downside of the employment-at-will law is that as long as an employer does not engage in an illegal action, employees do not

have much protection from being released from employment and experiencing unfair treatment.

▶ There are no legal standard for treating employees fairly except in the state of Montana and in Puerto Rico and the Virgin Islands.

▶ Individual state laws and company size affect what benefits a company must offer to its employees.

▶ Employers are not required to give their employees vacation time, although most employers choose to do so in order to keep productivity and morale high.

▶ Employers are not required by law to provide meal or rest breaks unless the workplace is unionized or state labor regulations indicate otherwise.

▶ Although sick leave is generally not a legally required benefit, many employers offer it either on a paid or unpaid basis.

▶ Discrimination in the workplace can occur for a variety of reasons, including age, disability, immigration status, language, marital status, sexual orientation, national origin, pregnancy, race, religion, and gender.

▶ Federal laws that protect individuals from discrimination include the Americans with Disabilities Act of 1990, Title VII of the Civil Rights Act of 1964, the Pregnancy Discrimination Act of 1978, the Family and Medical Leave Act of 1993, the Age Discrimination in Employment Act, and the Older Workers Benefit Protection Act of 1990.

▶ Any form of harassment is illegal and should not be tolerated in the workplace.

▶ State laws and Title VII of the Civil Rights Act of 1964 make it illegal for an individual to be sexually harassed in the workplace.

▶ Racial harassment is considered to be a form of race discrimination and so is covered under Title VII of the Civil Rights Act of 1964.

▶ Items that should be obtained prior to leaving an employer include letter of references, severance package, and copies of any signed contracts or agreements.

▶ If an involuntary termination has occurred through no fault of the employee's, then the employee is likely eligible for unemployment compensation.

▶ If possible, leave an employer on good terms and with no bridges burned.

LEARNING OBJECTIVES REVISITED

Review the learning objectives for this chapter and rate your level of achievement for each objective using the rating scale provided. For each objective on which you do not rate yourself as a 3, outline a plan of action that you will take to fully achieve the objective. Include a time frame for this plan.

1 = did not successfully achieve objective

2 = understand what is needed, but need more study or practice

3 = achieved learning objective thoroughly

	1	2	3
Understand what constitutes discrimination in the workplace.	☐	☐	☐
List and explain various laws that protect individuals from discrimination.	☐	☐	☐
Explain the importance for employees to understand their legal rights and obligations in the workplace.	☐	☐	☐
Discuss methods that employers use to diminish employee misuse of office computers.	☐	☐	☐
Describe the various types of monitoring systems available to employers to track employees' computer activities and general productivity.	☐	☐	☐
Explain the rights an employee has to privacy.	☐	☐	☐
Discuss the purpose of the law of employment-at-will and explain the pros and cons of this law.	☐	☐	☐
Explain the various benefits that employers are required and not required to offer employees.	☐	☐	☐
Discuss how an employee can determine if he or she has been discriminated against.	☐	☐	☐
Explain how employees report discrimination and harassment incidents.	☐	☐	☐
Provide examples of sexual and racial harassment.	☐	☐	☐

Steps to Achieve Unmet Objectives

Steps	Due Date
1. ____	__________
2. ____	__________
3. ____	__________
4. ____	__________

SUGGESTED ITEMS FOR LEARNING PORTFOLIO

Refer to the "Developing Portfolios" section at the front of this textbook for more information on learning portfolios.

- Monitoring Systems: The purpose of this activity is to increase your understanding of monitoring systems in the workplace.

- Discrimination Laws: The goal of this activity is to increase your understanding of discrimination laws.

- Internet Research: This activity provides the opportunity for you to explore topics that are of interest to you.

REFERENCES

Canter, J. (2005). Drawing the line on privacy at work [electronic version]. Wall Street Journal Executive Career Site: CareerJournal.com. Retrieved April 11, 2005, from http://www.careers.wsj.com/myc/legal/19990209-canter.html

CollegeGrad.com. (2005). Drug testing and other possible conditions of employment [electronic version]. Retrieved November 24, 2005, from http://www.CollegeGrad.com/jobsearch/24-2.shtml

Grossman, M. (1998–2006). Employees, the net, and trouble [electronic version]. Retrieved June 19, 2006, from http://www.ecomputerlaw.com/articles/show_article.php?article=2006_employees,_the_net,_and_trouble

Spolter, L. (2005). Are you a victim of workplace defamation? [electronic version]. The Wall Street Journal Executive Career Site: Career Journal.com. Retrieved April 8, 2005, from http://www.careerjournal.com/myc/legal/19990503-spolter.html

Towns, D. (2002). Legal issues involved in monitoring employees' Internet and e-mail usage [electronic version]. Retrieved April 8, 2005, from http://www.gigalaw.com/articles/2002-all/towns-2002-01-all.html

Weil, G. B. (2000). Company e-mail and Internet policies [electronic version]. Retrieved April 8, 2005, from http://www.gigalaw.com/articles/2000-all/gall-2000-01-all.html

Workplace Fairness. (2005a). General info: Invasion of privacy [electronic version]. Retrieved April 8, 2005, from http://www.workplacefairness.org/index.php?page=generalprivacy

Workplace Fairness. (2005b). Classifications [electronic version]. Retrieved April 8, 2005, from http://www.workplacefairness.org/index .php?page=classifications

Workplace Fairness. (2005c). Vacation pay [electronic version]. Retrieved April 8, 2005, from http://www.workplacefairness.org/index .php?page=vacationpay

Workplace Fairness. (2005d). Meal and rest breaks [electronic version]. Retrieved April 8, 2005, from http://www.workplacefairness.org/ index.php?page=breaks#5

Workplace Fairness. (2005e). Sick leave [electronic version]. Retrieved April 8, 2005, from http://www.workplacefairness.org/index .php?page=sickleave

Workplace Fairness. (2005f). Discrimination: General information [electronic version]. Retrieved April 8, 2005, from http://www .workplacefairness.org/index.php?page=generaldisc

Workplace Fairness. (2005g). Disability discrimination [electronic version]. Retrieved April 8, 2005, from http://www.workplacefairness.org/ index.php?page=disability

Workplace Fairness. (2005h). Pregnancy leave [electronic version]. Retrieved April 8, 2005, from http://www.workplacefairness.org/ index.php?page=pregnancyleave

Workplace Fairness. (2005i). Race discrimination [electronic version]. Retrieved April 8, 2005, from http://www.workplacefairness.org/ index.php?page=racedisc

Workplace Fairness. (2005j). Age discrimination [electronic version]. Retrieved April 8, 2005, from http://www.workplacefairness .org/index.php?page=age

Workplace Fairness. (2005k). Sexual harassment [electronic version]. Retrieved April 8, 2005, from http://www.workplacefairness .org/index.php?page=sex

Workplace Fairness. (2005l). Racial harassment [electronic version]. Retrieved April 8, 2005, from http://www.workplacefairness.org/ index.php?page=raceharassment

Workplace Fairness. (2005m). Leaving your job [electronic version]. Retrieved April 8, 2005, from http://www.workplacefairness.org/ index.php?page=leaving

Workplace Fairness. (2005n). Final pay [electronic version]. Retrieved April 8, 2005, from http://www.workplacefairness.org/index .php?page=finalpay

CHAPTER OUTLINE

Importance of Communication: An Overview

Effective Verbal Communication

Effective Written Communication

Tools to Assist with Writing

Technology and Written Communication

4

Communication Skills for Student Success

By the end of this chapter, you will achieve the following objectives:

- Explain the importance of good listening skills.
- List reasons why listening can be difficult.
- Explain the benefits and characteristics of assertive communication.
- Discuss considerations that should be made when sending an e-mail.
- Describe how professionalism is demonstrated in written communication.
- Explain the purpose of utilizing open-ended questions versus closed questions.
- Recognize the importance of body language.
- Explain the importance of effective communication.
- Demonstrate the ability to create a visual presentation.
- Demonstrate the ability to conduct professional correspondence.

TOPIC SCENARIO

After graduation Elizabeth Lanham began searching for a job. In the first two weeks she had sent out 25 resumes. She followed up appropriately, checking to find out when interviews might be taking place and if she was a candidate for consideration. Weeks went by, resumes continued to be sent, but Elizabeth still did not get any interviews. Over time Elizabeth began to wonder why she had not even gotten one call from all the resumes she had sent. She knew she was well qualified for the entry-level jobs she was applying for. After six months Elizabeth finally got her first interview. It wasn't until this first interview that Elizabeth finally found out why she had not been receiving any earlier calls for potential jobs. During the interview Elizabeth was informed that her resume and cover letter had spelling and grammar errors. The interviewee said that Elizabeth was very qualified for the job but that the lack of attention given to her resume and cover letter had indicated a lack of attention to detail that could affect her ability to perform the required job duties. Elizabeth did eventually get a job. By using the interviewee's feedback, Elizabeth made the necessary changes and corrections to her documents so they exhibited the professionalism required for employment. Based on this short description, answer the following questions:

▶ Is it right for employers to rule out applicants due to errors on the resume and/or cover letter? If so, why? If not, why not?

▶ How important do you think written and spoken communication will be in the job that you will be seeking after graduation?

▶ What can Elizabeth do in future written communication to make sure she shows professionalism?

▶ If you lack skills in either written or spoken communications, how do you plan on improving?

▶ What sources might be available to you for improving these skills?

IMPORTANCE OF COMMUNICATION: AN OVERVIEW

4

As illustrated in Elizabeth's story, it is important to develop excellent communication skills. The significance of effective written and spoken communication skills cannot be understated. In any profession, individuals are valued for their ability to communicate effectively. The focus of this chapter is to review the skills needed for effective communication in both academic and professional settings. Developing these skills while in school will make a difference to your success as a professional.

EFFECTIVE VERBAL COMMUNICATION

Effective verbal communication is a fundamental skill. Technical aptitude is more useful when it can be expressed clearly. Your success can depend on your ability to apply and communicate your knowledge. Learning how to speak effectively in the classroom and as a professional begins with understanding the basics of effective communication. Communication can be divided into two parts:

- The Sender: the individual expressing his or her needs, feelings, thoughts, and opinions
- The Receiver: the individual listening and understanding what is being communicated

Effective communication occurs when the receiver of the information interprets and understands the sender's message in the same way the sender intends it.

LISTENING

Listening is one of the most challenging aspects of communication. Ineffective listening can be caused by

- preoccupation and lack of attention
- thinking rather than listening
- closed-minded thinking
- prejudging the speaker or judging what is being said

It is important to make the distinction between hearing and listening. Effective listening begins with taking time to understand what the speaker is thinking and feeling from his or her perspective. To listen adequately involves actively participating in the communication process by focusing on what the speaker is saying; attending to spoken elements as well as unspoken elements, such as emotion and body language; and concentrating on the present moment. Active participation cannot be accomplished if you are preoccupied, thinking about other topics, or anticipating what the "right" answer will be to what the speaker is saying.

© BananaStock Ltd.

Effective communication requires careful and focused attention, clear expression of thoughts and feelings, and mutual respect.

EFFECTIVE LISTENING

1. Take the time to understand what the speaker is saying.

2. Take the speaker's perspective.

3. Attend to spoken as well as unspoken elements.

? CRITICAL THINKING QUESTIONS

Consider the following scenario and answer the questions that follow.

You are the group leader for a project at your place of employment. One of your team members contributes effectively during group meetings but does not look group members in the eye when speaking. You begin to hear comments and remarks—not all of them kind— about this individual and her lack of eye contact. You suspect that her lack of eye contact may be due to cultural influence.

4–2. How do you approach the group?

4–3. How do you address the issue with the individual?

? CRITICAL THINKING QUESTION

4–4. What other body language examples can you think of? What clues do you think these movements and behaviors reveal?

▶ REFLECTION QUESTION

• Think of a conversation you recently had. Did the individual you were speaking with exhibit any body language? If so, what do you think the body language was telling you?

BODY LANGUAGE

Individuals often communicate feelings or thoughts with their body language.

Arms folded across chest, lack of eye contact, and fidgeting are elements of body language that can be revealing. Arms folded may signal that the individual does not care about what is being said. Lack of eye contact can indicate that the individual feels uncomfortable. Evaluating how others perceive your body language is important. Understanding how others may be interpreting your gestures and movements may help you gain insight into the effectiveness of your communication.

It is important to remember that Western interpretations of body language may differ from interpretations in other cultures. For example, in many Asian cultures, making eye contact can be interpreted as a lack of respect for authority. Avoid jumping to conclusions and consider that if an individual has been raised with certain cultural expectations, these characteristics are deeply ingrained and are to be respected. If certain behavioral nuances interfere with communication, consider cultural diversity. Work collaboratively to achieve an understanding.

Although body language is important to consider during communication, caution should be taken to avoid overinterpretation or misinterpretation. Taking all aspects of communication into consideration is important, so be aware of the other components of communication as well. Use a combination of cues from listening, hearing, and interpreting body language to accurately understand what the receiver is communicating verbally and nonverbally.

INTERPRETING BODY LANGUAGE

1. Be aware of how your body language is being interpreted. You may be conveying an unintended message.

2. Consider that certain gestures and other body language can be interpreted differently by individuals from diverse cultures.

3. Be careful not to overinterpret the meaning of body language.

QUESTIONING TECHNIQUES

Asking appropriate questions is another important element of effective communication. Learning how to use questions effectively to discover information is a helpful tool in improving communication. There are two general types of questions: open-ended questions and closed questions.

Open-ended questions require more than a yes or no answer from the receiver. The purpose of asking open-ended questions is to gain more detailed information. An example of an open-ended question would be, "When should open-ended questions be used instead of closed questions?"

Closed questions are typically used to confirm information and often require one or two words to answer. For instance, "Did you go to the office on Monday or Tuesday?" or "Did you say that the test is on Wednesday?"

success steps

USING EFFECTIVE QUESTIONING TECHNIQUES

1. Use open-ended questions to gain detailed information.

2. Use closed questions to confirm information.

3. Use the appropriate type of question to facilitate communication.

ASSERTIVENESS

Assertiveness is the ability to express your beliefs, needs, feelings, and opinions in a manner that clearly makes your point, but that is not intimidating and demonstrates respect for the feelings and opinions of the receiver of your message.

To better understand assertive communication, it is helpful to compare it with other styles that are usually less effective. Consider the following communication styles:

▶ **Aggressive.** Aggressive communication typically conveys anger and impatience and is generally abrasive. Aggressive communication is typically characterized by a raised voice, strong gesturing, glaring eyes, and harsh words. Aggressive communication tends to alienate the receiver of the message and hinders communication.

▶ **Passive.** A passive communication style is characterized by a soft voice, lack of eye contact, and a tendency to avoid stating needs, feelings, and opinions. Passive communication can avoid immediate conflict, but can leave the passive sender feeling "walked on" and as if his or her feelings and wishes are not honored.

? CRITICAL THINKING QUESTIONS

Evaluate the following scenarios and determine what type of question needs to be asked. Indicate the type of question that should be used and then write an appropriate question for each scenario.

4–5. You're at the office and you can't figure out what software the manager wants you to download.
Type: __________
Question: __________

4–6. At your job you need to obtain a patient's history during a physical exam. What might you ask when obtaining a patient's history?
Type: __________
Question: __________

4–7. You are in class and you are really struggling with understanding what is on the board.
Type: __________
Question: __________

▶ **Passive-aggressive.** Passive-aggressive communication occurs when feelings of anger or discontent are expressed passively. An example is the individual who, following a meeting with a coworker, smiles and acts as though nothing is wrong. However, he is actually angry and walks out of the office, slamming the door to express his feelings.

▶ **Assertive.** The individual using an assertive communication style expresses his or her opinions and feelings directly using carefully chosen words. Tone of voice is firm, yet calm and nonabrasive, and is modulated at a conversational level. The sender of the assertive message actively listens to the response of the receiver and respectfully acknowledges the sender's position. Eye contact is direct, but not glaring or threatening.

Developing Assertive Communication Skills

There may be situations in which an aggressive or passive communication style is appropriate and effective. However, generally, and especially in the workplace, an assertive communication style is preferred and usually most effective. It is important to remember that using an assertive style does not necessarily get you what you want, but it may maximize your chances or promote a favorable compromise. Consider the following suggestions for communicating assertively:

▶ **Know what you want.** Clearly identify what you want from a specific communication. Doing so will help you express yourself more clearly and support you in knowing where you can compromise.

▶ **Understand your feelings.** Knowing your feelings will help you to express them clearly, which can serve to clarify a situation. For example, saying "I am confused about the messages I am receiving" conveys that you are open to hearing clarification and correcting any misunderstandings. Expressing feelings has the added benefit of humanizing the communication.

▶ **Use "I" statements.** The statement "I am confused about the messages I am receiving" puts the responsibility on the sender of the message. An "I" message avoids blame, which can be implied in messages that begin with "you." Consider the difference between "I am confused about the messages I am receiving" and "You are sending confusing messages." An "I" message indicates that the sender is taking responsibility, while a "you" message tends to sound accusatory and may put the receiver on the defensive, hindering the communication process. Use "I" statements to express your feelings, needs, opinions, and wishes.

▸ **Communicate from a "win-win" position.** Be prepared by knowing the points on which you are willing to compromise and be willing to negotiate when appropriate. Use "I" statements to express points on which you are unable or unwilling to compromise.

success steps

COMMUNICATING ASSERTIVELY

1. Clearly identify what you want or need.
2. Understand your feelings and how they relate to what you want.
3. Use "I" statements.
4. Approach the situation with a win-win attitude.

APPRECIATING DIVERSITY

Interacting effectively with others requires an appreciation of each person as an individual. Culture and environment can have a significant impact on communication patterns. Words can have different meanings depending on an individual's culture. Identifying the cultural background of individuals can minimize or avoid confusion or misunderstandings during communication. Home environment can also influence an individual's use of words. Grammar and concepts such as assertiveness can also vary depending on an individual's upbringing. When communicating with others, it is helpful to be considerate and not be too quick to judge an individual's word choice or communication abilities.

VERBAL COMMUNICATION IN THE CLASSROOM

Sending and receiving messages through listening, evaluating body language, and questioning are all parts of the communication process and are critical for successful interaction in the classroom. Learning to communicate effectively in the classroom provides good practice opportunities for developing professional interpersonal skills required for employment. Classroom communication involves both the written and spoken word. It is important to develop your skills in both areas.

There are many opportunities for verbal communication in the classroom, including group activities, discussions, questions, and presentations. To optimize the use of these forums, it is important to follow some simple rules.

▸ **Participate in group activities**. Group activities are successful for individual members and the group only if all members participate. Participation includes not only completing activities but

REFLECTION QUESTIONS

- Is your communication style usually passive, passive-aggressive, aggressive, or assertive? What examples can you give to support your observation?
- What changes might you make to improve your communication style? How would making a change enhance your communications?

REFLECTION QUESTIONS

- In your communication with others, how do you demonstrate appreciation for diversity in your audience?
- How can you increase your sensitivity to diverse communication practices?

Learning to communicate effectively in the classroom provides good practice opportunities for developing the professional interpersonal skills required for employment.

communicating clearly with team members as well. To facilitate group communication, it is helpful for group members to establish guidelines and standards for effective communication. Guidelines should also define group etiquette and expectations for respectful and professional communication between group members. Establishing acceptable methods for communication also supports effective communication. For example, the group may choose electronic forms such as e-mail and bulletin boards for communicating with group members and may limit telephone calls to certain hours.

▶ **Ask questions.** Opportunities to ask questions in class offer an excellent chance to confirm your understanding of material and clarify information. Different types of questions can be utilized in the classroom, but always understand your purpose prior to asking. For example, clarifying information may require a closed question, while further explanation of information may be achieved by asking an open-ended question. Although it is said "no question is stupid," do try to utilize class time appropriately. Some questions are best answered in a one-on-one meeting with the instructor rather than during class. Speaking up in class also provides an opportunity to practice making inquiries and speaking up in a group of colleagues, which will be expected in the workplace.

▶ **Develop listening skills.** Listening is an important element of asking and receiving information in class. Listening in class may involve skills other than those used in conversation. For example, in class you may listen for specific information. During the listening process, you may also be actively thinking about how information relates to your existing knowledge and writing notes accordingly. You will balance actively listening to the instructor with recording significant notes for meaningful study at a later time.

▶ **Participate in class discussion.** Instructors sometimes ask reflection questions and critical thinking questions to encourage students to share their opinions and ideas. In-class discussions work best if all students actively participate. Discussion is an excellent way to expand your thinking and understanding of the material and develop critical analysis and thinking skills. Students who develop critical thinking abilities gain a valuable tool that will be appreciated later in their careers. Developing respect for diverse opinions and viewpoints during discussions is also important for successful classroom interaction and is critical to success in the workplace. Demonstrating an appreciation for all opinions, regardless of whether or not you agree, as well as learning to disagree respectfully are basic professional communication skills.

▶ **Give presentations.** In-class presentations require both written and verbal communication skills, both of which improve and become easier with practice. Students need to embrace the opportunities to hone these skills in the classroom. You may find it helpful to practice your presentation in front of the instructor or a small group of peers to gain confidence prior to presenting to the entire class. Other factors in developing presentation skills include allowing enough time to become familiar with the material and revise as needed, maintaining the organization of material during preparation and presentation, and practicing speaking during class discussions. Pay attention to how classmates interact and speak, and learn from observing others. Use opportunities to speak outside of class as practice. When you speak, practice supporting your statements with verifiable facts. If possible, interact with the professional world by working or participating in internship opportunities. Developing confidence and skill at giving presentations will be a valued skill during your career (Gordon, n.d.).

To summarize, effective verbal communication skills are learned. As a student, take advantage of every opportunity to learn and grow in this area. Employers will expect excellent verbal communication skills, and your overall success depends on these skills.

success steps

COMMUNICATING EFFECTIVELY IN THE CLASSROOM

1. Actively participate in and contribute to group activities.

2. Ask questions in class.

3. Develop your listening skills.

4. Actively participate in class discussion.

5. Give presentations to develop both oral and written communication skills.

EFFECTIVE WRITTEN COMMUNICATION

Much like oral communication, communicating effectively in writing requires developing skills and taking the time to write correctly. Well-written communication delivers your message with clarity and effectiveness. Poorly written communication can cause confusion and misunderstandings. As with spoken communication, effective written communication is critical to success not only in school but also in the business environment.

WRITTEN COMMUNICATION IN THE WORKPLACE

Examples of written communication in the workplace include completing inventory forms, writing financial statements, completing work orders, filling out patient charts, sending electronic messages, and making sales or other types of presentations. Most importantly, daily interactions with colleagues and customers often require clear and effective written communication.

As a student, it is important to clearly understand the requirements that future employers will expect from you as a professional and to practice and apply these skills in the classroom. Written communication is effective when attention is given to the following elements:

> ▶ **Professionalism.** Professionalism is indicated by the appearance of the communication. For example, the appearance of a letter can indicate professionalism or a lack of care. Written communication that has grammatical errors or misspellings presents an unprofessional image. In correspondence, elements such as font selection, paper quality, organization, and neatness convey professionalism. Likewise, the manner in which an e-mail is written can either increase your professional credibility or diminish it.

> ▶ **Organization.** Organization is critical to professional image. If a term paper is disorganized, the information in the paper may be misunderstood, resulting in a poor grade. A business proposal that is well organized is more likely to achieve a business goal. Effective organization of written communication allows the information to flow, giving the reader a better opportunity to easily comprehend the ideas that are presented.

> ▶ **Quality.** Grammatical and punctuation errors, misspellings, smudges, and disorganization of information are examples of a lack of quality in written work. Errors that reflect a lack of quality reflect poorly on your ability to execute other tasks well. While this may seem presumptuous, impressions conveyed by written communication (particularly when your communication is your only introduction to another person) make a strong impact. Developing high standards of quality for written communication while you are in school will lay the foundation for continuing to apply care and attention to details in your future professional communications.

WRITTEN COMMUNICATION IN THE CLASSROOM

The classroom provides an excellent environment for developing your writing skills. Opportunities for developing writing skills in the classroom include note taking, tests, term papers, projects, and presentations. While some of these tasks seem a bit mundane, practicing clarity of written expression in each will contribute to your overall skill development, as well as enhance your learning.

It is important to be clear regarding what the instructor requires. Meet the requirements and go beyond them to cover your topic in a thorough manner that reflects high standards. Keep in mind that the quality of work done for classroom assignments should represent not only what is required in the classroom, but should reflect the type of work you would do on the job. Also, demonstrating writing capabilities in the classroom can be to your benefit if you use the instructor as an employment reference.

Plagiarism

Any discussion on written communication merits reference to the significance of plagiarism. When completing any written work in the classroom or the workplace, the ethical and legal ramifications of plagiarism are critical. Apply methods for avoiding plagiarism to all of your written work. methods for avoiding plagiarism to all of your written work.

apply it

Plagiarism Research

GOAL: To develop a better understanding of what plagiarism is and how to avoid it.

STEP 1: Using Internet or library sources, research more about what constitutes plagiarism and how you can avoid it as a student.

STEP 2: Write a short paper regarding your findings. Cite the material used in your research.

Presentations

Various software programs have significantly changed how the written component of classroom presentations is created. Software programs such as Microsoft PowerPoint, Macromedia Director, Corel Presentations, Lotus Freelance Graphics, and Harvard Graphics give individuals the opportunity to produce highly visual presentations. The written component is displayed visually in this type of presentation, making clearly written and precise communication all the more critical. The purpose of using a presentation tool is

4

to enhance the material and visually convey the message. Presentations that have a clear message, are well organized, and are visually appealing will be received more positively.

The following recommendations for creating electronic presentations are based on Hakim (2005):

- Know the purpose of the presentation and who your audience will be.

- Make sure the colors and font styles chosen for your presentation don't cause the audience to focus on the colors and styles versus the content. Colors and styles should be appealing and easy to read, but not the center of attention.

- Have a headline for each slide to focus your audience on each topic presented.

- Use background colors that affect your audience positively. Different colors can create different feelings.

- Make sure your lettering can be clearly seen. For instance, depending upon the background color, your ink may be more visible if it is white instead of black.

- Have your colors complement each other. Colors that do not go well together will be distracting to your audience.

- Use a font that is not too busy. Typically, Arial and Times fonts are chosen for their simple and plain appearance.

- Pay attention to font size. A general rule of thumb is to make sure your audience in the back of the room can read each line clearly. Less than 22-point font will be very difficult to read. Larger than 36 point may be overwhelming.

- As much as possible, limit bulleted items to one or two lines. Bulleted items should be written in phrases rather than full sentences.

- Make sure slides are not overwhelming with either images or text.

- Only use clip art, animations, and other visual aids if they strengthen your message. Remember the "KISS" rule: "Keep It Simple, Silly!"

- Review each slide for accuracy prior to presenting.

- Before the presentation, be familiar with the equipment you will use and have a backup plan, such as handouts, in the event the equipment malfunctions.

- When showing the slide presentation, be sure you are facing the audience.

success steps

GIVING EFFECTIVE ELECTRONIC PRESENTATIONS

1. Have a purpose that applies to your audience.

2. Use colors, design, and font styles that are appealing but not the focus of attention.

3. Select a plain font (such as Arial or Verdana) that is of an appropriate size (22–36 point).

4. Limit bullet points to one or two lines.

5. Write bullet points in phrases rather than sentences.

6. Use clip art and images only to illustrate your point. Too much embellishment detracts from the presentation.

7. Review carefully for accuracy before presenting.

8. Face the audience, not the slides.

REFLECTION QUESTIONS

- How much experience have you had in giving presentations?
- What strengths and weaknesses do you think your presentation skills have?
- How do you plan on improving your presentation skills?

apply it

Presentation Tool Analysis

GOAL: To demonstrate the ability to effectively communicate within a team environment, to analyze a presentation tool, and to produce a good presentation.

STEP 1: Form a group of no more than four students.

STEP 2: Each group should research one presentation tool. For instance, Group 1 may research everything about PowerPoint. Group 2 can research what the presentation tool Macromedia Director offers. Group 3 would research Lotus Freelance Graphics.

STEP 3: After each group has conducted its research, students should write a brief analysis of their findings.

STEP 4: Each group should prepare a presentation of its brief analysis. If possible, have each group use the tool it researched as its presentation tool. If only one tool is available in the classroom, all students should use that tool for their presentations.

STEP 5: Consider putting this Presentation Tool Analysis project in your Learning Portfolio.

4

TOOLS TO ASSIST WITH WRITING

In addition to the numerous articles on effective writing that can be found on the Internet, there are a variety of available tools that are worthwhile for use in the classroom and later in business. A few of these tools include:

- dictionary
- thesaurus
- *The Elements of Style* by Strunk and White
- *Modern Language Association Handbook* (MLA style)
- *Publication Manual of the American Psychological Association* (APA style)
- Turabian's *A Manual for Writers of Term Papers, Theses, and Dissertations* (simplified Chicago style)
- software programs such as ScholarWord
- campus resources, such as writing labs, tutors, and your instructor

IMPROVING YOUR WRITING SKILLS

Employers often indicate that writing is one of the most desirable skills a job applicant can possess. Kaplan (2004) offers the following suggestions for improving writing skills:

- Prepare an outline. Use the outline to indicate what needs to be included in the finished piece of writing and to organize its content.

- Write a draft. A draft is just that. At the draft stage, don't worry about spelling, word choice, or grammar. Simply express your thoughts and ideas.

- Correct spelling and review the document for improvement on word choice. Planning ahead and managing your time will leave you ample time to review and revise.

- Use the tools mentioned previously to assist in improving word choice, grammar, and style.

- Write the final draft, paying attention to choice of words and important details such as spelling and grammar. Allow ample time to set the final draft aside for a day or so and review it with a fresh perspective. Make revisions as needed based on your final review. If the content is not of a confidential nature, you might ask a trusted colleague to proofread the document.

- Write as often as possible and consider writing to be a skill that can be worked on and developed. Competence and confidence develop with practice.

success steps

COMMUNICATING EFFECTIVELY IN WRITING

Step 1: Budget your time so that you have time to write several drafts as well as review and modify the final copy.

Step 2: Prepare an outline to organize your thoughts.

Step 3: Write a draft to get your thoughts down on paper. Don't worry about spelling, grammar, and neatness at this point—just get the thoughts recorded.

Step 4: Review your draft, correct errors, and modify word choice as needed.

Step 5: Use tools such as those mentioned in this chapter (dictionary, thesaurus, and style guides) to assist in word choice and other aspects of composition.

Step 6: Write the final draft.

Step 7: Set the final draft aside for a day or so and review it with fresh eyes.

Step 8: Ask a trusted colleague to review the final draft if the material is not of a confidential nature.

Step 9: Take advantage of every opportunity to practice writing.

TECHNOLOGY AND WRITTEN COMMUNICATION

Advancements in technology have made effective written communication an even greater requirement. The speed at which electronic communication takes place requires thoughtfulness and attention to tone, choice of words, and accuracy.

E-MAIL

With the increased use of e-mail as a communication tool, knowing how to use e-mail effectively is important. As with any type of written communication, attention should be paid to who the audience is and the purpose of the e-mail. A social e-mail will be different from an e-mail sent for business. Dowling (n.d.) suggests the following tips for writing e-mail:

▶ Prior to sending an e-mail, review it to determine if it is clear, concise, useful, and necessary.

▶ Remember that you can be held accountable for whatever you write.

Using electronic communication, such as e-mail, requires attention to accuracy, detail, and rules of etiquette.

▶ Be aware of the length of the e-mail. At times, it might be more effective to write a short note with more detailed information included as an attachment.

▶ E-mail is not always confidential. Send only that which you don't mind having shared. Select other forms of communication, such as a face-to-face meeting or regular mail, for certain types of communication.

▶ As with any correspondence, be professional. E-mail is not to be used for disciplining the reader.

▶ Make sure your e-mail is necessary. If you send too many unnecessary e-mails containing jokes and other trivial communications, receivers of your e-mail may choose to ignore messages from you that may be important. Be aware that in the workplace, sending e-mails of a nonprofessional nature may violate company technology use policy.

▶ Use grammar and punctuation that reflects traditional written communication. Appropriate punctuation makes the message easier to read and reflects on your professionalism.

▶ Observe e-mail etiquette (also called *netiquette*). There are expectations that apply uniquely to e-mail. For example, using all capital letters is considered to be "yelling at" or responding aggressively to your reader. When appropriate, carefully placed capitals can provide emphasis. Using all lowercase does not follow the rules of English grammar and usage.

▶ Use the Subject line appropriately to catch the attention of the receiver. The subject line should accurately (but briefly) describe the content of the e-mail.

▶ Always proofread your e-mail before sending it. Make sure it represents you professionally.

success steps

SENDING PROFESSIONAL E-MAIL

1. Remember that you are accountable for what you write in e-mail.

2. Keep the e-mail brief, with concise information. If a more detailed explanation is needed, consider sending it as an attachment.

3. Send only necessary e-mail. Sending jokes and trivial communications may cause recipients to ignore your e-mail.

4. Know your organization's e-mail policy. There may be consequences for sending e-mail that is not job related.

5. Remember that e-mail is not confidential and that records are available.

6. Use traditional grammar and spelling rules.

7. Observe netiquette.

8. Use the subject line to communicate what the e-mail is about.

9. Maintain professionalism. Do not write an e-mail when you are angry or to discipline someone.

10. Proofread your e-mail before sending.

REFLECTION QUESTION

- When writing professional e-mail, how might you change your writing style from that used for social e-mails?

apply it

Style Research

GOAL: To develop a clearer understanding regarding requirements stated in the MLA and APA handbooks.

STEP 1: Research the requirements set forth by the MLA and APA style books (the *Modern Language Association Handbook* and the *Publication Manual of the American Psychological Association*).

STEP 2: Compare and contrast the style suggestions and write a brief explanation of both styles.

STEP 3: Prepare to share your thoughts with the class.

STEP 4: Consider placing this worksheet in your Learning Portfolio.

CHAPTER SUMMARY

This chapter introduced elements of communication that are important to success in school and in the workplace. Listening, nonverbal gestures, questioning, and assertive communication were emphasized as significant elements of oral communication. Professional presentation, quality, and clarity were emphasized as aspects of effective written communication. Considerations specific to electronic communications and presentations were also reviewed.

Effective communication is a skill that is foundational to many other skills and to success in school and the workplace. Your development of all of the skills addressed in *100% Student Success* can be enhanced by effective communication abilities. You are encouraged to consider how developing your communication skills can support all of your academic and professional endeavors.

POINTS TO KEEP IN MIND

In this chapter, the following main points were discussed in detail:

- Communication has two participating parties: the sender and the receiver.
- Lack of attention and closed-minded thinking can reduce the effectiveness of listening.
- By listening, hearing, and interpreting body language, the receiver may more accurately understand what the sender is communicating verbally and nonverbally.
- Two general types of questions are open ended and closed.
- Respect for individual diversity is essential for effective communication.
- Learning how to communicate effectively in the classroom offers good practice for the professional communication skills required for employment.
- In-class group activities are successful only if all team members participate.
- Listening well facilitates learning from in-class questions.
- Giving attention to professionalism, organization, and quality of the material makes written communication more effective.
- Plagiarism is using another person's ideas or words without giving the author appropriate credit.
- The purpose of using presentation tools is to enhance the material and visually convey the message.

LEARNING OBJECTIVES REVISITED

Review the learning objectives for this chapter and rate your level of achievement for each objective using the rating scale provided. For each objective on which you do not rate yourself as a 3, outline a plan of action that you will take to fully achieve the objective. Include a time frame for this plan.

1 = did not successfully achieve objective

2 = understand what is needed, but need more study or practice

3 = achieved learning objective thoroughly

	1	2	3
Explain the importance of good listening.	☐	☐	☐
List reasons for why listening can be difficult.	☐	☐	☐
Explain ways to avoid plagiarism.	☐	☐	☐
Discuss considerations that should be made when sending an e-mail.	☐	☐	☐

	1	2	3
Describe how professionalism is demonstrated in written communication.	☐	☐	☐
Explain the purpose of utilizing open-ended questions versus closed questions.	☐	☐	☐
Recognize the importance of body language.	☐	☐	☐
Explain the importance of effective verbal communication.	☐	☐	☐
Demonstrate the ability to create a visual presentation.	☐	☐	☐
Demonstrate the ability to conduct professional correspondence.	☐	☐	☐

Steps to Achieve Unmet Objectives

Steps	Due Date
1. ______________________________	__________
2. ______________________________	__________
3. ______________________________	__________
4. ______________________________	__________

SUGGESTED ITEMS FOR LEARNING PORTFOLIO

▶ Reflection and Critical Thinking Questions: Include your written responses to these questions. Use them to review your development over time.

▶ Presentation Tool Analysis

▶ Style Research

REFERENCES

Dowling, E. (n.d.). 10 tips for effective e-mail. Mind Tools. Retrieved February 10, 2005, from http://www.mindtools.com/email.html

Gordon, D. E. (n.d.). Five keys to acquiring better verbal communication skills. CollegeRecruiter.com. Retrieved February 10, 2005, from http://www.collegerecruiter.com/pages/articles/article146.htm

Hakim, C. (2005). Essentials of effective PowerPoint presentations— PowerPoint presentations that work. Retrieved May 24, 2006, from http://www.unleash.com/chakim/essentials/index.asp

Kaplan, R. M. (2004). You can improve your written communication skills. Retrieved February 20, 2005, from http://www.job-resources.com/0103tip.htm

CHAPTER OUTLINE

Communication: An Overview

Getting along with Others

Customer Service

Business Writing

5 Business Communication

LEARNING OBJECTIVES

By the end of this chapter, you will achieve the following objectives:

- Define *communication* and explain when communication is considered successful.
- Discuss the characteristics of effective verbal communication.
- Describe the characteristics of effective listening.
- Explain methods to strengthen communication between employers and employees.
- Discuss how to establish and maintain positive relationships in the workplace.
- Explain how conflict can be resolved.
- Discuss how employee satisfaction is reflected in customer satisfaction.
- Compare and contrast effective and ineffective customer service.
- List and explain the steps of responding appropriately to criticism.
- List and explain the "Seven Cs" of effective business writing.
- Discuss the general format of a business letter.
- Explain the basic format of a memo.
- Discuss considerations to be made when using e-mail and composing e-mail in the workplace.

TOPIC SCENARIO

Jean started her new job three months ago and has had difficulty getting along with one of her coworkers ever since. Jean doesn't feel as though the problem is a result of anything specific that the coworker is doing, but rather that the trouble is the coworker's personality, which is generally irritating to her. Jean is unsure what to do, but she believes her work is being affected by this personality clash.

Based on this scenario, answer the following questions:

- Should Jean just learn to live with the situation or should she confront the coworker?

- If Jean is to confront the coworker, what should the expected outcome be?

- How should Jean confront the coworker if the problem is personality based?

- Can Jean change in order to make the situation more acceptable?

- Should Jean involve her manager?

COMMUNICATION: AN OVERVIEW

Verbal and nonverbal communication in the workplace occurs in many situations, including one-on-one discussions, group meetings, conference calls, e-mails, and written correspondence. Your satisfaction at work relies to a great extent on your ability to use excellent communication skills. Effective communication makes interactions with others more satisfying and often increases productivity.

According to Accel-Team (2005a, p. 2), "Communication is a two-way process in which people transmit (send) and receive ideas, information, opinions, or emotions. In the world of business, the aim should be to develop communication patterns between individuals and groups that are meaningful, direct, open, and honest." Given the importance of effective communication, how best can it be accomplished?

Communication is greatly impacted by an individual's verbal and nonverbal messages and is successful only if all parties involved clearly understand the message that has been conveyed. Waughfield (2002) states that effective communication results under the following conditions:

- The sender uses clear and well-understood words to convey the message.

The ability to communicate clearly and effectively with a variety of people is critical to workplace success.

▶ The receiver hears the message that the sender intends.

▶ Verbal and nonverbal messages are consistent with each other.

▶ The receiver is receptive to the message.

FACTORS OF EFFECTIVE COMMUNICATION

Listening is a critical factor to effective communication. The following are guidelines to more effective listening are defined by Accel-Team (2005b, p. 2):

▶ Make eye contact with the speaker.

▶ Question the speaker to clarify meanings.

▶ Show concern about the speaker's feelings.

▶ Occasionally repeat what you are hearing to confirm your understanding.

▶ Do not rush the speaker.

▶ Maintain poise and emotional control.

▶ Respond with a nod, smile, or frown.

▶ Pay close attention.

▶ Do not interrupt.

▶ Stay on the subject until the speaker finishes his or her thoughts.

Communication at work involves a variety of individuals, including coworkers, supervisors, and customers. The success of any business can be measured by employee and customer satisfaction, which is greatly influenced by positive interactions. The impact of satisfying communication between employer and employee is likely to be reflected in successful relationships with customers.

Successful employers work diligently to ensure that communication is effective with their employees. McNamara (1999) suggests using the following devices to build strong internal communication:

▶ Written status reports on current projects submitted from all employees to supervisors

▶ Monthly employee meetings

▶ Weekly or biweekly department meetings

▶ Monthly one-on-one meetings between supervisor and employees

Other forums may be appropriate and effective depending on your individual work setting. For example, individual work teams often hold regular meetings to track projects and communicate progress.

5

Getting along with others makes the workplace more pleasant and contributes to productivity.

GETTING ALONG WITH OTHERS

Getting along with others is important to your overall career success. Improving your daily interactions with others at work contributes to productive professional relationships and requires consistent use of effective communication skills. Observing the simple guidelines listed below supports strong relationships in the workplace.

- **Be a positive person.** Negative or moody people eventually drain the office environment of positive emotional energy.

- **Observe and listen to others.** By doing so, you can learn a lot about your supervisor's and your coworkers' likes and dislikes. Draw on this knowledge to establish positive relationships.

- **Avoid unprofessional behavior.** For example, silliness and poor manners may irritate coworkers and distract them from the task at hand. Be receptive to feedback from others and alter your behavior as needed.

- **Learn to avoid "pushing people's buttons."** Be aware of issues and behaviors to which your coworkers are sensitive. Consciously avoid subjects and actions that annoy or anger colleagues.

- **Avoid rushing to react to others' actions or words.** Think through your responses logically rather than reacting emotionally. Too often people are quick to anger and to pass judgment. Hastily expressing emotions eventually works against you.

- **Have a genuine and caring attitude.** Develop a genuine concern for your coworkers' well-being. Approach colleagues with a helpful and collaborative attitude. For example, offer assistance if it appears to be needed.

- **Help others feel good about themselves.** Recognize your colleagues' accomplishments. Always give credit to the deserving individual. Offer genuine words of encouragement and congratulations for a job well done.

success steps

BUILDING STRONG WORKPLACE RELATIONSHIPS

- Be a positive person.
- Observe and listen to others.
- Avoid unprofessional behavior.

- Learn to avoid "pushing people's buttons."
- Avoid rushing to react to other's actions or words.
- Have a genuine and caring attitude.
- Help others feel good about themselves.

CONFLICT RESOLUTION

Conflict in the workplace occurs for a variety of reasons and can adversely affect productivity if it is not resolved. Conflict is often due to a simple misunderstanding that can be quickly resolved through discussion. Conflicts that occur due to personality differences, however, can be more challenging to deal with.

There are a variety of ways that an employee can help to de-escalate a conflict. The following are suggestions for conflict de-escalation are offered by Anderson (2004):

Step 1. Consider what you are really trying to accomplish: What needs are you trying to fulfill? How important is making your point in the greater scheme of things? Is it worth damaging the working relationship you have established with the individual?

Step 2. Avoid considering the other individual as an adversary. Resentment creates more conflict.

Step 3. Remain objective. Do not let strong emotions cloud your judgment.

Step 4. Demonstrate effective listening skills and your ability to put your needs aside to hear what others are saying. Avoid interrupting others.

Step 5. Repeat to the other speaker what he or she has said to confirm that you are hearing and understanding his or her position.

Step 6. Avoid overpowering the situation. If you do, you are likely to escalate the negative conditions and antagonize the other party.

Step 7. Strive to be fair to all parties involved when proposing solutions and remain flexible to consider a variety of solutions.

Step 8. Recruit an uninvolved person as a mediator if necessary. A fair and neutral party may be helpful in resolving the conflict.

REFLECTION QUESTIONS

- What feedback have you received regarding your communication abilities?
- In what areas could you improve those abilities?

? CRITICAL THINKING QUESTION

3–1. Can an individual get to a point where he or she is proficient as a communicator or is there always room for improvement? Explain your answer.

CONFLICT RESOLUTION STEPS

1. Know what you are trying to accomplish by resolving the conflict.
2. Maintain a positive relationship throughout the resolution process.
3. Remain objective and control emotional responses.
4. Use effective listening skills and avoid interrupting.
5. Repeat what you hear to confirm understanding.
6. Avoid attempting to overpower the situation.
7. Strive for fairness and compromise.
8. Use mediation as necessary.

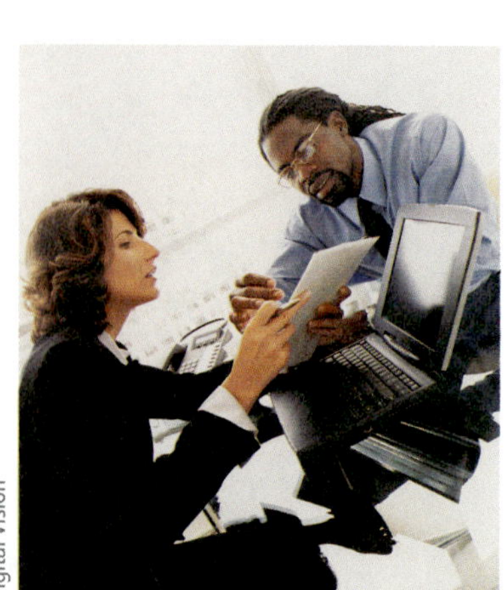

©Digital Vision

Being able to use corrective feedback to problem solve and set goals is an important part of your professional development and long-term success.

HANDLING CORRECTIVE FEEDBACK

How you deal with corrective feedback (commonly known as constructive criticism) makes a significant statement regarding your desire to grow personally and professionally. While some individuals are threatened by criticism regardless of its intention, others learn how to accept criticism and to select the comments that are important to incorporate into their development. Learning how to hear corrective feedback and respond to it constructively is a useful skill. Study the following process for responding to criticism (Anderson, n.d.):

Step 1. Acknowledge the feedback verbally or nonverbally. For example, a nod of the head or saying, "Yes, I remember that situation" lets the speaker know that you are listening to what he or she is saying.

Step 2. Control your emotions. Do not assume that the individual giving the criticism has bad intentions. People are sometimes well intentioned even though their approach is not the best. Responding with anger prevents you from hearing something that may be important for your own growth and limits or eliminates your opportunity to present your perspective. If feelings of anger become apparent on the part of either party, pause or take a brief "timeout" to allow emotions to cool.

Step 3. Clarify the feedback and encourage discussion by requesting additional information. Really listen during this time. Do not allow personalities or feelings to get in the way of an important message. Focus on what you can learn from the feedback. Be aware of the speaker's feelings and motives for giving the feedback. By listening, you can learn a lot about the real purpose of the encounter.

Step 4. Find something on which you and speaker agree and call attention to this point of agreement. Use it as a starting point for discussion. Doing so often helps the person feel as if you are hearing the message that he or she is sending and de-escalates any emotions that have become charged during the interaction.

Step 5. Provide your perspective respectfully and tactfully. State what you agree with in the other party's feedback and offer a plan for what you will do in response to the criticism. It is important to apologize if an apology is appropriate. Then, state your perspective, identifying it as your viewpoint and pointing out which elements of the criticism you disagree with. Responding assertively and responsibly gains respect from the person giving the criticism.

Step 6. Incorporate the feedback into daily activities. Ultimately, what feedback you accept is your choice. You may not agree with the criticism; however, it is still your responsibility to apply it to performing according to the expectations of your position. Consider how you can use corrective feedback as a tool for your growth and development.

success steps

ACCEPTING CORRECTIVE FEEDBACK

1. Acknowledge that you have heard the feedback by nodding or verbally responding to it.

2. Control your emotions.

3. Ask for additional information. Remain focused on the issue. Avoid finding fault with an individual or personality.

4. Find common ground on which you and the other person agree. Use that point of agreement as a basis for discussion.

5. Provide your perspective of the situation respectfully and tactfully.

6. Incorporate the feedback into your daily activities.

REFLECTION QUESTIONS

- How do you handle criticism?
- When someone criticizes you, what is your natural reaction?
- How can you improve how you handle criticism?

? CRITICAL THINKING QUESTION

5–2. What is your reaction to the following statement: "If you have nothing good to say, don't say anything"?

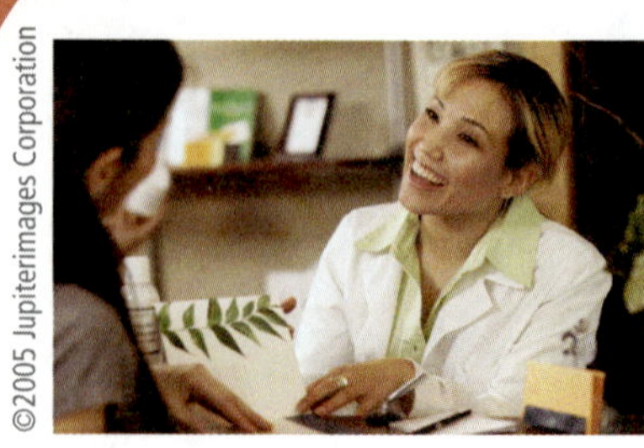

Having a professional demeanor means that you are courteous, you are honest yet tactful with customers, and you put customers' interests first.

CUSTOMER SERVICE

As stated earlier, the success of any business is reflected in employee and customer satisfaction. Employee satisfaction is achieved when each employee believes that he or she is respected and appreciated by the employer. In turn, employers indicate their satisfaction with an employee's performance through formal and informal communication methods. Employers who openly communicate employees' importance to the organization discover that employees feel positively about the company and are likely to pass on those feelings to the company's customers.

"Customer service is key to any successful business that deals with the public or even in a business-to-business environment" (Stovall, 2002, p. 1). Regardless of whether the communication with the customer is by phone, in person, or in writing, good customer service skills are essential to any company's success. When customers feel respected and appreciated by a business, they are loyal to that business, which, in turn, establishes repeat business from customers. A company's value is measured both by the quality of its products and by the way it treats each customer.

A large part of demonstrating respect for customers is interacting with them in a professional manner, which is conveyed by your appearance, demeanor, and behavior. General guidelines for professional dress stipulate clean, neat clothing that follows the stipulations of your company's dress code. For example, if you work in a setting where casual dress is acceptable, your clothing can be casual, but it should be tidy and well cared for. You, like your clothing, must also be clean and well groomed.

Having a professional demeanor means that you are courteous and honest yet tactful with customers, and you put their interests first. Professional demeanor when dealing with customers is demonstrated through the behaviors noted in the following list (Loeffler, 2003):

- **Make a good first impression.** Whether the communication is by phone, in person, or in writing, demonstrate professionalism and courtesy through your choice of words. For example, use a formal title, such as Ms. Smith or Dr. Jones. Do not use first names unless instructed to do so by your company or the customer. Use common courtesies, such as saying "please" and "thank you." Be respectful of the caller's time by avoiding or minimizing wait times. Offer as much information as you can within appropriate guidelines and offer to research information that you do not have immediately available. Follow up with the caller.

- **Let customers know they are valuable during your exchanges.** Customers want to know they are more than just a number and that they are individually valued. Learn what the customer needs and wants and make every effort to provide effective information and service. Meet customers' needs creatively. Assist customers in problem solving and offer suggestions and ideas. You are the expert in your field, and customers will appreciate your efforts to apply your knowledge to their interests.

- **Have a professional appearance.** Customers are drawn to individuals who present themselves as a professional in both attire and in conduct. Look and act professional in all of your exchanges.

- **Enjoy your customers.** Smile and demonstrate a genuine interest in people. Be professional and sincere, but be friendly and have fun. Use your customers' cues and responses to help you determine an appropriate level of interaction.

- **Discover customers' needs by utilizing good listening skills.** Use effective listening skills, such as clarifying, asking questions, and focusing on the speaker, to understand customers' needs. Applying good listening skills is a critical component of good customer service.

- **Develop a trusting relationship over time.** Customers return to those with whom they have developed a rapport. Build relationships with customers by being sincere and honest (even if this means not getting the sale this time), following through on what you say you will do, and using your expertise to help customers solve problems and meet their needs.

- **Acknowledge a customer's presence through use of good eye contact and a smile.** If you cannot leave what you are doing when a customer arrives, let the customer know you will be with him or her as soon as possible. Never ignore a customer, regardless of how busy you are.

- **Treat customers with respect.** Even if you are angry or frustrated about a situation, never express those feelings to a customer.

- **Avoid arguing with a customer, even if the customer is wrong.** Offer reasonable options within your limitations with an explanation, as appropriate. Arguing only escalates the situation. Avoid eating, drinking, or chewing gum in front of customers: If you wish to freshen your breath, use a breath mint.

- **Avoid making excuses or using negative phrases when working with customers.** Comments such as "It's not my job" and "I can't help you with that" can offend customers and be detrimental to business. If you are engaged in a task that cannot be interrupted, acknowledge the customer's presence and politely let the customer know you will be with him or her as soon as possible.

▶ **Ask questions to learn customers' needs.** If you do not know the answer to a customer's question or cannot resolve a problem, say so and let the customer know that you will get back to him or her as quickly as possible. Be sure to follow through, even if that requires a phone call at a later time.

▶ **Keep personal or professional frustrations to yourself.** Address these concerns with the appropriate individuals. Customers and clients expect your focus to be on them and their needs.

▶ **Do not waste customers' time.** Avoid small talk unless the customer indicates a desire for it. Most customers would rather receive quick and efficient service than chat.

▶ **Be aware of your demeanor and unspoken messages.** Avoid arrogance, a condescending attitude, rudeness, and curtness. Be aware of how you are perceived by others and strive to improve behaviors that are interpreted as negative traits.

▶ **Use professional telephone etiquette.** When placing a call, identify yourself and explain your reason for calling. Respect the recipient's time by asking whether this or another time would be better to talk. When taking an incoming call, answer using company protocol. (Follow the same guidelines for interacting in person with customers.) If you need to put a customer on hold, ask whether doing so is acceptable or offer the customer the option to call back.

success steps

PRACTICING PROFESSIONAL DEMEANOR

1. Make a good first impression.
2. Treat customers with value during your exchanges.
3. Have a professional appearance.
4. Enjoy your customers.
5. Use good listening skills to discover the customer's needs.
6. Develop a trusting relationship with customers over time.
7. Acknowledge a customer's presence with good eye contact and a smile.
8. Treat customers with respect.
9. Avoid arguing with a customer, even if the customer is wrong.
10. Avoid eating, drinking, or chewing gum in front of customers.

> **11.** Avoid making excuses or using negative phrases when working with customers.
>
> **12.** Ask questions to learn the customer's needs.
>
> **13.** Keep personal or professional frustrations to yourself.
>
> **14.** Do not waste customers' time.
>
> **15.** Be aware of your demeanor and unspoken messages.
>
> **16.** Use professional telephone etiquette.

BUSINESS WRITING

Effective business communication encompasses both the spoken and the written word. Those who develop the skills required to compose high-quality written business communications are more efficient and productive. Business letters, memos, and e-mails are examples of written communication that occurs in the workplace.

BUSINESS LETTERS

Business writing is effective when individuals pay attention to and incorporate the following concepts into their writing: **C**lear, **C**oncise, **C**orrect, **C**ourteous, **C**onversational, **C**onvincing, and **C**omplete, also known as "The Seven Cs of Business Letter Writing" (*Business Letter Writing,* 2003a, p. 1). In business situations, your reader's time is precious. So your correspondence must be succinct and accurate to avoid creating confusion, wasting the reader's time, or failing to achieve its goal. To help eliminate confusion, use short sentences and simple words, and avoid using wordy phrases, jargon, technical terms and abbreviations, and abstract words and phrases (*Business Letter Writing,* 2003b). Use courteous language to convey professionalism and a caring, thoughtful attitude. Carefully select your words to effectively convey important points to the reader. The information you supply must be complete enough for the reader to draw correct conclusions from the message, but be free of unnecessary details that may cause confusion.

When writing, it is critical to consider who your reader(s) is (are). "If you keep your readers in mind when you write, it will help you use the right tone, appropriate language and include the right amount of detail. If you imagine yourself in your reader's position, you're more likely to write a good letter" (*Business Letter Writing,* 2003c, p. 1). By asking the following questions based on suggestions from the book *Business Letter Writing,* you will be better equipped to meet the needs and expectations of your audience.

- What are the backgrounds of my readers?
- What is their level of expertise on this subject?
- What additional information do they need to know?
- What information might be interesting for them to know?
- Will I need to use technical terms? If so, which ones will I need to define?
- What are the readers' biases and prejudices? How should I take those into consideration?
- What are the audiences' concerns? How should I take these into consideration?
- Will I need to persuade the audience to a point of view? How can I accomplish this?
- What reactions can I anticipate?

Professionalism is conveyed not only through your choice of words, but also through your letter's appearance. Study the following suggestions for formatting a business letter (Colorado State University, 1997–2005):

- The sender's contact information should be provided on the company's letterhead. The information should include the sender's name, address, and phone number. Cell phone numbers and fax numbers may also be provided.
- Include the recipient's company's name, reader's name and title, and address. Courtesy titles should be used when appropriate. For example, *Dr. Russell Smith.*
- If the reader's name is unknown, an attention line should be used. For example, *Attention: Director of Lab Department.*
- A subject line that indicates the content of the letter may be used. For example, *Subject: Time Sheets.*
- A salutation should always be used in a business letter. The typical salutation is "Dear" followed by the reader's courtesy title and last name. For example, *Dear Dr. Smith.*
- Business letters are typically single spaced. A general rule for length is three paragraphs: an introductory paragraph, a paragraph that contains the main theme and points of the letter, and a concluding paragraph.
- *Sincerely, cordially,* and *yours truly* are appropriate closes for a business letter. The first word of the close is capitalized (others are not) and followed by a comma. For example, *Yours truly,*

▶ The writer of the letter should type his or her name and title four lines after the complimentary close. Above the typed name the writer should sign his or her name.

▶ End notations are needed if someone else has typed the letter. The end notation identifies this individual by his or her initials. For example, if Kathy Priest wrote the letter but Jan Jones typed it, the following end notations would be utilized: *KP/jj*. The end notation *Enclosure* indicates if the envelope contains any documents in addition to the letter. The word *enclosure* should be used, followed by a number indicating how many documents are present. Typically, the names of the enclosures are noted in the body of the letter. For example, *The agenda for Tuesday's meeting and the proposal for the new training program are enclosed for your review* would be included in the letter body. The end notation would appear as *Enclosure (2)*.

▶ If a copy of the letter is being sent to other readers, this is indicated in the copy line. For example, *cc: John Smith, Judith Tanker.*

Spacing requirements are standard and are indicated in the letter example presented in Figure 5–1.

MEMOS

Business memos can be simple or complex, depending on the information they convey. Typically, the purpose of a memo is to inform readers about new information, such as policy changes, price increases, and so on, or to request the reader to take an action, such as attending a meeting (Purdue University Online Writing Lab, 1995–2004). Memos generally are shorter in length than business letters. To facilitate ease of reading, consider using bullet lists when appropriate (Purdue University Online Writing Lab, 1995–2004).

A memo typically opens with the following information:

▶ TO: (recipients' names and job titles)

▶ FROM: (your name and job title)

▶ DATE: (current date)

▶ SUBJECT: (what the memo is about)

The body of the memo can include one paragraph or more, depending on the complexity of the information. The first section of the memo should clearly state its purpose by explaining the issue at hand and the related task or assignment. More in-depth information may be included as needed, such as a discussion segment that provides details supporting the stated ideas, or a summary that emphasizes the memo's main points. The second section of

Regency Center
248 Samuel Avenue
Santa Barbara, CA 92418
Telephone: 928-467-0298
Fax: 928-461-0137

May 24, 2005

Nathan Right
Right Corporation
2834 E. Smith Road
Franktown, MA 21345

Dear Mr. Right:

Thank you for your time. It was a pleasure speaking with you today. Enclosed are some promotional materials that will help further acquaint you with our facilities and services.

In regards to your upcoming company event, we are looking forward to the opportunity to provide you with the quality of service that Regency Center offers to their customers.

Once you have reviewed the enclosed information, we look forward to speaking with you further regarding how we might be of service.

Thank you for choosing the Regency Center.

Sincerely,

Sara Duncun
Promotions Manager, Regency Center
928-467-0297
sduncan@pm.regencycenter.com

Enclosure (3)

FIGURE 5–1.   A business letter requires professional wording and attention to details such as spacing and appearance. Figure 5–1 is an example of a professionally written letter that illustrates the appropriate spacing.

the memo should clearly state what steps the reader is to take. In addition, explain the benefits of the action and provide information about any support that is available to the reader to help him or her achieve the stated goals. For lengthier assignments or in situations where more extensive information is required, an attachment (similar to an attachment to a business letter) may be used. If an attachment is provided, include the following notation at the end of the memo: *Attached: [Name of the attachment]* (Purdue University Online Writing Lab, 1995–2004).

As with a business letter, make sure to adhere to the "Seven Cs." An example of a memo can be found in Figure 5-2.

MEMORANDUM

TO: Brent Lloyd

COPIES TO: Jon Dwight, Chris Marshall

FROM: Jane Lucy (her signed initials would go next to her name)

DATE: May 24, 2006

SUBJECT: New Construction

Brent, we have just been informed that your department will be under new construction starting on June 1, 2005 and will last for about 4 days.

We are sorry for the inconvenience but once the new construction is completed the new equipment for your department will be installed.

Please inform your staff and address any arrangements that must be made to accommodate your staff during this time. If any assistance is needed to make these arrangements, please let me know.

FIGURE 5–2. Although less formal than a business letter, a business memo also must meet certain criteria. Figure 5–2 illustrates the appropriate format for a business memo.

E-MAILS

E-mail has significantly impacted workplace communication among employees, among businesses, and between businesses and their customers. Today, fewer business letters and memos are created, while the use of e-mail continues to increase, and the appropriate use of e-mail can save time and expense. As with the traditional forms of written business communication, however, e-mail has its own set of standards. Study the following suggestions for using e-mail appropriately and effectively (Brody, 2005):

- **Keep e-mails brief, concise, and to the point.** Strive to keep the entire message visible in the window that appears when you click the *Compose new message* button (or whatever "new message" button your e-mail software uses). If it is necessary to provide lengthy support information, include it as an attachment. Be aware that large attachments take longer to download and take up more space on the recipient's hard drive. Faxing lengthy documents is an alternative to sending them as e-mail attachments.

- **Address one topic per message.** Doing so allows recipients to focus on a single issue as well as to file e-mails according to topic. Considering the amount of information received daily via e-mail, including one topic per message maximizes the effectiveness of your e-mail.

- **Avoid being antagonistic or critical.** Online, this behavior is known as "flaming." Constructive criticism or corrective comments are more appropriately done in person. Do not use words presented in all capital letters, as this is the e-mail equivalent of shouting.

- **Ensure that all e-mails you send have value for the recipient.** If messages lack value, they may be considered "spam" and deleted. When you send jokes and similar content, you stand the risk of losing credibility with professional colleagues and of violating your company's computer use policy. Use judgment regarding what you send.

- **Be aware that there is no such thing as a private e-mail.** Information technology (IT) staff can use software and online services to access messages even after they have been deleted.

- **Check spelling and punctuation for accuracy.** E-mail correspondence is sometimes considered to be less formal than hard-copy correspondence, but e-mail messages should follow the same rules

> ### *success steps*
>
> **COMPOSING EFFECTIVE E-MAILS**
>
> 1. Keep e-mails brief, concise, and to the point.
> 2. Address one topic per e-mail.
> 3. Avoid being antagonistic or critical.
> 4. Ensure that all e-mails you send have value for the recipient.
> 5. Be aware that there is no such as a private e-mail.
> 6. Check spelling and punctuation for accuracy.
> 7. Include a meaningful subject line.
> 8. Respond to e-mails within 24 hours.
> 9. Communicate your unavailability.

REFLECTION QUESTIONS

- What is the quality of your writing skills? What areas of writing do you find challenging?
- Do you ever find receiving e-mails annoying? If so, what about it is annoying? How can you make sure your e-mails do not irritate or annoy others?

? CRITICAL THINKING QUESTION

5–3. How can miscommunications occur with e-mail and how can these miscommunications be avoided?

of clarity and correctness as other correspondence. Most e-mail software has a spelling and grammar check. Use these tools if they are available, but realize that they catch only certain errors. You should carefully proofread your message before sending it, just as you would any other letter.

- **Include a meaningful subject line.** A relevant subject line that conveys the main point of the e-mail allows busy professionals to organize and prioritize their messages.

- **Respond to e-mails within 24 hours.** Doing so is considered professional and courteous. If you need more time to compose an in-depth answer or retrieve information, make this clear in your reply.

- **Communicate your unavailability.** Let people know if you will not be checking e-mail for an extended period of absence, such as during a vacation. Use the automated "out of office" reply that lets senders know that you are away and when you plan to return.

CHAPTER SUMMARY

Communication is a critical factor in professional success. This chapter introduced elements of communication that contribute to effective relationships with colleagues and customers. Listening skills were emphasized as a major factor in resolving conflict, hearing corrective feedback, and in other professional interactions.

POINTS TO KEEP IN MIND

In this chapter, several main points were discussed in detail:

- Your satisfaction at work greatly relies on your ability to use effective communication skills.
- Communicating effectively with others leads to increased employee satisfaction and productivity.
- Communication is successful only if all parties involved clearly understand the message that is being conveyed.
- Listening is a critical factor to effective communication.
- The success of any business is reflected in employee and customer satisfaction.
- The influence of satisfying interactions between employer and employee is reflected in communications with customers.
- Learning how to get along with others is important for overall career success.
- Employees can de-escalate conflict in a variety of ways.
- Regardless of whether communication with the customer is by phone, in person, or in writing, effective customer service skills must be demonstrated.
- The manner in which one deals with criticism makes a significant statement regarding one's desire to grow personally and professionally.
- Your reader's time is precious, so information must be communicated clearly, concisely, and correctly.
- When writing, it is critical to consider who your reader(s) is (are) and to adjust your tone, language, and amount of detail accordingly.
- Correct use of the various elements of a business letter, its appearance, and word choice all contribute to a professional image.

apply it

Writing a Business Letter

GOAL: *To develop a better understanding of the content of a business letter.*

STEP 1: Write a business letter utilizing the various elements discussed in this chapter.

STEP 2: Submit the first draft of the letter to the instructor to be reviewed. Have the instructor provide feedback regarding areas that can be improved and rewrite the letter for a final submission.

STEP 3: Consider placing the business letter in your Learning Portfolio.

apply it

Handling Criticism

GOAL: *To help develop a deeper understanding of how to handle criticism effectively.*

STEP 1: Divide the class into pairs. In each pair, one student should take the role of "supervisor," and the other the role of "employee."

STEP 2: Each "employee" should perform a short task that the "supervisor" will critique.

STEP 3: After the "supervisor" has critiqued the performance/task, the "employee" should respond to how he or she felt about what was said and how it was said. (The "employee" is actually critiquing the critique.) Have the "supervisor" respond to what has been shared. When the exercise is complete, the students should switch roles and repeat the exercise.

Web Research Report

GOAL: To gain further understanding of topics discussed in this chapter.

STEP 1: Conduct further research on at least one topic from this chapter.

STEP 2: Write a brief report on what Web sites you used in your research and what you learned.

STEP 3: Consider placing this report in your Learning Portfolio.

LEARNING OBJECTIVES REVISITED

Review the learning objectives for this chapter and rate your level of achievement for each objective using the rating scale provided. For each objective on which you do not rate yourself as a 3, outline a plan of action that you will take to fully achieve the objective. Include a time frame for this plan.

1 = did not successfully achieve objective

2 = understand what is needed, but need more study or practice

3 = achieved learning objective thoroughly

	1	2	3
Define *communication* and explain when communication is viewed as successful.	☐	☐	☐
Discuss what is involved in achieving effective verbal communication.	☐	☐	☐
Describe how effective listening can be achieved.	☐	☐	☐
Explain methods to increase strong internal communication between employers and employees.	☐	☐	☐
Discuss how to establish and maintain positive relationships in the workplace.	☐	☐	☐
Explain how conflict can be de-escalated.	☐	☐	☐

Discuss how employee satisfaction is reflected in customer satisfaction.	☐	☐	☐
Describe the do's and don'ts of customer service.	☐	☐	☐
List and explain the steps involved in responding to criticism.	☐	☐	☐
List and explain the Seven Cs of effective business writing.	☐	☐	☐
Discuss the general format of a business letter.	☐	☐	☐
Explain the basic format of a memo.	☐	☐	☐
Discuss issues to consider when using e-mail and composing e-mail in the workplace.	☐	☐	☐

Steps to Achieve Unmet Objectives

Steps   Due Date

1. ____   ____________

2. ____   ____________

3. ____   ____________

4. ____   ____________

SUGGESTED ITEMS FOR LEARNING PORTFOLIO

Refer to the "Developing Portfolios" section at the front of this textbook for more information on learning portfolios.

- Business Letter: This activity will give you experience writing an effective business letter.

- Web Research Report: Use this activity to explore a topic discussed in this chapter that you would like to learn more about.

- Handling Criticism: Write in your journal about your responses to this activity to help you develop your skills in using feedback effectively.

REFERENCES

Accel-Team. (2004a). Business communications: Conceptual model [electronic version]. Retrieved May 5, 2005, from http://www.accel-team.com/communications/busComms_00.html

Accel-Team. (2004b). Business communications: Why all this fuss about listening [electronic version]. Retrieved May 5, 2005, from http://www.accel-team.com/communications/busComms_02.html

Anderson, K. (n.d.). Handling criticism with honesty and grace [electronic version]. *Speaker's Platform*. Retrieved May 5, 2005, from http://www.speaking.com/articles_html/KareAnderson_622.html

Anderson, K. (2004). Resolving everyday conflicts sooner [electronic version]. Retrieved May 5, 2005, from http://www.pertinent.com/articles/communication/kareCom91.asp

Brody, M. (2005). Rules for the wired: Effective customer service in an age of electronic communication [electronic version]. *4Hoteliers: Hospitality and Travel News*. Retrieved May 5, 2005, from http://www.4hoteliers.com/4hots_fshw.php?mwi=518

Business Letter Writing. (2003a). The seven Cs of business letter writing [electronic version]. Retrieved May 6, 2005 from http://www.business-letter-writing.com/writing-a-business-letter-examples/7Cs-of-business- . . .

Business Letter Writing. (2003b). Writing your business plan in plain English [electronic version]. Retrieved May 6, 2005, from http://www.business-letter-writing.com/writing-a-business-letter-examples/writing-your-bus . . .

Business Letter Writing. (2003c). Putting your reader first [electronic version]. Retrieved May 6, 2005, from http://www.business-letter-writing.com/writing-a-business-letter-examples/putting-your-rea . . .

Colorado State University. (1997–2005). Writing@CSU: Writing guides. Introduction: business letters [electronic version]. Retrieved May 6, 2005, from http://writing.colostate.edu/references/documents/bletter

Loeffler, B. (2003–2005). Good service: A matter of "do's and don'ts" [electronic version]. Retrieved May 5, 2005, from http://www.enspiron.cc/article.asp?ID=28

McNamara, C. (1999). Free basic guide to leadership and supervision: Basics of internal communications [electronic version]. Retrieved May 5, 2005, from http://www.mapnp.org/library/mgmnt/prsnlmnt.htm

Purdue University Online Writing Lab. (1995–2004). Memo writing [electronic version]. Retrieved May 6, 2005, from http://owl.english .purdue.edu/handouts/pw/p_memo.html

Stovall, J. (2002). Customer service [electronic version]. Retrieved May 5, 2005, from http://refresher.com/!jsservice.html

Waughfield, C. G. (2002). *Mental Health Concepts* (5th ed.). Clifton Park, NY: Thomson-Delmar, a division of Thomson Learning, Inc.

CHAPTER OUTLINE

What Is Networking?

Networking Venues

Steps in the Networking Process

Other Networking Techniques

6 Networking and Self-Promotion

LEARNING OBJECTIVES

By the end of this chapter, you will achieve the following objectives:

- Define *networking* and describe what it is not.
- Describe the purposes of networking.
- Describe various networking venues and how each is best utilized.
- Practice steps of effective networking in various settings.
- Implement strategies to increase the effectiveness of networking.
- Implement additional networking techniques such as informational interviewing.

TOPIC SCENARIO

Roger McPherson has been job hunting for several months, but with few results. His frustration reached an all-time high when he heard from a career counselor that many advertised jobs are filled long before they are advertised in print or on the Internet. The career counselor told him that he needed to network and make connections in the field as a way to promote himself effectively.

Based on Roger's situation, answer the following questions:

- What did the career counselor mean by "networking" and "making connections"?
- What did the career counselor mean when he told Roger to "promote himself effectively"?
- Where are some places that Roger might begin his networking?
- What are some important points for Roger to remember as he begins networking?
- How should Roger organize his networking efforts?

WHAT IS NETWORKING?

There are many definitions and descriptions of networking. "Networking is about meeting people . . . and finding that person or persons who has an interest in your skills, background, and what you can bring to a company" (Kovar, n.d.(a)). Bguides.com (2005) states that "networking is simply building relationships . . . with the understanding that each of you represents a valuable resource with expertise to share." Essentially, networking is establishing relationships and contacts, sustained over time, that benefit both parties in the professional world. In the case of seeking job referrals and a niche in the professional workplace, networking is typically directed at establishing relationships that can lead to employment opportunities and professional growth.

Briefly, networking involves meeting people who can provide you with pertinent information and referrals and to whom you can provide the same or something comparable. Obtaining information and getting referrals may involve face-to-face meetings, telephone conversations, or e-mail correspondence (Kovar, n.d. (b)). The remainder of this chapter will focus on how to engage in successful networking.

WHAT NETWORKING IS *NOT*

Effectively describing networking may begin with an explanation of what it is not. Several sources describe common misconceptions of networking. Networking is not:

▶ Calling the people you know when you need a job (Flantzer, n.d.). You may get lucky using this approach, but results are not likely to be as effective or long term as they can be with true networking.

▶ Telling people how wonderful you are (Bjorseth, as cited in Kovar, n.d.(b)). While a part of networking does involve promoting yourself and your skills, self-promotion is directed at demonstrating how your skills can meet the needs and support goal achievement of others.

▶ Getting a referral from everyone you talk to Kovar (n.d.(b))). You can expect a certain number of rejections and/or individuals who are unable or unwilling to assist you in your networking efforts. Effective networking takes time, patience, and persistence.

▶ All about you (Kovar, n.d.(a); Flantzer, n.d.; Welch, n.d.; Kurow, 2002). Although you are likely to benefit from networking, it also involves giving support to others. Networking relationships are mutually beneficial. You must add value to your networking relationships by giving in return to people you meet during the networking process.

Professional networking results in mutually beneficial relationships in which you give and receive information that supports professional development.

WHAT NETWORKING IS

Networking is the establishment and maintenance of mutually supportive professional relationships over time. Establishing a network to belong to that provides mutually beneficial results takes time, commitment, and attention. Networking means having relationships with a variety of people who can provide information and resources to each other. Consider the following aspects of successful networking, recommended by Kovar (n.d.(b)) and others:

> **Successful networking depends on long-term relationships.** Bguides.com (2005) emphasizes that in order to successfully network, you must think beyond specific events and one-time contacts. Networking entails building relationships that are sustained and involve mutual exchange between people over time.

> **Networking occurs over a sustained time period.** It is unlikely that you will achieve a lead for employment (or other information) during a single contact or at one particular time. Patience and persistence are necessary for successful networking. Establishing the effective relationships upon which successful networking is built requires time as well as maintaining contact with the individual.

> **Successful networking requires courtesy and respect.** Courtesy and consideration are of paramount importance in professional networking. You demonstrate consideration in part by being respectful of busy schedules, offering something of value in return, demonstrating effective listening skills, and expressing appreciation.

> **Research and knowledge are critical elements of networking.** It is important to research the industry or organization in which you have interest or with which your contact is involved. Kovar (n.d.(b)) suggests the Internet as a tool for conducting effective research.

---

tips and tricks

GUIDELINES FOR SUCCESSFUL NETWORKING

- Successful networking depends on long-term relationships.
- Networking occurs over a sustained time period.
- Success in networking requires courtesy and respect.
- Research and knowledge are critical elements of networking.

THE PURPOSE OF NETWORKING

Networking can serve a variety of purposes. Although as a college student your main focus for networking is likely to be finding employment, keep in mind that the concepts of networking can be applied to a variety of situations and may serve you well at various times throughout your career. The following purposes of networking are adapted from Flantzer (n.d.):

- **Networking provides knowledge.** If you have a working knowledge of your field and its trends, you are more likely to be prepared to present yourself effectively to potential employers. Also, if corporate downsizing affects you at some time in your career, current knowledge of trends in your field will prepare you to be more aware of your options.

- **Networking provides contacts for employment.** Networking puts you in contact with individuals who may be able to hire you or refer you to a potential employer. Use your knowledge of your field to present yourself as informed and skilled. Networking provides the opportunity for you to communicate how your skills can benefit a potential employer's organization.

- **Networking establishes mutually beneficial relationships.** The networking process also introduces you to individuals who might benefit from your connections and knowledge and with whom you can establish mutually beneficial relationships. By positioning yourself in a way that allows you to help others, you set the stage for exchanging information that can benefit you and your contacts. Professional organizations are excellent resources for obtaining current industry knowledge, as well as for making professional contacts.

NETWORKING VENUES

Networking venues are typically of two types: those that exist and those that you create (American Association of Retired Persons, n.d.). Existing venues include established businesses and organizations where your skills might be needed. Networks that you create might include contacts that you make at networking or social events and that represent a wide variety of organizations.

EXISTING NETWORKS

Using an existing network means going to an event sponsored by a specific organization or conducting an informational interview with an individual at the organization. Utilizing an existing network offers a more focused approach to networking but may not present the diversity that created networks can provide. Existing networks are most useful when you are pursuing a position in a specific organization or seeking a niche in a particular field. The following are examples of existing networks:

- an existing business or organization
- an industry-specific career fair
- your field's professional organization

Networks can be created and developed from a variety of social and business settings.

CREATED NETWORKS

Created networks are those that you develop from a wide variety of sources. For example, you may attend a social event, attend a conference, and go to dinner with friends in another industry. You establish a relationship with an individual from each of these venues. You follow up appropriately and take the steps to maintain effective networking relationships (these steps will be discussed later in this chapter). By taking these steps, you have created a network. Created networks may take longer and more energy to establish than existing networks but can be richer in what they can offer because of their diversity. They are most useful for someone who wishes to explore different fields, is looking for a change, or would like to apply his or her skills in a new area. Created networks can be formed from any activity or venue where you are interacting with other people. Some of the more formal venues include:

- non-industry-specific career fairs
- professional organizations outside of your field
- networking groups and mixers
- Chamber of Commerce events

REFLECTION QUESTION

- What other networking venues can you think of? List as many as you can.

CRITICAL THINKING QUESTION

6–1. How can you learn about upcoming and organized networking events in your area?

STEPS IN THE NETWORKING PROCESS

Incorporating the elements of successful networking can be accomplished by following basic steps and organizing your endeavors around those steps. Recall the steps of the networking process as it relates specifically to the job search process. The same steps will be reviewed here and then be described in greater depth and applied in a more general manner. Consider how you can ensure that each of the elements of successful networking can be integrated into your networking plan.

Here are suggestions for successful networking from Bguides.com (2005) discussed in detail:

- **Have a networking plan.** Know what you are seeking and have a goal in mind. Clarify the information you need and steps you need to take to achieve your objective. Know the types of people who can provide you with valuable information, and seek to meet those individuals. Determine the types of settings and events where you can best achieve this. From this information, devise a plan for your networking.

- **Be aware of and prepared for networking opportunities as they present themselves (often in unexpected places).** It is important to be prepared for networking opportunities as they present themselves. You are more likely to recognize opportunities when you have prepared an effective networking plan. Based on your plan, be prepared with a personal introduction, questions that will engage the individual and encourage conversation, open-ended questions that will lead to the information you are seeking, and a closing statement that expresses appreciation for the person's time and information. You may or may not request an opportunity for follow-up.

Networking can occur in any situation, including those where you might not expect it. For example, social events and informal gatherings can present excellent networking opportunities.

▌ **Put yourself in situations where you will meet people.** Effective networking requires interaction with others. Involve yourself in activities where you are likely to meet new people. Activities can be professional or social.

▌ **Communicate effectively.** Effective communication requires effective nonverbal and verbal messages. Be aware of how others perceive your facial expressions, eye contact, general energy level (which should not be too low and yet not overwhelming), and gestures. Rely on your plan and the questions you have prepared to sound polished and professional. (Avoid sounding like a recording.) Use effective listening skills and ask pertinent, open-ended questions. Remember that both nonverbal and verbal communication can have different meanings to individuals from diverse cultures. Be sensitive to cultural preferences and perceptions.

▌ **Develop quality relationships.** The key to effective networking is the quality of relationships rather than the quantity of relationships. Keep your goals in mind so that you can foster relationships that support them. Quality relationships are based on developing a mutual understanding of individual needs and goals and providing information that supports them. Remember to add value to your relationships by giving back.

▶ **Stay organized and support individuals who assist you.** Be organized. After you meet someone, make notes regarding his or her affiliation, expertise, and interests, along with other pertinent information about your meeting. In addition to supporting your goals, you will have information about the person and may be able to offer something related to his or her interests and goals.

▶ **Follow up appropriately.** It is essential to follow up any networking activity with a handwritten thank-you note. Thank your contacts for referrals, information, and other assistance that they provide. It is also courteous to express appreciation for someone's time and effort, even if no specific referrals or leads came from the information. If you are in doubt regarding whether to send a thank-you note, it is best to err on the side of sending one. Expressing appreciation is always acceptable.

▶ **Enjoy yourself and have fun with the networking process.** Meeting people is fun and can support your current interests as well as spark new ones. You may discover new aspects of yourself or your profession. Approach networking with an open mind and spirit of adventure.

success steps

NETWORKING STEPS

1. Have a networking plan.
2. Be aware of and prepared for networking opportunities as they present themselves (often in unexpected places).
3. Put yourself in situations where you will meet people.
4. Communicate effectively.
5. Develop quality relationships.
6. Stay organized and support individuals who assist you.
7. Follow up appropriately.
8. Enjoy yourself and have fun with the networking process.

apply it

A Networking Plan

GOAL: *To establish a plan for successful networking.*

STEP 1: On a sheet of paper or in an electronic document, list the elements of preparing to network. These steps, adapted from Bguides.com (2005), include the following:

   a. your goal

   b. steps you need to take to achieve your objective

   c. information you need,

   d. types of people you need to meet

   e. types of settings and events where you might meet these people

STEP 2: From your list, and based on the resources available in your locale, determine specific networking venues, identify people who fit the types you have defined, and research information that you will need to be well prepared.

STEP 3: In preparation for actually networking, record contact information for individuals and registration information for events.

MAXIMIZING YOUR NETWORKING SUCCESS

Sustaining relationships over time requires investment of time and energy. In today's busy world, it is unreasonable to expect that someone you have met briefly will remember you. However, if you have stayed in touch and given back it may be more likely that people will think of you when they encounter someone who might be helpful to you. Consider the following suggestions for maintaining your visibility with the contacts that you make:

- **Make others feel valued.** Welch (n.d.) tells us that "people may not remember what you say or do. They will always remember how you make them feel." Pay attention to contacts' accomplishments and attributes that merit recognition. Give sincere compliments and respect for achievement and successes.

- **Demonstrate thoughtfulness.** Considerate actions can make an impression. Gestures that are done in another's best interest and without expectation for reward are typically appreciated and remembered. Zucker (n.d.) gives the example of sending someone information about a conference in his or her field with a brief note stating that you thought the person might be interested in learning about it. Another thoughtful gesture is to send an article or Internet link to someone on a topic of interest. If you have done and organized your networking notes on the contacts you have made, this should be a fairly easy task.

▶ **Stay connected.** Zucker (n.d.) emphasizes the importance of staying in touch with people on a continual basis. Sending holiday cards with an update on your activities is one way to accomplish this. Another way to keep in touch with contacts is to send an e-mail or other correspondence regarding changes you have made or other information about your professional life that your contacts might find interesting. People are flattered that you included them in your correspondence, and doing so keeps your name in front of them.

▶ **Focus on what you can offer others.** Let your contacts know what you can bring to their organization. Kurow (2002) reminds us that people are typically most interested in how you can help them. Maintain a clear picture of the contributions you can make based on your skills and talents and be able to express how these meet your contacts' needs. Use what you have learned in your research to understand your contacts' needs and be prepared to demonstrate how you can help them.

▶ **Get involved.** Being involved in a variety of organizations outside of your profession can benefit you by increasing your visibility, exposing you to a variety of new people, and showcasing your abilities (Zucker, n.d.). Consider taking prominent roles in community and other organizations of your choice.

success steps

MAXIMIZING YOUR NETWORKING SUCCESS

1. Make others feel valued.
2. Demonstrate thoughtfulness.
3. Stay connected.
4. Focus on what you can offer others.
5. Get involved.

❓ CRITICAL THINKING QUESTION

6–2. How can you begin to implement networking steps and activities to create a strong network for your job search?

apply it

Networking Preparation

GOAL: To prepare for effective networking.

STEP 1: Prepare a list of topics related to your field on which you would like information. Also, prepare a brief introduction of yourself and your goal.

STEP 2: Prepare a list of open-ended questions related to your topics that would be appropriately asked of a networking contact. If you need help with questions, conduct an Internet search using "professional networking" as your search term and look for articles that suggest effective open-ended questions.

STEP 3: Familiarize yourself with the questions you decide on so that you are comfortable and effective using them when the appropriate situation arises.

STEP 4: Practice with classmates, friends, or other individuals who will give you honest and constructive feedback.

apply it

Simulated Networking

GOAL: To practice presenting yourself effectively during a networking opportunity.

STEP 1: Set aside a time with classmates to hold a "networking event." You may set this up as part of a class activity or as an event held after school hours either on or off campus. You may find it effective to involve other students by requesting the assistance of your career services department.

STEP 2: Make appropriate arrangements according to the plans you have made.

STEP 3: Attend the event as you would any other networking event. Practice the steps outlined in this chapter and use them during the event.

STEP 4: Although this is a *simulated* activity, be aware of opportunities that can present themselves. Remember that opportunities can be found anywhere.

OTHER NETWORKING TECHNIQUES

There are other techniques that can add to your networking skills. Networking opportunities can present themselves at any time, and you will need to be prepared. Other situations may require a more formal approach. Methods that you can use in both of these circumstances are presented here.

THE ELEVATOR SPEECH

An elevator speech is a "short (15–30 second, 150-word) sound bite that succinctly and memorably introduces you" (Kurow, 2002). The name *elevator speech* is derived from the idea that you should be able to deliver your introduction and make a lasting impression in the time it takes to ride an elevator. Elevator speeches are also sometimes called "30-second commercials." You should highlight your unique qualities and their benefits in your elevator speech, and do so in an assured and conversational manner.

You can use your elevator speech anytime and anywhere you wish to introduce yourself to a potential contact and spark his or her interest. Typically, you can use your elevator speech when anyone asks you the question, "What do you do?" Elevator speeches can be used in a variety of settings from formal networking events to standing in line at the grocery store. Kurow (2002) makes the following suggestions for devising an elevator speech:

- **Consider the benefits that you can deliver.** You are more likely to evoke interest if your elevator speech clearly identifies the benefits of what you do. The advantages you can deliver are likely to capture the attention of your contact and lead to further conversation. List all your services and their benefits.

- **Create a captivating opening line based on benefits.** Your opening line should capture attention as well as raise the listener's curiosity. The listener should want to hear more. For example, a woman who sells jewelry might say, "I'm Suzanne Smith, and I help women to shine and sparkle." It is not necessary to include your title in your opening line.

- **Practice!** Your elevator speech should flow easily. Practice your speech until you come across as confident, sincere, and engaging.

---

success steps

CREATING AN ELEVATOR SPEECH

1. Consider the benefits that you can deliver.
2. Create a captivating opening line based on benefits.
3. Practice!

Having your "elevator speech" prepared and practiced will allow you to create interest in your abilities and provide opportunities for networking in many places.

apply it

Elevator Speech Preparation

GOAL: *To prepare an effective elevator speech.*

STEP 1: Individually, follow the steps for preparing an elevator speech listed in this chapter. Prepare several introductory statements that are engaging, summarize the benefits of your skills, and stimulate further interest.

STEP 2: After individuals have prepared their elevator speeches, gather in small groups and share your speeches. Share feedback and suggestions for improvement. You may find ways to combine the statements that you have prepared to make an even greater impact.

STEP 3: Practice your elevator speech with a classmate until you can deliver it smoothly and effectively.

THE INFORMATIONAL INTERVIEW

The informational interview is conducted to obtain information about a field or specific company. It is more formal than networking and chance encounters in that it is a scheduled appointment for which you must thoughtfully prepare. The Career Center at Florida State University (2004) and Crosby (2002) list the following purposes of the informational interview:

- to gain information about a career or profession
- to gain information about a specific organization
- to improve your general interviewing skills and ability to communicate with a variety of professionals
- to use as a networking tool to broaden your base of professional contacts
- to gain insight into the realities of the workplace
- to learn effective methods of preparing for a specific career
- to discover new careers and fields that may be of interest

Steps in Informational Interviewing

The steps of an informational interview are similar to preparing for networking opportunities. Research, question preparation, and courteous professional skills are all of paramount importance. Consider the following steps for preparing a productive informational interview, adapted from Crosby (2002):

- **Do your research.** As was the case with networking, effective research will provide you with a strong basis for your interviewing and will allow you to ask more effective questions and acquire more in-depth information. Consider professional organizations, instructors, and the career placement department at your school as sources for your research.

- **Select a person to interview.** Your research sources may also be able to suggest individuals to interview. Consider the following considerations when selecting a person to interview:

  - Select individuals in the field in which you are interested. Crosby points out that these individuals will know more about your field than human resource personnel do.

  - Select individuals who have approximately the same level of responsibility that you would have upon entry into the field.

- **Set up the interview.** Interviews can be arranged by telephone, letter, or e-mail, with a letter being the most common method. If you make contact with a letter or e-mail, follow up with a telephone call. Indicate in the written correspondence that you will be following up on a specific date and be sure to do so. Include the following information in your request for an informational interview:

- If making contact by telephone, ask if this is a good time to talk. If not, arrange a better time.
- Provide your name and a brief introduction.
- Give the name of the referring person or how you found the individual.
- Present your request for a meeting and a brief description of what you hope to accomplish.
- Provide information regarding the follow-up telephone call if you are writing a letter.

- **Prepare effectively.** Research the organization as thoroughly as possible. Being knowledgeable demonstrates a genuine interest and increases your credibility. Bring your current resume. A general resume may be more effective so that you can revise it based on the outcome of the informational interview. Prepare the questions that you will ask at the interview. Try to ask questions that will help you to gain an understanding of what the job is really like.

- **Dress appropriately.** Although less formal than a job interview, the informational interview requires that you present yourself professionally. Chapter 6 discusses professional dressing in depth.

- **Pay attention to time frames.** Typically, informational interviews last 20–30 minutes. As with any professional appointment, it is imperative that you arrive on time and respect the time limitations you or your interviewee have set. Effective preparation will allow you to maximize your interview time by having prepared and focused questions.

- **Write a thank-you note.** Follow up with a handwritten note expressing your appreciation for the time that the individual spent with you. The note can be brief; it might include appreciation for the time and advice you received along with a summary of the most helpful information. Send the thank-you note within a day or two of the interview.

success steps

INFORMATION INTERVIEWS

1. Do your research.
2. Select a person to interview.
3. Set up the interview.

4. Prepare effectively.
5. Dress appropriately.
6. Pay attention to time frames.
7. Write a thank-you note.

apply it

Informational Interview Preparation

GOAL: *To prepare for an effective informational interview.*

STEP 1: Prepare a list of individuals in your field whom you would like to interview. Consider those who are employed at an organization in which you are interested. Prepare a brief introduction of yourself and your goal.

STEP 2: Prepare a list of topic-related, open-ended questions that would be appropriately asked during an informational interview. Research "informational interview" on the Internet and look for examples of questions that you might use in your interview.

STEP 3: Practice your interview with a classmate, instructor, or other colleague. Ask these people to critique your performance; set goals to improve based on their feedback.

apply it

Informational Interview Practice

GOAL: *To prepare for an effective informational interview.*

STEP 1: Prepare a list of individuals in your field whom you would like to interview. Consider those who can offer information about a job in which you are truly interested.

STEP 2: Prepare a list of questions that you would like to ask each individual. Meet with a group of students who are completing this activity and share ideas for effective interviewing questions.

STEP 3: Team up as pairs and practice your informational interviewing skills. Consider making the practice as realistic as possible by dressing professionally and writing a thank-you note.

STEP 4: Throughout the process, provide constructive feedback and suggestions to your interviewing partner.

CHAPTER SUMMARY

Networking as a means of developing professional contacts was the main theme of this chapter. You learned what networking is as well as what it is not, and you explored formal and informal networking techniques. Etiquette and follow-up were stressed as important components of the networking process. Variations on networking, such as informational interviews and elevator speeches, were also emphasized.

POINTS TO KEEP IN MIND

In this chapter, several main points were discussed in detail:

- Networking is the establishment and maintenance of mutually supportive professional relationships over time.
- Networking is *not* getting a referral every time you speak to someone.
- Successful networking depends on long-term relationships and giving back to others.
- Networking can serve a variety of purposes, although as a college student your main purpose for networking is likely to be finding employment.
- Networking venues are typically of two types: those that exist and those that you create.
- It is critical to write thank-you notes and express appreciation for assistance.

LEARNING OBJECTIVES REVISITED

Review the learning objectives for this chapter and rate your level of achievement for each objective using the rating scale provided. For each objective on which you do not rate yourself as a 3, outline a plan of action that you will take to fully achieve the objective. Include a time frame for this plan.

1 = did not successfully achieve objective

2 = understand what is needed, but need more study or practice

3 = achieved learning objective thoroughly

	1	2	3
Define *networking* and describe what it is not.	☐	☐	☐
Describe the purposes of networking.	☐	☐	☐
Describe various networking venues and how each is best utilized.	☐	☐	☐
Practice steps of effective networking in various settings.	☐	☐	☐
Implement strategies to increase the effectiveness of networking.	☐	☐	☐
Implement additional networking techniques such as informational interviewing.	☐	☐	☐

Steps to Achieve Unmet Objectives

Steps   Due Date

1. _______________________________________   __________

2. _______________________________________   __________

3. _______________________________________   __________

4. _______________________________________   __________

SUGGESTED ITEMS FOR LEARNING PORTFOLIO

▶ Reflection and Critical Thinking Questions: Include your written responses to these questions. Use them to review your development over time.

▶ Networking Plan: This activity will guide you in developing skills for successful networking.

▶ Networking Preparation: Record the outcomes of this activity in your portfolio and update this resource for your networking events and activities as you develop additional questions and gather information.

▶ Networking Simulation: Keep notes from these practice sessions to help you develop your networking skills.

> ▌ Elevator Speech Preparation: Record ideas for your elevator speech. As you use them, keep notes regarding their effectiveness.

> ▌ Informational Interview Preparation: This activity is intended to prepare you for developing informational interviewing skills that will support your professional development.

> ▌ Informational Interview Practice: Keep records of your practice sessions and feedback that you receive. Make notes regarding changes that you can make to improve your performance.

REFERENCES

American Association of Retired Persons (n.d.). Networking for a job: What it is and how to do it. Retrieved April 6, 2005, from http://www.aarp.org/money/careers/findingajob/communityresources/a2004-05-10-networkingjob.html

Bguides.com. (2005). The 9 essentials of networking with people and creating more opportunity (2nd ed.). Bguides: Guides to get business done™. Richmond, VA: MaxPitch Media, Inc. Retrieved May 22, 2006, from http://www.bguides.com

The Career Center, Florida State University. (2004). Information interviews. Retrieved April 8, 2005, from http://www.career.fsu.edu/ccis/guides/infoint.html

Crosby, O. (2002, Summer). Informational interviewing: Get the inside scoop on careers [Electronic version]. *Occupational Outlook Quarterly, 46*(2). Bureau of Labor and Statistics. Retrieved April 8, 2005, from http://www.bls.gov/opub/ooq/2002/summer/art03.pdf

Flantzer, H. (n.d.). Networking for career success. Networking for Professionals: The Best in Professional Networking. Retrieved April 4, 2005, from http://www.networkingforprofessionals.com/NFCS.php

Kovar, R. (n.d.(a)). Networking—A key factor in a successful job search. Networking for Professionals: The Best in Professional Networking. Retrieved April 4, 2005, from http://www.networkingforprofessionals.com/NJS.php

Kovar, R. (n.d.(b)). People know people. Networking for Professionals: The Best in Professional Networking. Retrieved April 4, 2005, from http://www.networkingforprofessionals.com/RK.php

Kurow, D. (2002). Preparing your elevator speech. *Networking for Professionals: The Best in Professional Networking*. Retrieved April 4, 2005, from http://www.networkingforprofessionals.com/DK.php

Welch, T. (n.d.). When you connect with others you move mountains. *Networking for Professionals: The Best in Professional Networking*. Retrieved April 4, 2005, from http://www.networkingforprofessionals.com/MM.php

Zucker, R. (n.d.). Staying networked. *Networking for Professionals: The Best in Professional Networking*. Retrieved April 4, 2005, from http://www.networkingforprofessionals.com/SN.php

6

CHAPTER OUTLINE

Purpose of the Resume

Types of Resumes

Resume Formats

Guidelines to Creating a Resume

Utilizing Technology to Send Resumes

Cover Letters

References and Recommendations

7 Resume and Cover Letter Development

TOPIC SCENARIO

As a college graduate, Mike Lanham has become very successful in his profession. In his newly acquired position as a manager, Mike's first task is to hire individuals to fill a number of vacant positions within his department. This will be Mike's first experience in hiring. The positions Mike must fill range from highly technical to clerical. To begin the process of hiring, Mike reviews the received resumes. In addition to the technical skills and abilities that are listed, Mike also pays close attention to the appearance of the resume. From the appearance Mike believes he can more easily identify organized individuals.

Based on this short description of Mike's task, answer the following questions:

- How can a resume indicate if an individual is organized, detailed, and professional?
- How much weight should the appearance of a resume carry in the selection process?
- Do you think Mike is being unfair to applicants who do not exhibit these skills through the appearance of their resumes? Should Mike consider these individuals anyway?
- If you have developed a resume, do you think your resume indicates that you are an organized, detailed, and professional individual? If so, how? If not, why not?

PURPOSE OF THE RESUME

The purpose of a resume is to demonstrate to the reader that you are qualified or have the appropriate skills for a position. The goal of submitting a resume is to lead to an interview. Because employers have many responsibilities and limited time, applicants need to understand that resumes must say a lot in a very short and concise manner. Typically, an employer will spend no more than 30 seconds reviewing a resume. Within those 30 seconds, resumes can be either thrown aside or kept for further review.

The resume should be a statement summarizing your abilities, skills, and professionalism. The words and appearance provide the employer with a first impression of the applicant.

The National Association of Colleges and Employers (n.d.) suggests the following general guidelines for preparing a resume:

- **Know your skills and abilities.** Take a self-assessment test in order to be clear on what you can offer future employers.
- **Have your information outlined prior to writing your resume.** Outlining your skills, abilities, and work experience will simplify the task of writing your resume.

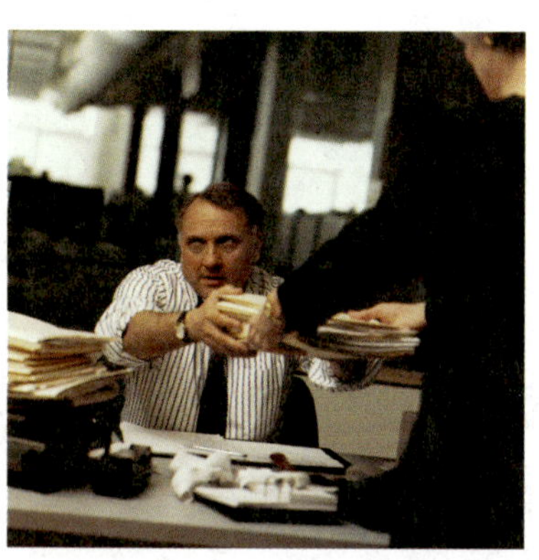

Employers may receive hundreds of resumes for one position and will spend a minimal amount of time reviewing each. Make sure your resume is professional in its appearance and conveys your skills and abilities at a glance.

▶ **Be clear on the position for which you are applying.** Review your resume prior to each submission to ensure that you are providing information relevant to the position.

▶ **Utilize appropriate tools to give your resume a professional appearance.** Paper size, paper weight, envelope size, and strength of ink are elements to consider.

▶ **Choose an appropriate resume for the job.** Be clear on what type of resume will work best for the job you are applying for.

success steps

PREPARING TO WRITE A RESUME

1. Know your skills and abilities.

2. Have your information outlined prior to writing your resume.

3. Be clear on the position for which you are applying.

4. Utilize appropriate tools to give your resume a professional appearance.

5. Choose an appropriate resume for the job.

REFLECTION QUESTIONS

- How thorough is your knowledge regarding preparation of a resume?
- What else would you like to learn about the process of resume writing?

CRITICAL THINKING QUESTION

7–1. How can you determine if a resume contains enough material, too much, or too little?

TYPES OF RESUMES

There are a variety of different resumes from which individuals can choose. These include:

▶ chronological resume

▶ functional resume

▶ combination resume

▶ curriculum vitae

The choice of resume type depends on the applicant's experience and the amount of information the employer is seeking.

THE CHRONOLOGICAL RESUME

The chronological resume lists professional experience in reverse chronological order. Chronological resumes are typically preferred by employers because they are perceived as fact based and can be easily reviewed. Due to its format, the chronological resume works best for individuals with "solid experience and a logical job history" (JobStar Central, 2006(a)). Those who have experienced career changes and lack experience may find the chronological resume more difficult to use. Figure 7–1 is an example of the chronological resume.

Resume Sample: Chronological Format

Jesse Three Crows
23 First Street ■ Albany, NY 12208
(518) 555-3647 ■ jthreecrows@aol.com

WORK EXPERIENCE:

September 2002 to Present — Assistant Bookkeeper, Achievement Office Sales/Service, Albany, NY. Aid in bookkeeping, payroll services, and tax preparation.

September 2003 to May 2004 — Internship at Goldworthy & Ames Certified Public Accountants, Albany, NY. Provided tax preparation assistance for five major clients.

September 2001 to April 2002 — Tutor, Teaching and Learning Center, The College of Saint Rose, Albany, NY. Provided tutoring assistance in Math 121, 122 and Statistics I and II to students on an individual basis.

May 2000 to September 2004 — Groundskeeper. Albany High School, Albany, NY. Maintained school grounds during summer break.

EDUCATION:

September 2000 to May 2004 — The College of Saint Rose, Albany, NY
Bachelor of Science degree in Business Administration conferred in May 2004
Accounting GPA: 3.8
Overall GPA: 3.5

COMPUTER SKILLS: — Microsoft Office and Apple applications

LEADERSHIP EXPERIENCES: — Supervisor and team leader of client audits Co-captain 1999–2000 State Championship basketball team. Two gold medals and one bronze–Team Handball–Empire State Games

REFERENCES: — Available upon request.

FIGURE 7–1.   A chronological resume lists the applicant's experience in the order in which it occurred.

THE FUNCTIONAL RESUME

The functional resume lists experience by type rather than chronologically. For example, on a functional resume management experience from several positions would be grouped in one section. Computer skills would be grouped in another. Some employers may feel that the functional resume is more difficult to review, as it is less structured than a chronological resume and it is more difficult to associate experience with a specific job.

JobStar Central (2006(b)) states that the functional resume works best for those individuals

- whose work history is varied, with no clear career link between each job
- who are new college graduates entering the workforce with little work experience
- whose past job titles do not clearly indicate the level of skills used
- who are trying to make a career change

Figure 7–2 illustrates the functional resume.

Resume Sample: Functional Format

Jesse Three Crows
23 First Street ■ Albany, NY 12208
(518) 555-3647 ■ jthreecrows@aol.com

SKILLS / ACHIEVEMENTS: Supervisor and team leader of client audits.

Excellent computer skills, including Microsoft Office and Apple applications.

Working with clients and interpreting their needs.

Working under the pressure of deadlines.

EMPLOYMENT HISTORY: Assistant Bookkeeper, Achievement Office Sales/Service, Albany, NY. 2002 to present.

Intern, Goldworthy & Ames Certified Public Accountants, Albany, NY. 2003 to 2004.

Tutor, Teaching and Learning Center, The College of Saint Rose, Albany, NY. 2001 to 2002.

Groundskeeper, Albany High School, Albany, NY. 2000 to 2004.

EDUCATION: Bachelor of Science degree, Business Administration, The College of Saint Rose, Albany, NY, May 2004.

RELEVANT COURSES: Financial Accounting, Behavioral Science in Business, Urban Economics, Managerial Economics, Financial Information Systems, Taxation, Strategic Marketing Planning, Investment Theory, New Business Ventures and the Entrepreneur, Performance and Financial Auditing.

REFERENCES: Available upon request.

FIGURE 7–2. A functional resume presents the applicant's experience by type.

COMBINATION RESUMES

A combination resume blends features of both chronological and functional resumes. Figure 7–3 is an example of a combination resume.

Resume Sample: Combination Format

Jesse Three Crows
23 First Street ■ Albany, NY 12208
(518) 555-3647 ■ jthreecrows@aol.com

SKILLS / ACHIEVEMENTS:

Supervisor and team leader of client audits.

Excellent computer skills, including Microsoft Office and Apple applications.

Working with clients and interpreting their needs.

Working under the pressure of deadlines.

WORK EXPERIENCE:

September 2002 to Present — Assistant Bookkeeper, Achievement Office Sales/Service, Albany, NY. Aid in bookkeeping, payroll services, and tax preparation.

September 2003 to May 2004 — Internship at Goldworthy & Ames Certified Public Accountants, Albany, NY. Provided tax preparation assistance for five major clients.

September 2001 to April 2002 — Tutor, Teaching and Learning Center, The College of Saint Rose, Albany, NY. Provided tutoring assistance in Math 121, 122 and Statistics I and II to students on an individual basis.

May 2000 to September 2004 — Groundskeeper. Albany High School, Albany, NY. Maintained school grounds during summer break.

EDUCATION:

September 2000 to May 2004 — The College of Saint Rose, Albany, NY
Bachelor of Science degree in Business Administration conferred in May 2004
Accounting GPA: 3.8
Overall GPA: 3.5

REFERENCES:

Available upon request.

FIGURE 7–3.   A combination resume uses features of both the chronological and functional resumes.

THE CURRICULUM VITAE

Depending on the profession, the curriculum vitae may be most appropriate. The curriculum vitae (CV) is a detailed description of all academic and professional pursuits, including educational endeavors, professional positions and their related duties, publications, presentations given and attended, volunteer work, organizational memberships and positions held, and honors and recognition that have been received. While the chronological or functional resume is no more than one or two pages, a curriculum vitae can be 15–20 pages. The CV is most commonly used in academic and research settings. The detail of a CV makes it appropriate mainly for individuals who have extensive experience and credentials.

RESUME FORMATS

Resume formats will depend on your field and the requirements of the employer. Consider the following formats.

ELECTRONIC RESUMES

An electronic resume is intended to be delivered via e-mail or through an online application form. The electronic resume has no text formatting, making it scannable, or able to be read by any e-mail or resume tracking program. For example, using all capital letters in a standard font such as Times or Helvetica for headings eliminates formatting that might be specific to your word processing program.

The following guidelines to facilitate electronic processing of a resume are suggested by Seneca College of Applied Arts and Technology Career Services (2001) and The Santa Clara University Career Center (n.d.):

- Use plain fonts, such as Arial, Verdana, Helvetica, or Courier.
- Do not use italics, boldface, or underlined text.
- Use 10- or 12-point font.
- Do not use graphics, decorative borders, or other visual elements.
- Avoid using indentations to minimize the problem of misalignment and document asymmetry. Separate sections using capitalized headings and an additional line of space.
- Adjust margins so that the resume fits into a standard e-mail window. The left margin should be set at 1 inch and the right margin at 3 inches.

- Save your document as "Text Only with Line Breaks." Your word processing program may warn you that you will be losing some of the formatting. Click "OK."
- Edit and clean up your document by opening it in a text editor program such as Notepad®.
- Use a bulleted list to present information clearly and concisely.
- Cut and paste your resume into the body of an e-mail rather than sending it as an attachment.
- Conduct a trial run by sending the resume to a friend with a different e-mail program to test its legibility. Ask the friend to print the document to ensure that it prints accurately.

WEB RESUMES

A Web resume is posted on the Internet and is typically used to display an individual's skills in designing hypertext markup language (HTML) documents. It is beneficial to individuals seeking art or graphics positions and has the capacity to include electronic media such as video, audio, and advanced graphics.

SELECTING A RESUME FORMAT

Experts recommend keeping copies of your resume in various formats so that you will be prepared to respond to a specific employer's request. Dikel (2004) recommends the following formats:

- A printable version completed in a word processing program that can be printed and mailed in hard copy. A printable version of your resume can include elements such as boldface type, bullets, and graphics.
- A plaintext (ASCII) version appropriate for pasting into online forms. This version follows the guidelines for an electronic resume.
- An e-mail version (also ASCII) that is formatted for the length-of-line restrictions in e-mail and meets the requirements for an electronic resume.

GUIDELINES TO CREATING A RESUME

Regardless of the resume format, employers typically need similar information. Include the following information on the resume, not necessarily in

REFLECTION QUESTIONS

- With which of the resume formats are you familiar? With which would you like to become more familiar?
- If you have an existing resume, how do you think your chosen format has served you in the past? If it has been effective, why? If not, why not?

CRITICAL THINKING QUESTION

7–2. What is your reaction to the following statement? "Since it takes a lot of extra work to create various versions of the resume, I don't think that is necessary."

this order (Hess, 1999):

- contact information, including name, address, telephone number, and e-mail address
- summary of qualifications
- education, including names and locations of schools, dates attended and date of graduation, major course of study, and degree earned
- work history (paid experience)
- volunteer work history (unpaid experience)
- specialty certifications, credentials, or licenses
- military experience
- professional memberships and positions held
- information regarding special skills, recognition, and achievements

The following are some simple guidelines to follow when compiling your resume:

- **Customize your resume.** A resume targeted at a specific job is most effective. Customize your resume so that your skills and achievements support the job for which you are applying. This does mean that you will need to adjust your resume each time you apply for a job, but better results are worth that extra effort.
- **Be prepared with the information you need to write your resume.** Collect all pertinent information such as job history, transcripts, certifications, and other documents that contain data that you will include on your resume. This eliminates or minimizes the need to search for information and will make more efficient use of your time.
- **Select the best resume type for your needs.** Be clear on which resume type is the best choice for effectively presenting your information relative to the job requirements. Make sure to check if an electronic resume is required.
- **Use available resources to help with the composition of your resume.** There are a variety of resources that provide sample copies and suggestions for resumes. Conduct an Internet search using "resumes" or "resume writing" as your search term. Also, seek assistance from the career center on your campus.
- **Consider additions to your resume based on your field.** Depending on the job for which you are applying, additions to the resume can be helpful. For example, in the graphic arts field, added visual interest can demonstrate creativity. Follow the standards of your field. Whatever you add should be simple and professional. Your words should be the focus.

? CRITICAL THINKING QUESTIONS

7–3. What other action verbs can you think of? Compile a list and refer to it when writing your resume.

7–4. Which action verbs are most appropriate for your field and experience?

7

▸ **Limit the length of functional or chronological resumes.** A length of one or two pages is ideal. Pages should be added only if they are absolutely necessary to effectively represent your experience.

▸ **Use bullets for an easy read.** Avoid using long sentences and being too wordy. Use phrases that convey your points clearly and concisely.

▸ **Use action verbs and phrases to describe your accomplishments and skills.** Select words that convey precise and efficient action when describing your accomplishments. According to Barthel and Goldrick-Jones (n.d., "Consider Word Choice Carefully"), your resume should "sound positive and confident; neither too aggressive, nor overly modest." Examples of action verbs include *created, modified, directed, supervised, wrote, illustrated,* and *managed.*

▸ **Use a professional tone.** Avoid extensive use of pronouns such as "I" or "me," especially at the beginning of paragraphs. Write in a formal conversational tone. Avoid contractions (use "do not" instead of "don't") and avoid abbreviations and slang.

▸ **Use a professional e-mail address.** E-mail addresses that are used socially, intended to be fun and amusing, may not be appropriate for professional correspondence. Thoughtfully consider your e-mail address. If it in any way presents an unprofessional image or can be interpreted as offensive, consider creating another account for professional use. Your Internet service provider (ISP) may offer additional mailboxes with your subscription or you may use one of the free services offered on the Internet. A professional e-mail would be your name or a variation on it. An example is susan.smith@yourISP.com.

▸ **Include all important information that employers will want.** For example, a job history must include the name of the employer, your job title, job location, and dates of employment. Reasons for leaving a job should not be included.

▸ **Check for accuracy.** Make sure your address, phone numbers, and e-mail address are correct. Use only permanent addresses. Ensure that your outgoing voice mail message is professional and appropriate for an employer to hear.

▸ **Represent well-rounded skills.** Include both technical and soft skills on your resume.

▸ **Use discretion with personal interests.** Personal hobbies and activities should not be listed unless they are related to the job you are seeking.

▶ **Be honest about your abilities.** Never embellish your experience or skills. You do not want to mislead employers to assume you are more qualified than you actually are.

▶ **Include only postsecondary experience.** As a college graduate, list only your college experience. High school graduation should not be listed.

▶ **Do not list personal information on your resume.** Information pertaining to religion, marital status, and ethnicity should not be listed on the resume.

▶ **Limit lengthy experience.** If your work experience spans more than 10 years, it is acceptable to list the most recent 10 years only. List more only if the experience relates directly to the job.

▶ **Pay attention to mechanics.** Make sure your resume is professional by paying close attention to spacing, spelling, and grammar. Barthel and Goldrick-Jones (n.d., "Evaluate Your Resume") suggest that you assess the appearance of your resume and ask the following questions:

   ▶ Is the page too busy with different type styles, sizes, lines, or boxes?

   ▶ Is there too much white space? (White space is the area on the resume that does not contain any writing or graphics.) White space should be sufficient to allow easy reading, but not so much that the content appears sparse.

   ▶ Is important information quick and easy to find?

▶ **Get a professional opinion.** Ask a professional, such as the personnel in your campus career center or a colleague in the field, to review your resume. Be open to constructive criticism. You want your resume to be the best it can be.

▶ **Include a thoughtful career objective.** Include a career objective that is stated as a goal and reflects the characteristics of the position you are seeking. An example of a career objective is "Seeking a position as a medical assistant in a medium-size family practice." The career objective is placed at the beginning of the resume, following your contact information.

▶ **Check for legibility.** If providing a hard copy to the employer, make sure the printed copy of your resume is easy to read and that the paper is of good quality. High-quality white paper is the most appropriate.

▶ **List references separately.** Speak to people who know you and your work about being a reference for you. List them on a separate reference sheet.

COMPLETING A RESUME

1. Be prepared with the information you need prior to writing your resume.
2. Select the best resume type for your needs.
3. Use resources on the Internet to help with the composition of your resume.
4. Consider additions to your resume based on your field.
5. Try to limit functional or chronological resumes to one page.
6. Use bullets for an easy read.
7. Use action verbs and phrases to describe your accomplishments and skills.
8. Use a professional tone.
9. Don't leave out important information that employers will want.
10. Check for accuracy.
11. Represent well-rounded skills.
12. Use discretion about including personal interests.
13. Be honest about your abilities.
14. Include only postsecondary experience.
15. Do not list personal information on your resume.
16. Limit lengthy experience.
17. Pay attention to mechanics.
18. Check for legibility.
19. List references separately.

REFLECTION QUESTIONS

- What did you learn from the resume guidelines?
- If you have an existing resume, how might your resume change based on what you have learned from the guidelines?

? CRITICAL THINKING QUESTION

7–5. Do you think it is important to follow these guidelines or do you think more individuality should be allowed when it comes to content and style on one's resume?

©Digital Vision

Today, resumes are commonly sent via e-mail or posted on the Internet. Remember that in some situations, however, it is a good practice to also send a hard copy via surface mail.

UTILIZING TECHNOLOGY TO SEND RESUMES

In addition to the more traditional methods of mailing and faxing, e-mailing or posting a resume on the Internet have become common practice today. Using these methods requires only a slight change to the format of the resume.

SENDING RESUMES VIA E-MAIL

The following are guidelines to follow when e-mailing a resume (Minnesota Department of Employment and Economic Development, 1994–2004):

- Usually, unsolicited resumes should not be sent by e-mail.

- Conducting mass e-mailings of your resume is not an effective marketing tool.
- After e-mailing your resume, follow up with a phone call.
- It is recommended that you send a hard copy in the mail. Indicate in your original e-mail that you have also mailed a hard copy.
- Be sure that the employer can receive attachments if you are including attachments.
- Be sure that the employer has the correct software version to receive your resume.
- Always include a cover letter with your e-mailed resume.
- Address your cover letter to a specific person. Avoid using the phrase "To whom it may concern."

POSTING RESUMES ON THE WEB

Entering the resume into a job database is another way to respond to a job opportunity. Today, there are job search sites and placement services where resumes can be posted and are available to employers. The following are typical steps for displaying a resume on a Web database, based on criteria from Seneca College Career Services (2001):

1. Register with the Web site, by providing
   - contact information, including name, address, e-mail address, and so forth.
   - other demographic information that is requested.
2. Follow the instructions for setting up a password.
3. Register for e-mail services, such as job alerts.
4. Post your resume.

Displaying the resume on your own Web site is also an option. It is easier to upload the resume to a Web site if certain composition elements have been considered. Choose one of the following alternatives for simplifying the upload process (Seneca College Career Services, 2001):

- Compose the resume in Notepad or another text editor and manually encode it using HTML.
- Create the resume in Microsoft Word® and save it as HTML.
- Prepare the resume using a Web page authoring tool that is part of your Web browser, such as Netscape Composer.
- Format the resume using Web page authoring software, like Dreamweaver® or ColdFusion®.

It is relatively easy to post a resume on a Web site. Many Internet service providers (ISPs) offer a personal home page with a subscription to the service. If this is not available from the ISP as part of a subscription, space can be rented.

SAFETY ON THE WEB

With the growing use of Internet technologies, individuals need to take some precautions to remain cyber-safe. The following are some safety considerations recommended by Dikel (2004):

> ▮ **Limit where you post your resume on the Internet.** Avoid "overposting." Limit your postings to three or four job sites.

> ▮ **Pay attention to privacy policies.** Ensure that your personal information will not be released without your knowledge.

> ▮ **Expect a trial period.** Use sites that allow you to view and evaluate the usefulness of the site before making a long-term commitment.

> ▮ **Carefully consider your contact information.** Be wise about how much contact information you provide. For example, consider only providing e-mail information rather than your name, address, and phone numbers.

> ▮ **Give general information.** Use general information and descriptions to present employment history. Avoid using company names and dates of employment.

> ▮ **Keep information current.** Repost your resume every 14 days so that it appears as a fresh submission. If a response is not received in a month or so, remove it and find another posting site.

> ▮ **Remove promptly when appropriate.** Once you are hired, delete all posted resumes.

▶ REFLECTION QUESTION

- What concerns might you have regarding the use of some of these more advanced methods for sending your resume? What might you do to overcome these concerns?

? CRITICAL THINKING QUESTION

7–6. How might technology continue to change how resumes are sent to employers?

---

success steps

BEING CYBER-SAFE

1. Limit where you post your resume on the Internet.
2. Pay attention to privacy policies.
3. Expect a trial period.
4. Carefully consider your contact information.
5. Give general information.
6. Keep information current.
7. Remove your resume promptly when appropriate.

apply it

Utilizing Technology to Send Resumes

GOAL: To develop a clearer understanding of how to use technology to send resumes.

STEP 1: Conduct research on the Web to further understand how technology can be used to send your resume.

STEP 2: If technology is not your strength, schedule a meeting with someone who is more knowledgeable in this area to help clarify areas that are unclear.

STEP 3: Write a report of your findings and what you learned.

STEP 4: Consider placing this report in your Learning Portfolio.

COVER LETTERS

The cover letter is a tool for introducing yourself to an employer and is a required element when submitting a resume. The cover letter provides the opportunity to give additional information regarding your skills and experience and to summarize how they relate to the desired job. The cover letter should clearly convey what you have to offer to the employer. Do not focus on yourself; avoid statements such as, "this would be a great opportunity for me." The cover letter should not exceed one page in length. Princeton University Career Services (n.d.) provides the following general guidelines to consider when developing a cover letter:

 Each cover letter should be written in response to the specific job requirements. Sending a generic cover letter is strongly discouraged.

- Keep copies of all cover letters in order to refer back to as needed.

- The cover letter must provide information that clearly illustrates how your skills and experiences match what the organization is seeking.

- Whenever possible, cover letters should be addressed to a specific person.

- If the job comes through a referral, mention this in the cover letter. Include this information in the opening paragraph. A familiar name is more likely to capture and hold the interest of the reader.

- Professionalism in the cover letter is as critical as in the resume. Pay attention to elements such as spelling, grammar, spacing, professional tone, and paper quality. Elements of the cover letter should match those in the resume.

A well-written cover letter can provide the prospective employer with information about an applicant's personality, ability for being detailed, communication skills, enthusiasm, and intelligence.

The cover letter can also provide the prospective employer a glimpse into who the applicant is as an individual.

The Writing Center at Rensselaer Polytechnic Institute (n.d.) recommends that the format of the cover letter include the following:

- ▶ Paragraphs should reflect a formal conversational tone.
- ▶ The first paragraph usually is brief and tells which job you are applying for as well as where you learned about the position.
- ▶ The body of the letter can range from one to three paragraphs. These paragraphs provide the opportunity to elaborate on your qualifications and experiences. Being specific regarding how these abilities and experiences match well with the desired job is critical.
- ▶ The last paragraph contains a request for further contact and states how this contact can be achieved.

Figure 7–4 shows a sample cover letter.

William Running Deer
432 East Brooks Avenue
Denver, CO 80000

November 3, 2005

Ms. Christina Chung
Human Resources Director
Everett Technologies
10067 Mountain View Road
Broomfield, CO 82222

Dear Ms. Chung:

Enclosed please find my resume in support of my interest in the office manager position that was advertised in the October 30, 2005 edition of the *Denver Gazette* and posted on Everett Technologies' Web site.

The experience that I would bring to Everett Technologies includes a background as an assistant office manager, overseeing the streamlining of various office procedures, and implementing data tracking systems. My qualifications effectively support your stated company goal of developing and putting into practice a new client data management system.

I would very much like to discuss ways in which my experience could contribute to a smooth and efficient transition to a new system and would value the opportunity to further explore how I might support your efforts in the office manager position. Thank you for your consideration and I look forward to hearing from you.

Sincerely,

William Running Deer

FIGURE 7–4.   An effective cover letter provides the employers with a concise yet clear overview of your skills and goals.

apply it

Job Search Materials

GOAL: *To demonstrate the ability to develop a resume, cover letter, and reference sheet.*

STEP 1: Use the information from this chapter and other available resources to develop a resume, cover letter, and reference sheet.

STEP 2: Share your resume with a respected professional and ask for constructive criticism.

STEP 3: Redo areas as instructed by the reviewer and submit to the instructor for review.

STEP 4: Consider putting this project in your Learning Portfolio.

OTHER TYPES OF CORRESPONDENCE

There are other types of correspondence frequently utilized by the job seeker. These include:

- thank-you letters sent following phone or in-person interviews
- letters of inquiry sent to request more information regarding job opportunities or a specific advertised position
- letters requesting withdrawal of one's application
- acceptance letters to indicate acceptance of an offer
- letters to decline an offer
- e-mail correspondence

As with the cover letter, these letters continue to represent the applicant's professionalism. The same attention given to the cover letter should be given to any of these types of correspondence. Various resources, such as the Internet, provide a wealth of information to help individuals produce each of these types of correspondence.

REFLECTION QUESTION

- How effective are your professional letters? Where might you go for help in developing these skills?

CRITICAL THINKING QUESTION

7–7. What is your reaction to the following statement? "A generic cover letter is sufficient, as writing a customized letter for each potential job is too time-consuming."

REFERENCES AND RECOMMENDATIONS

Employers usually request the names of individuals who are familiar with your professional performance and will attest to your skills, abilities, and overall professionalism. Include the name, title, address, phone number, and e-mail address of each reference. List the elements of each reference on separate lines, as you would when addressing an envelope. Michigan State University Career Development Center (1996) makes the following suggestions for locating individuals who will consent to being listed as references and provide positive recommendations:

- Never list an individual who has not given you permission to be listed as a reference. It is critical that you contact and request permission from each person you wish to use as a reference.

- Be sure that individuals you list as references can match your experience with the job for which you are applying. Prepare them for questions that they may be asked.

- Make sure that the information offered by each reference will place you in the best possible light. Ask each reference directly if he or she will provide a positive recommendation. If someone asks not be used as a reference, respect his or her wishes and substitute someone else.

- References must have good communication abilities. Choose references wisely and select those who are able to present themselves professionally.

- Send your selected references a copy of your resume. This will assist them in discussing your background and answering questions posed by the employer.

- Avoid using photocopies when sending recommendation letters.

- Make sure the letters contain all the necessary information the employer will need to contact the reference. Check the address and phone numbers for accuracy.

- Letters of recommendations are usually offered to the employer separately from the resume and cover letter package. Providing too much material at the beginning might overwhelm the employer.

- Stay in touch with your references during your job search. It is professional and courteous to keep them up to date regarding the jobs for which you are applying, as well as the outcome of each application.

- Always thank your references as they provide recommendations for you. Follow up with a telephone call and personally thank them. Sending a handwritten thank-you note is also appropriate.

REFLECTION QUESTIONS

- What individuals would you use as references? Why did you select these individuals? How will they present you in the best possible light?
- What concerns might you have about finding references? How can you effectively address these concerns?

? CRITICAL THINKING QUESTION

7–8. What specific questions might you ask an individual who you are considering using as a reference?

▶ Provide references on a sheet separate from your resume. Select quality paper and use a full sheet. It is typical to list three to eight references, depending on the employer's request. Review your reference list to ensure that its appearance is neat and clean. Include your name and personal contact information on the top of the sheet in case it is separated from your resume.

apply it

Preparing Professional Correspondence

GOAL: *To demonstrate the ability to develop a variety of letters used to correspond during the job search.*

STEP 1: The instructor should divide the class into two groups. Each group should be given at least three different types of correspondence letters.

STEP 2: Each group should conduct research regarding group members' letters and the appropriate content, layout, and purpose of each. A short report on these findings should be compiled by the group and presented to the class. Handouts or overheads should be encouraged.

STEP 3: Each group member must also write one letter of each type he or she has researched. These are to be turned in to the instructor for review.

STEP 4: Consider putting the correspondence examples from this activity in your Learning Portfolio.

CHAPTER SUMMARY

This chapter provided the foundations for preparing a resume, cover letter, and other types of professional correspondence used during the job search process. You learned how to select content for each type of correspondence, as well as how to present it professionally and effectively. Various formats for submitting resumes were reviewed, and you received guidelines for selecting the most appropriate format for your needs.

 POINTS TO KEEP IN MIND

In this chapter, several main points were discussed in detail:

- The purpose of a resume is to spark an interest with the potential employer by pointing out your abilities, skills, and professionalism.

- Resumes must be short, concise, yet full of details.

- Resume types include chronological, functional, combination, and the curriculum vitae.

- Recent college graduates typically choose to use either the functional or combination resume.

- Various formats of resumes include printed, scannable, plaintext, e-mail, and Web versions.

- Standard guidelines for creating a resume include using bullets for an easier read, avoiding long sentences and wordiness, and using action verbs and phrases to describe your accomplishments and skills.

- Items that should not be included on your resume include use of personal pronouns, temporary addresses and phone numbers, and lists of personal hobbies and activities that are unrelated to the job.

- Your resume can be sent to an employer in several ways, ranging from traditional methods such as mailing and faxing to more contemporary methods such as e-mailing or posting on the Internet.

- The cover letter, which must always accompany the resume, should provide further details regarding your skills and experience and how these directly relate to the desired job.

- Other types of correspondence you may utilize include thank-you letters, letters of inquiry, letters of withdrawal, acceptance letters, letters to decline an offer, and e-mail.

- References need to be individuals who offer a positive recommendation, present your skills effectively, and exhibit good overall communication skills.

 LEARNING OBJECTIVES REVISITED

Review the learning objectives for this chapter and rate your level of achievement for each objective using the rating scale provided. For each objective on which you do not rate yourself as a 3, outline a plan of action that you will take to fully achieve the objective. Include a time frame for this plan.

1 = did not successfully achieve objective

2 = understand what is needed, but need more study or practice

3 = achieved learning objective thoroughly

	1	2	3
List the elements that are typically required on a resume.	☐	☐	☐
Explain the purpose of a resume.	☐	☐	☐
Discuss some general guidelines for preparing a resume.	☐	☐	☐
Compare and contrast the various types of resumes.	☐	☐	☐
Describe the various formats that resumes can be prepared.	☐	☐	☐
Explain the general guidelines for making a resume scannable.	☐	☐	☐
Discuss how to appropriately e-mail a resume.	☐	☐	☐
Explain how resumes can be entered into Web site databases.	☐	☐	☐
Understand how to be more cyber-safe.	☐	☐	☐
Demonstrate the ability to write a variety of types of correspondence letters.	☐	☐	☐
Demonstrate the ability to prepare a professional resume.	☐	☐	☐
Demonstrate the ability to prepare a reference sheet.	☐	☐	☐
Demonstrate the ability to write a cover letter.	☐	☐	☐

Steps to Achieve Unmet Objectives

Steps	Due Date
1. ____	_________
2. ____	_________
3. ____	_________
4. ____	_________

SUGGESTED ITEMS FOR LEARNING PORTFOLIO

▶ Utilizing Technology to Send Resumes: This activity is intended to help you develop a clearer understanding of how to use technology to send resumes.

▶ Job Search Materials: By completing this activity, you will gain experience in developing a resume, cover letter, and reference sheet.

▶ Preparing Professional Correspondence: The goal of this activity is to provide practice in creating a variety of letters used to correspond during the job search.

REFERENCES

Barthel, B. & Goldrick-Jones, A. (n.d.). Resumes [Electronic version]. *The Writing Center at Rensselaer Polytechnic Institute.* Retrieved March 15, 2005, from http://www.rpi.edu/web/writingcenter/resume.html

Dikel, M. F. (2004). Prepare your resume for emailing or posting on the Internet. Retrieved March 15, 2005, from http://www.rileyguide.com/eresume.html

Hess, P. M. (1999). *Career Success: Right Here Right Now!* (pp. 80–85). Thomson Delmar Learning: Clifton Park, NY.

JobStar Central. (2006(a)). What is the right resume for me? Chronological. Retrieved May 26, 2006, from http://jobstar.org/tools/resume/res-chro.cfm

JobStar Central. (2006(b)). What is the right resume for me? Functional. Retrieved May 26, 2006, from http://jobstar.org/tools/resume/res-func.cfm

Minnesota Department of Employment and Economic Development. (1994–2005). Internet job search strategies—The electronic resume. Retrieved March 18, 2005, from http://www.deed.state.mn.us/cjs/cjsbook/internet3.htm

Michigan State University, Career Development Center. (1996). Establishing references: A guide for jobseekers. Retrieved March 18, 2005, from http://www.msu.edu/user/leedyjen/reflet.htm

National Association of Colleges and Employers. (n.d.). Your guide to resume writing. Retrieved March 15, 2005, from http://www.jobweb.com/Resumes_Interviews/resume_guide/how_to.htm

Princeton University Career Services. (n.d.). Resume guide. Retrieved March 15, 2005, from http://web.princeton.edu/sites/career/Undergrad/JobSearch/resume_guide.html

The Santa Clara University Career Center. (n.d.). Resumes. Retrieved November 3, 2005, from http://www.scu.edu/careercenter/resources/publications/resumes.pdf

Seneca College of Applied Arts and Technology, Career Services. (2001). Using the Internet to apply for jobs. Retrieved March 18, 2005, from http://ilearn.senecac.on.ca/careers/apply/resume/e_resume.html

The Writing Center at Rensselaer Polytechnic Institute. (n.d.). Cover letters. Retrieved March 15, 2005, from http://www.rpi.edu/web/writingcenter/cover_letter.html

7

CHAPTER OUTLINE

The Importance of Etiquette in the Job Search

Job Search Etiquette

Etiquette in Special Situations

8 Professional Courtesies in the Job Search

LEARNING OBJECTIVES

By the end of this chapter, you will achieve the following objectives:

- Explain the importance of utilizing proper etiquette during the job search.
- Discuss ways that job applicants can demonstrate good manners.
- Describe the considerations that a job applicant should make when using a cell phone for an interview.
- Discuss the standards of effective phone interviewing.
- Explain important considerations to make when an interview is conducted over a meal.
- Demonstrate the ability to use good phone manners during a phone interview.

TOPIC SCENARIO

Nearing the end of her college education, Joan has sent out letters of application to a number of employers. Today, Joan received a call from an employer who had received her information and wants to conduct an initial interview by phone. The interview is scheduled for tomorrow at 2:00 p.m.

Based on this scenario, answer the following questions:

▶ How should Joan prepare for the phone interview?

▶ Would Joan prepare differently for the phone interview as opposed to an in-person interview? If so, how?

▶ What considerations should Joan make to ensure that the interview runs smoothly?

▶ What phone courtesies should Joan demonstrate?

▶ If Joan is using a cell phone, what are the additional considerations? What should she do differently?

THE IMPORTANCE OF ETIQUETTE IN THE JOB SEARCH

Something as simple as etiquette—good manners—can seem like an insignificant thing. However, the social appropriateness that you demonstrate in the job search speaks to your professionalism and how you will manage your conduct on the job. An employer appreciates being treated courteously, and doing so makes a favorable impression. In addition, consider the messages that etiquette sends.

▶ **How you will represent the organization.** The consideration and courtesy that you demonstrate during the job search process provides the employer with an example of how you will treat customers or clients. The way in which clients are treated forms the public image of the company and either attracts business or discourages it. Employers want to hire individuals who will represent their company in a positive manner.

▶ **Messages about you as a person.** The consideration that you show others contributes to the reputation you are building as a professional. Professional circles are frequently small, and word travels. Even if you are not hired by a particular employer, your reputation is being established based on your interactions and your manners.

Etiquette and courtesy demonstrated during the job search reveals much about how you treat other people and how effectively you work with others.

8

apply it

The Importance of Proper Etiquette

GOAL: *To gain an understanding of the importance that employers place on applicants utilizing proper etiquette.*

STEP 1: Schedule an interview with a professional in your chosen field. The purpose of the interview is to inquire as to the importance that the employer places on proper etiquette and how proper etiquette should be exhibited by job applicants.

STEP 2: Write a short report regarding your findings and be prepared to share it with the class.

STEP 3: Consider placing the report regarding the Importance of Proper Etiquette in your Learning Portfolio.

JOB SEARCH ETIQUETTE

Professionalism can be demonstrated in various ways, including the use of proper etiquette. There are many opportunities for job applicants to demonstrate proper etiquette throughout the application process. It is important to remember that employers not only seek a technically qualified individual, but also look for an individual who has the capability to follow general principles of good manners and professionalism. The following are some general guidelines that a job applicant can utilize to demonstrate good manners (Caroselli, 2000):

> ◗ **Respond immediately to any communication received from an employer.** Follow up the employer's call, letter, or e-mail and inform the employer if you are accepting or declining his or her invitation. Do not be rude by neglecting to follow through. Even if you are not interested in continuing with the company, you need to inform the employer of this decision. It is important to do so graciously and maintain a positive professional relationship throughout the process of withdrawing an application or declining an offer.

> ◗ **Never be late.** If an employer tells you to call at a certain time, then make sure you call on time. Show up for the interview on time or even a little early. Being on time demonstrates respect for the other person's time.

> ◗ **Demonstrate politeness.** Politeness can be demonstrated by saying words such as *please, thank you,* and *excuse me.* Say "thank you" and

8

"please" to the receptionist and other individuals with whom you have contact. Remember the importance of establishing good first impressions.

▶ **Pay attention to time.** Be aware of rambling. Employers are busy individuals who want applicants to answer questions clearly and concisely. During your conversations and interviews with the employer, be mindful of his or her time. Glancing discreetly at one's watch is appropriate. Quickly come to a stopping point if you see time is running out. The employer will greatly appreciate your attention to this matter. If the employer chooses to extend the time, that is his or her choice. The job applicant should be willing to stay as long as the employer requires.

▶ **Listen well.** Employers want to share information about the company and the job with applicants. Although some of the information may be public knowledge, show an interest. Never yawn or stare off into space, as doing so demonstrates poor manners.

▶ **Be aware of your body language.** Sit up and demonstrate attentiveness. Straight yet relaxed posture with a slightly forward lean, direct eye contact, and an occasional nod communicate enthusiasm and interest. In addition to interest, direct eye contact indicates honesty. Avoid crossing your arms, as doing so can be interpreted as anger or a closed attitude. Positive body language communicates much about your attitude and how you are approaching the employment opportunity.

▶ **Demonstrate passion and interest in the company and the job.** Actions such as making follow-up calls to learn the status of the interviewing and decision-making processes demonstrate your investment. Take the initiative to bring to the interview items such as a portfolio of your work to demonstrate your abilities and dedication to your work. The more you demonstrate passion for the company and the job, the more the employer will see you as a potential candidate.

▶ **For any interview, be prepared.** A lack of preparedness can indicate a lack of interest. If an employer asks if you have any questions, make sure you do! Those who fail to ask questions can be viewed as uninterested.

▶ **Perform a job-related task if asked.** Some employers will have applicants perform a job-related task to see if the applicant is qualified for the job. Graciously perform the task to the best of your ability and never refuse to perform the task requested by the employer. Refusal indicates lack of confidence and lack of ability.

▶ **Send a postinterview thank-you note.** A survey conducted by the staffing firm Accountemps found that "more than 76% of employers like receiving a post-interview thank-you note, but only 36% of applicants write them" (Caroselli, 2000). Thank-you notes should be sent immediately after the interview. The content of the thank-you note should include thanking the interviewer for his or her time, offering to provide additional material as needed, and stating an interest in working for the company.

▶ Never renege on an agreement you make with a company. When you have accepted a position with an organization, you must stop interviewing with other companies. The employer is depending on you and has possibly lost the chance to hire their second choice, due to the time that has passed. In addition, word travels in the professional world and you may be hurting your reputation.

REFLECTION QUESTIONS

- Do you typically demonstrate good manners?
- With what areas of etiquette could you become more familiar?

? CRITICAL THINKING QUESTION

8–1. How do you respond to the following statement? "As an employer I would never hire an individual who demonstrates poor manners."

---

success steps

PROPER ETIQUETTE IN THE JOB SEARCH

1. Respond immediately to any communication received from an employer.

2. Be on time for any interview or appointment with an employer.

3. Demonstrate politeness by demonstrating courtesies such as saying "please," "thank you," and "excuse me," and waiting to be offered a seat.

4. Pay attention to time and be aware of rambling. Speak succinctly and to the point.

5. Listen well. Pay attention to information about the organization and show interest in what the employer tells you.

6. Be aware of your body language.

7. Demonstrate passion and interest in the company and the job.

8. For any interview, be prepared. Use the research you have completed on the company and have questions ready to demonstrate your interest.

9. Some employers will have applicants perform a job-related task to see if the applicant is qualified for the job. Graciously perform the task.

10. Send a postinterview thank-you note.

11. Never renege on an agreement you make with a company.

©Image Source Limited

Although telephone interviews can be more casual in some respects (such as attire), they should be treated as a professional appointment by minimizing distractions and having relevant documents in front of you. Pay particular attention to your verbal communication, as the interviewer does not have the benefit of responding to non-verbal behaviors.

ETIQUETTE IN SPECIAL SITUATIONS

General etiquette considerations are important in all professional interactions and activities. There are situations that may arise during the job search process that require attention to specific details that are unique to the situation. The following less traditional interviewing methods are included here because of their unique demands and the special etiquette considerations they require.

PHONE INTERVIEW ETIQUETTE

Demonstrating phone etiquette is an important element of the job search process. Initial contact with a company often occurs by phone. Employers call the contact numbers job applicants provide on their resumes. The importance of this information being accurate is critical to job search success. Voice mailboxes and answering machines are frequently used to receive messages. Job applicants must ensure that these devices are set up with an appropriate message that demonstrates both professionalism and proper manners. Entertaining messages that may be amusing to your friends are not always appropriate when you are expecting return calls from prospective employers. Change any whimsical messages to something straightforward and professional. Proper messages include examples such as (Crawford Hentz, n.d.(a), "Pre-contact"):

- "You've reached Brenda, Cathy, and Mark. Please leave a message."
- "You've reached the Sizemores. Please leave a message."
- "You've reached 617-973-5235. Please leave a message."

If you rely on other people to take messages for you, it is your responsibility to ensure that these individuals also understand and use proper phone etiquette and take messages accurately.

When you receive a message from an employer, phone etiquette requires you to return the message in a timely manner. When returning the call, it is important to give your full first and last name, along with the reason for your call. Always be polite and repeat information as required. Be aware of rate of voice and pitch. Speak clearly and distinctly.

If you receive a call from an employer directly, don't defer the employer. It is best to put aside what you are doing and take the call promptly. However, there may be circumstances when you are preoccupied with another task or rushing to get to an appointment and are truly unable to give your undivided attention. In this case, it may be best not to take the call and return the call when you are able to focus. If you answer the phone, good phrases to use in this situation would be " 'I'm so happy you called. I have about 10 minutes before I have to run out the door. Is that enough time, or can I call you back later this afternoon?' This way, you are expressing your interest, being clear about the time you have, and suggesting a time to connect later" (Crawford Hentz, n.d.(a), "When you're there for the contact").

CELL PHONE INTERVIEWS

With the increased use of cell phones versus land lines, job applicants do need to make sure that cordless phones and cell phones are fully charged when possible. If the battery is low, inform the employer at the beginning of the call and ask if you can call him or her back immediately using a different phone. If you use a cell phone as your primary phone, inform the employer at the time of the call and indicate that a call back will be immediate if a disconnect occurs. Make sure to get correct callback numbers. If hearing the employer is difficult due to a poor cell phone signal, check that you understand each other. Crawford Hentz (n.d.(a), "When you're there for the contact") suggests saying, "I'm having trouble hearing you. Can you hear me clearly?" It is less acceptable to ask the employer to speak up, which can sound abrupt and demanding. At the end of the call, make sure to thank the employer for his or her time and follow up the phone call with a thank-you letter.

Phone interviews should be treated with as much care and attention as you would give to an in-person interview. Although getting hired solely from the phone interview is unlikely, it does offer the opportunity for the employer to get to know you and to draw conclusions about whether further conversations should occur.

For further information regarding successful phone interviewing, consider the following recommendations from Crawford Hentz (n.d.(b)):

- Ensure that the contact information in your cover letter and resume is correct.
- Make sure your answering machine or voice mail message is professional.
- Keep by the phone a list of companies to which you have sent your resume. That way, you will not be caught off guard when an employer calls.
- Be prepared for a telephone interview just as you would for an inperson interview. Do your research just as you would for a traditional interview.
- Find a location where you will not be disrupted during the phone interview.
- Take notes of your conversation as you would during an in-person interview. Make sure note taking does not get in the way of good listening skills.
- Indicate if you are not able to hear the employer. Do so in a courteous manner.

▶ Smile during your interview. It will make a difference in how your voice sounds.

▶ Never interrupt the interviewer.

▶ Accept silence. If you have sufficiently answered a question, silence is acceptable while the interviewer prepares for the next question. Do not fill the silence with meaningless chatter, but you might ask a question that is related to your last response.

▶ Avoid sneezing or coughing. If these are unavoidable, say "excuse me." Never yawn, chew gum, eat, or drink during an interview.

▶ Always say "thank you" at the end of the phone interview, indicate your interest, and ask when to expect further word regarding other possible interviews.

success steps

TELEPHONE INTERVIEW ETIQUETTE

1. Ensure that the contact information in your cover letter and resume is correct.

2. Have a professional-sounding message on your answering machine or voice mail.

3. Keep a list of companies you have contacted by the phone.

4. Prepare by researching the company and writing down questions.

5. Find a location where you will not be disturbed during the phone interview.

6. Take notes.

7. Courteously let the employer know if you cannot hear what he or she is saying.

8. Smile during your interview. Your voice will convey a pleasant demeanor.

9. Never interrupt the interviewer.

10. Accept silence. If you have sufficiently answered a question, allow the interviewer to prepare for the next question. You may ask a question related to your last response, but do not fill the silence with meaningless chatter.

11. Avoid sneezing or coughing. If these are unavoidable, say "excuse me."

12. At the end of the phone interview, say "thank you," indicate your interest, and ask when to expect word regarding other possible interviews.

apply it

Phone Interview Role-Play

GOAL: *To demonstrate the ability to use good phone manners during a phone interview.*

STEP 1: Form pairs with other students in your class.

STEP 2: With scenarios provided by the instructor, role-play a phone interview. One student will be the employer and the other student the job applicant. Treat the role-playing seriously, since this activity can help prepare you for real-life phone interviews. After the role-playing is accomplished, the student playing the employer should constructively critique the job applicant on his or her phone manners and phone interviewing abilities. Where could the job applicants improve? What did they do right? If needed, redo the role-playing so you can practice and improve on your phone interviewing abilities. Reverse roles to allow for each student to represent the employer and the job applicant.

STEP 3: Write a brief report on what you learned from this activity and consider putting this information in your Learning Portfolio.

REFLECTION QUESTION

- Do you think you would do well in a phone interview? What areas might you be able to improve in order to be more effective in a phone interview?

? CRITICAL THINKING QUESTION

8–2. How would individuals with some hearing loss deal with potential phone interviews? How might technology assist in responding to this issue?

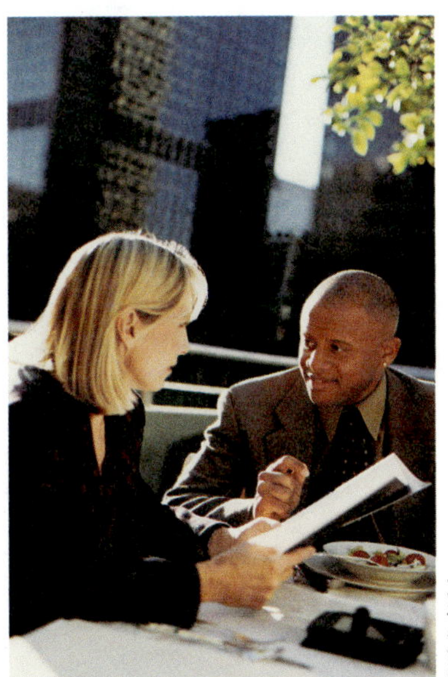

Interviews that take place over a meal require specific etiquette considerations and special attention to manners.

MEALTIME INTERVIEWS

Some employers may choose to have one of the interviews scheduled over breakfast, lunch, or dinner. If this occurs, consider the following:

- Do not choose the most expensive item on the menu. Even though the meal will be paid for by the employer, be reasonable with your selection.
- Choose an item on the menu that will not be messy. Avoid finger foods or items that can be sloppy, such as spaghetti and barbecued ribs.
- Avoid using black pepper. Pepper can get stuck in teeth.
- Use good table manners, such as placing the napkin in your lap prior to beginning the meal, keeping elbows off the table, and using the appropriate utensils.
- Never talk with your mouth full. Take small bites and swallow before answering a question.
- Use your napkin often to wipe your mouth.

> Do not order alcoholic beverages during an interview meal.

> After the meal, excuse yourself to go to the restroom. Check for food particles in teeth before returning to the table.

Further information regarding general table manners can be located on the Internet.

SUCCESSFUL MEALTIME INTERVIEWING

1. Do not choose the most expensive item on the menu.

2. Choose an item on the menu that will not be messy.

3. Avoid using pepper, as it can become stuck in your teeth.

4. Use good table manners. Place the napkin in your lap prior to beginning the meal, keep elbows off the table, and use the appropriate utensils.

5. Take small bites and swallow before answering a question. Never talk with your mouth full.

6. Keep your professional appearance by using your napkin to wipe your mouth frequently.

7. Do not order alcoholic beverages.

8. After the meal, excuse yourself to go to the restroom. Check for food particles in teeth before returning to the table.

apply it

Mealtime Interviewing

GOAL: *To develop a better understanding of how to effectively interview over a meal.*

STEP 1: Conduct research on the Internet and/or at the library regarding how to effectively interview over a meal.

STEP 2: Write a brief report regarding your findings.

STEP 3: Consider placing the report on Mealtime Interviewing in your Learning Portfolio.

CHAPTER SUMMARY

This chapter focused on acceptable etiquette in the job search process. The importance of etiquette cannot be overstated, as employers appreciate high standards of behavior. The manners that you demonstrate are not only appealing to an employer, but represent how you will treat clients in the future. In addition to emphasizing the importance of etiquette to your success in the job search and in the impression you make as a professional, general etiquette guidelines were provided. Then, etiquette requirements for specialized interview situations, including telephone and mealtime interviews, were reviewed.

POINTS TO KEEP IN MIND

In this chapter, several main points were discussed in detail:

▶ Employers seek technically qualified individuals who also demonstrate good manners.

▶ Demonstrating phone etiquette is an important element of the job search process.

▶ Phone interviews are just as important as in-person interviews and should be treated with as much care and attention.

▶ Interviews conducted on cell phones require specific etiquette and considerations.

▶ General table manners need to be followed during a mealtime interview.

LEARNING OBJECTIVES REVISITED

Review the learning objectives for this chapter and rate your level of achievement for each objective using the rating scale provided. For each objective on which you do not rate yourself as a 3, outline a plan of action that you will take to fully achieve the objective. Include a time frame for this plan.

1 = did not successfully achieve objective

2 = understand what is needed, but need more study or practice

3 = achieved learning objective thoroughly

	1	2	3
Explain the importance of utilizing proper etiquette during the job search.	☐	☐	☐
Discuss ways that job applicants can demonstrate good manners.	☐	☐	☐
Describe the issues that a job applicant should pay attention to when it comes to using a cell phone for an interview.	☐	☐	☐
Discuss standards associated with effective phone interviewing.	☐	☐	☐
Explain important considerations to make when an interview is conducted over a meal.	☐	☐	☐
Demonstrate the ability to use good phone manners during a phone interview.	☐	☐	☐

Steps to Achieve Unmet Objectives

Steps	Due Date
1. ____	__________
2. ____	__________
3. ____	__________
4. ____	__________

SUGGESTED ITEMS FOR LEARNING PORTFOLIO

▶ Importance of Proper Etiquette: This activity will familiarize you with the importance placed by employers on appropriate etiquette in the job search.

▶ Phone Interview Role-Play: This activity will give you an opportunity to practice telephone interview skills.

▶ Mealtime Interviewing: This activity will help you develop effective mealtime interview skills.

REFERENCES

Caroselli, M. (2000). Nine etiquette tips for job seekers. Retrieved April 6, 2005, from the Dow Jones Career Journal Web site: http://www .careerjournal.com/jobhunting/strategies/20000301-caroselli.html

Crawford Hentz, M. (n.d.(a)). Phone interview etiquette can propel you to the next step in the hiring process. Quintessential Careers. Retrieved April 6, 2005, from http://www.quintcareers.com/phone_interview_etiquette.html

Crawford Hentz, M. (n.d.(b)). Phone interviewing do's and don'ts. Quintessential Careers. Retrieved April 6, 2005, from http://www.quintcareers.com/phone_interviewing-dos-donts.html

CHAPTER OUTLINE

First Impressions

Dressing for Success

Dressing for the Interview

Building a Professional Wardrobe on a Budget

9 Dressing for Success

LEARNING OBJECTIVES

By the end of this chapter, you will achieve the following objectives:

- Describe appropriate clothing to be worn to an interview.
- Understand how first impressions can affect the opinions of others.
- Explain how appearance can be improved by paying attention to dressing for body type and skin tone.
- Explain how outward appearance can affect internal confidence.
- Discuss considerations that should be given to interviewing attire.
- Discuss grooming tips that are important to adhere to as a professional.

● TOPIC SCENARIO

Jim has always prided himself on demonstrating his individuality through his clothing and general appearance. Jim's clothing style has always been one that involves a variety of colorful items. His favorite outfit consists of loose-fitting denim jeans, a bright green shirt, and boat shoes with no socks. Jim also shows his personality via his long dreadlocks, one earring, and a tattoo on his forearm. Jim strongly believes that these items demonstrate his individualism and are important for others to accept. As a recent college graduate, Jim has been called for his first job interview. In reviewing his wardrobe, Jim begins to select items that he thinks will be appropriate for the interview. Knowing he is uncomfortable in a tie, and does not even own one, Jim decides not to wear a tie. In considering comfort, Jim also decides not to purchase other shoes but to stay with the boat shoes. He does conclude that he should wear socks. Jim decides that other necessary purchases include one pair of casual black pants and a loose-fitting yellow dress shirt. The weather is warm, so Jim decides long sleeves and a jacket are out.

Based on this short description of Jim's interviewing attire, answer the following questions:

- Do you think that Jim should be allowed to demonstrate his individualism through his choice of attire for the interview? If not, why not? If so, what do you think is appropriate? Would your answer change if you knew what type of job Jim was applying for? If so, how and why?

- Other than Jim's clothing issues, what other areas of Jim's appearance should he consider?

- If you were interviewing Jim, would you have any objections to Jim wearing short sleeves? Would the tattoo or earring be an issue? Why or why not?

- If Jim was an African American, do you think it would be more appropriate for him to wear dreadlocks than for a Caucasian male? If so, why?

- Would Jim be wise to change his hairstyle for the interview?

- What is your best advice to Jim regarding his wardrobe and appearance?

- Do you think employers pay too much attention to appearance and clothing? Explain your answer.

Casual and comfortable dress may be fine for campus life, but to make a positive first impression on potential employers, professional attire is a must. Casual campus dress such as that in the picture is not appropriate for an interview.

FIRST IMPRESSIONS

When pursuing a job, it is important to recognize the critical nature of making a good first impression. First impressions begin as soon as contact is made with a company of interest. This contact can occur through either written or spoken communication. Impressions are made through your resume, cover letter, and initial phone call; at the moment you visit to pick up an application; when you walk in for the interview; and when the first and subsequent interviews occur. During all these times the applicant is being scrutinized and evaluated. Conclusions are being drawn about one's professionalism and personality based on appearance, mannerisms, communication style, attitude, confidence level, and social skills.

Although some individuals may not like the idea that they are being judged by their appearance, it is important to accept that

- dress and grooming are important and are a critical factor in getting hired.

- first impressions do matter.

- overall dress does affect one's professional success.

Given these facts, it is critical for those who seek success both in obtaining a job and advancing in their careers to work toward improving their fashion sense, style, and grooming habits.

---

success tips

DRESSING TO MAKE A GOOD IMPRESSION

1. Remember that dress and grooming are both critical factors in getting hired.

2. Keep in mind that first impressions *do* matter.

3. Accept that overall dressing and grooming habits have an impact on professional success.

Understanding and accepting that your personal appearance does make a difference is the first step in presenting yourself effectively to potential employers. Developing the skills and presentation necessary to make a good impression is the second step and will be what differentiates a successful individual from one who is less successful. Dress and grooming are significant factors in being hired for a job as well as being considered for advancement within the organization (Wisconsin Department of Workforce Development, n.d.).

©Image 100 Ltd.

Dressing for success in the interview typically requires a conservative business suit for both men and women.

DRESSING FOR SUCCESS

For some individuals, dressing for success is not a difficult task. These individuals have learned what clothing items best suit their body type and make the most effective presentation. For others, learning how to polish one's appearance is more challenging.

Have you ever had someone say, "You look particularly nice today"? Compliments such as this may be attributed to the design and color of clothing that is especially fitting to individual coloring and body type. Patterns, colors, and material of clothing can make a significant difference in your appearance. For example, knowing what colors complement your skin tone allows you to choose color combinations more wisely. By paying attention to your clothing and color selections, you can enhance your outward appearance and in turn feel more internally confident. Confidence contributes to overall success.

apply it

Dressing for Success Research

GOAL: To develop further appreciation regarding what dressing for success means.

STEP 1: Select at least one or two articles that are used as a reference for this chapter or find other articles that are of interest to you.

STEP 2: Read the article(s) and write a brief report on what you learned.

STEP 3: Consider placing this Dressing for Success Research report in your Learning Portfolio.

BODY TYPE

Dressing for success and selecting clothes that contribute to a positive impression and self-confidence involve understanding your body type. Certain clothing styles are more flattering to some body types than others. Careful selection of clothes can enhance the positive. The following are suggestions for clothes that work best for various body types (Pages, 2005):

▶ **The inverted triangle.** Individuals with this body shape are broader in the upper body than in the lower body. Clothing advice for these individuals includes:

   ▶ Wear shirts with V-necks or open-neck shirts.

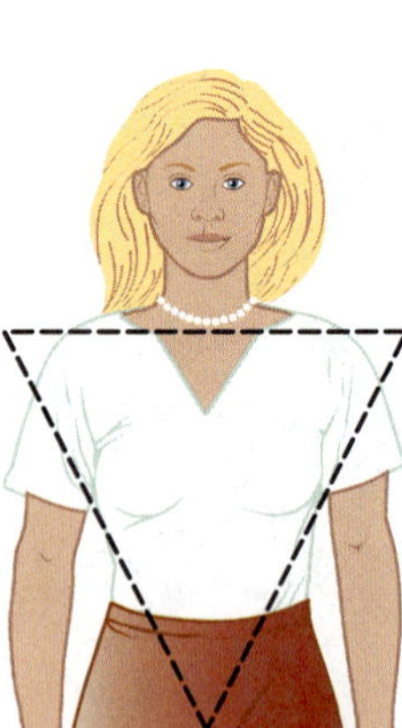

The inverted triangle body type is broader in the top half of the body.

▶ Avoid large patterns and bright colors on all clothing items and stick with one color (monochromatic outfits).

▶ For women, wear a long skirt that flares on the bottom to balance broadness in the upper body.

▶ Avoid tight shirts and shirts that have a lot of detail on the front.

▶ **The pear or diamond shape.** These individuals are essentially the opposite of the inverted triangle and are broader in the lower body than in the upper. These individuals may also have shoulders that slope. Clothing advice for this body shape includes:

▶ Wear well-tailored pants and shirts with simple lines. Women should avoid gathered or full skirts. A skirt with a center seam can help to diminish wide hips. Longer skirts also can be more complimentary to a woman with heavy legs.

▶ Wear long jackets with shoulder pads to balance the lower body.

▶ Avoid wearing tight pants or skirts that are too tight.

▶ Wear plain rather than decorative hosiery.

▶ Wear colors that are not too dark.

▶ **The rectangle.** Individuals with a rectangle shape have evenly distributed weight between the upper and lower body. They may need to select clothing that gives the illusion of more shape. Clothing for individuals with this body shape includes:

▶ Choose simple belts.

▶ Layer garments.

▶ For women, choose jackets, tunics, or vests over long skirts. Jackets should not end at the waist.

▶ Select pants that are straight with stiff or pressed-down pleats.

▶ Choose materials that retain their shape, such as crisp linens, cottons, twill, or tweed.

▶ Materials with vertical patterns should be avoided.

▶ Loose-fitting, oversized garments should be avoided.

▶ **Full figure.** Individuals with a full-figured shape or rounded figure will want to create the illusion of long, slim lines. Clothing selections should contribute to a shaped appearance. These can be accomplished as follows:

▶ Avoid clothing that is too tight and hugs the body.

▶ Avoid clothing that is too loose or too baggy, which can lead to a "dumpy" appearance.

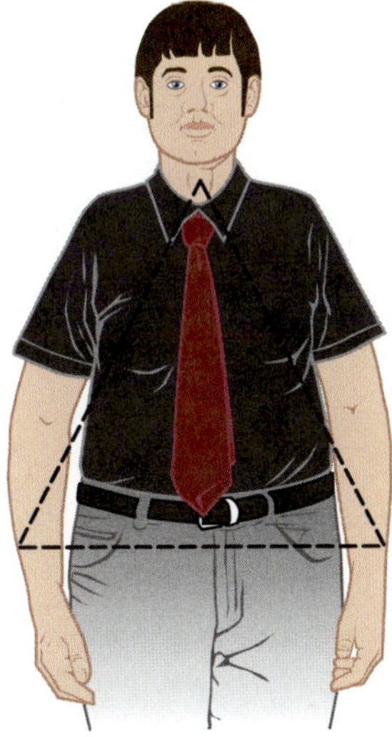

The individual with a pear- or diamond-shaped body type is broader in the lower half of the body.

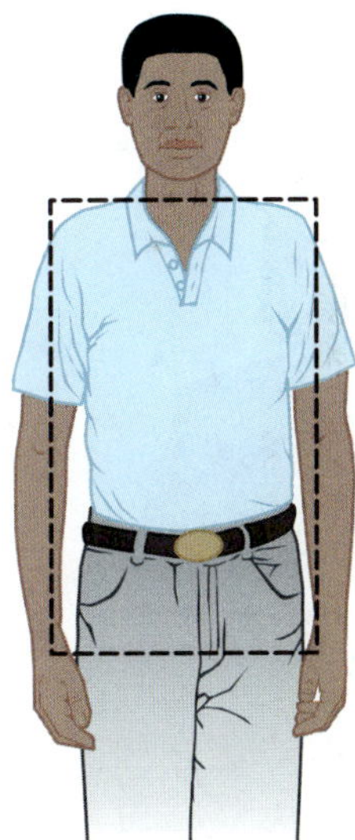

The rectangle body type is evenly proportioned between the upper and lower body.

> Select colors and textures that offer balance, as well as soft designs such as multicolored weaves.

> Wear skirts or pants with inverted pleats at the waist.

> Use belts that blend in with the outfit.

> Choose jackets that have straight lines and are defined at the waist.

Be aware that these body types are guidelines based on general categories, and most people find they are a combination of body types. Try various styles based on the type you think you are and use your best judgment to make your decisions. For any body type, the goal in selecting clothing is to look and feel your best. Let that be your guide.

apply it

Body Type and Skin Tone Appreciation

GOAL: To help develop an understanding of how to dress for success, appreciating body type and skin tone.

STEP 1: Form two groups of students. Have one group conduct research regarding body types and the other group research skin tones.

STEP 2: Look for information that can be presented to the class to provide insight into how to work effectively with the various body types and skin tones.

STEP 3: Give a presentation to the class using visual aids and activities that help individuals gain insight into their body type and skin tone.

STEP 4: Consider putting this Body Type and Skin Tone Appreciation report in your Learning Portfolio.

DRESSING FOR THE INTERVIEW

When deciding on appropriate dress for interviewing, the general consensus is that it is best to dress conservatively. A common standard is to dress one step up from the typical daily attire at the organization. It may be important to investigate the company where the interview will be taking place to confirm what attire will be appropriate. This can be accomplished by calling and asking someone in the human resource office or by visiting the company prior to the interview. Other considerations that affect dress choice are

The full figure or rounded body type is equally proportioned between the upper and lower body, but lines are less angular than the rectangle body type.

the type of job being applied for and the company dress expectations. For example, someone who is going to work as an airline mechanic will dress differently for the interview than someone who is applying for an executive position. If the airline mechanic applicant showed up in a three-piece suit, the employer might hesitate in hiring this individual, who is more than likely overdressed for the position. That is not meant to say that the airline mechanic should wear jeans to the interview. In fact, many employers find jeans to be unacceptable interview attire no matter what the job is. Much of the choice regarding what is worn to an interview depends on some common sense and having researched the corporate environment, culture, and the employer's preference.

So, what is acceptable? What if the company employees dress in office casual? Does their dress code affect how you dress for an interview or as a new employee? Does the interviewer's attire determine what you should be wearing? Here are some general thoughts from some professionals:

- No matter what your potential employer is wearing, the majority of employers will expect the interviewee to wear traditional interview attire (Larson, 2000).

- "The safest look for both men and women in an interview is traditional and conservative" (Brookhaven College Career Development Center, 2004, p. 1).

- "Even though the company may not require you wear a suit or professional wardrobe, you must put your best foot forward and wear it to the interview. Remember, it is a competitive market right now, and anything you can do to put yourself one step ahead of the competition is helpful" (Career Clinic, n.d.).

The most important thing to remember regarding the clothing you select for your interview is that your clothing must not get in the way of your presentation. You are there to sell your skills and abilities. You do not want your clothes to be the focus of the conversation!

GROOMING CONSIDERATIONS

Appropriate interviewing attire does include elements other than a good suit. A neat and clean appearance is perceived by many employers as being as important as the choice of dress. The following are grooming suggestions for before the interview:

- Hair style and care contribute to overall appearance. Hair should be clean and combed into an attractive style. If needed, get a haircut a week or two before the interview. For budget-conscious individuals, find a local beauty school that offers free or discounted haircuts.

9

> For men who choose to have facial hair, is important that facial hair be groomed and trimmed.

> Fresh breath during the interview is critical. Teeth should be brushed prior to the interview. Carry breath mints and use them before the interview as needed. Eating a small amount of food prior to the interview may also help maintain fresh breath by controlling unchecked stomach activity, but select mild foods that do not contribute to breath issues.

> Use deodorant. Avoid perfumes and scents.

> Appearance of fingernails can convey a professional image for both men and women. If money for manicures is a concern, see if a local beauty school in the area offers free or discounted manicures. If fingernail polish is worn, it should be clear or a soft, neutral color.

---

success steps

GROOMING FOR THE INTERVIEW

1. Keep hair neat and clean.

2. Select a hair style that complements your face shape and skin tone.

3. Make sure facial hair is groomed or removed.

4. Use deodorant and avoid perfumes and scents.

5. Make sure nails are manicured and appropriately colored if polish is used.

©Digital Vision

Well-selected interview attire for men includes a neutral color two-piece suit, solid color shirt in a neutral color, tie in complementary color, polished shoes, and minimal jewelry. Hair and nails should be well groomed. Cover tattoos and remove any body jewelry from piercings.

CLOTHING FOR THE INTERVIEW

Preparing for an interview and selecting clothing should be done as soon as the interview has been scheduled. Having at least two interviewing outfits is important. By keeping both outfits clean and ready, you will be prepared for any potential accidents that may occur. If the interviewing outfits have not been worn for a while, try each outfit prior to the interview day to make sure it fits properly. Dry clean or wash items as needed and complete any repairs such as missing buttons and frayed cuffs (Newberger, n.d.). Take care of other considerations prior to the interview, such as ensuring that shoes are polished and briefcase and/or purse is cleaned, polished, and well organized. If a winter coat will be needed, make sure that it is clean and ready to be worn.

Men's and women's clothing suggestions for interview attire are as follows (Brookhaven College Career Development Center, 2004; King's College Career Planning and Placement Office, n.d.):

Men:

▶ Suits are the most preferred outfit for interviewing. Common colors for suits are navy, brown, or shades of gray. Black is acceptable, but some may find it too dark or gloomy. Most professionals indicate that a two-piece suit is most appropriate.

▶ Shirts should always be long sleeved and be of solid colors: light blue, cream, or white. The fabric typically preferred is either a cotton-polyester blend or 100% cotton. Shirts must be clean and lightly starched.

▶ Tie colors should complement or blend with the overall outfit. The preferred fabric is 100% silk with a simple pattern. Once tied, the tie should have a small knot and extend down to the trouser belt. The acceptable width of ties is usually between 2¾ inches and 3½ inches. Bow ties should be avoided.

▶ Shoes should be well polished and in good condition, with no apparent scuff marks or other flaws. Black, brown, or burgundy leather shoes work best with business suits. Socks need to be dark, complement the suit, and be of calf length so that skin is not revealed when sitting down and crossing legs.

▶ Accessories such as belts should be selected to complement the shoes being worn. Jewelry should be minimal and typically include only items such as a wedding band, tie tack, watch, and cuff links. No earrings or other facial piercing rings should be worn to the interview. No accessories or clothing should have any words or images that indicate personal beliefs or political views. Tattoos should be covered when possible. Carry a leather briefcase that is in good condition. Make sure all of these items present a professional image.

success steps

MEN'S DRESSING TIPS

1. Select a neutral color, two-piece suit.

2. Select a long-sleeved shirt in a neutral color that complements the suit.

continued

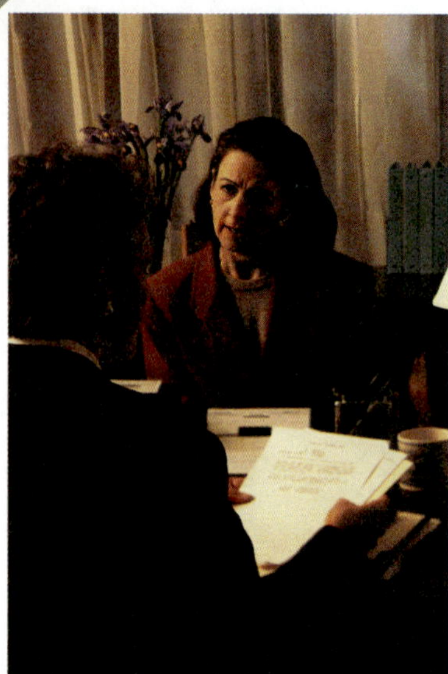

Well-selected interview attire for women includes a neutral color, two-piece suit; a solid color blouse without added frills; polished, neutral color pumps; neutral color hose; and accessories that complement the shoes. Avoid plunging necklines and dramatic make-up. Do not carry both a briefcase and a purse; select one or the other. A briefcase is preferable. Cover tattoos and remove any body jewelry from piercings.

continued

3. Select a tie in a color that complements the shirt and suit.

4. Ensure that shoes are polished and scuff free.

5. Wear dark-colored, calf-length socks.

6. Keep jewelry to a minimum.

Women:

▶ Skirt suits are the recommended attire for women for an interview. Dresses are acceptable but are less appropriate than a suit. If a dress is worn, then a matching jacket is highly recommended. Casual slacks should never be worn unless research of the company has indicated otherwise. Color choices for suits are typically beige, charcoal, gray, black, or navy blue. Skirts of knee length or 2 inches above the knee are recommended, but skirt length may be selected according to body type.

▶ Blouses in solid colors that complement the skirt should be selected. White or cream is recommended. Styles chosen should be selected to complement one's body type. Avoid blouses with front frills or lace and plunging necklines.

▶ Generally, basic pumps with low or medium heels work best. Shoes need to be polished and in good condition. Colors that typically coordinate well with women's business suits include solid black, brown, navy, taupe, and burgundy. Panty hose must be new or in excellent condition and fit well to avoid any bagging at the ankles. Carry an extra pair just in case of an emergency. A neutral color that matches your skin tone is best.

▶ Accessories such as belts should be selected to complement or match the shoes being worn. Carry a briefcase rather than a purse. Carry a small, professional appearing purse if you do not have an acceptable briefcase. Do not carry both. Make sure the briefcase appearance and its contents, such as pen and paper, represent a professional image. Jewelry should be minimal and should only include items such as a wedding or engagement ring, necklace, earrings, bracelet, and watch. No more than one ring per hand should be worn. Earrings should not be dangly but close to the ear and should complement the entire outfit. No more than one set of earrings should be worn. Eyebrow or any other facial piercing jewelry should be removed. No piece of jewelry worn should draw too much attention.

◗ Make-up should be worn but needs to complement your skin tone rather than overwhelm your natural appearance. Dark eye shadows should be avoided. If nail polish is worn it should be a subtle tone, such as pale pink or a clear gloss.

success steps

WOMEN'S DRESSING TIPS

1. Select a neutral color, two-piece suit with a skirt of appropriate style for your body type.
2. Choose a suit over a dress. If a dress is worn, a jacket should be added.
3. Select a solid color blouse without added frills. Avoid plunging necklines.
4. Wear polished, neutral color pumps with a low to medium heel.
5. Wear neutral color hose.
6. Select accessories that complement the shoes.
7. A briefcase is preferred to a purse. Do not carry both a briefcase and a purse.
8. Select make-up that complements your skin tone and features but does not overwhelm.

◗ REFLECTION QUESTIONS

- What clothing do you own now that is appropriate for professional attire?
- What more can you learn about your skin tone and body type that might help enhance your appearance?

❓ CRITICAL THINKING QUESTION

9–2. What is your reaction to the following statement? "It isn't the clothes that make a person."

9

apply it

Interview a Professional

GOAL: To develop further appreciation of what is entailed in dressing for success.

STEP 1: Contact a professional in your field and arrange an interview. The purpose of the interview is to discuss the type of dress most appropriate for the profession.

STEP 2: For the interview, dress in clothing you believe is appropriate for interviewing with this individual. During the interview, ask the professional to critique your choice of dress and to offer suggestions for improvement.

STEP 3: Write a brief report on what you learned. Set goals for developing your professional wardrobe.

BUILDING A PROFESSIONAL WARDROBE ON A BUDGET

Often, college students find themselves without much additional cash. Consequently, budgeting for the eventual purchase of professional outfits needs to begin as soon as possible.

The Department of Apparel, Merchandising, Design and Textiles at Washington State University (n.d.) makes the following suggestions for dressing professionally on a tight budget:

- Don't wait until the last minute to start looking for the outfits you need to purchase. Since you are on a tight budget, finding the best clothes you can get for your money may take some time. Take your time and make wise purchases.

- Keep in mind that you are not just purchasing these outfits for the interview, but that these two outfits may need to serve you until you receive your first paycheck. Because of this, make sure the outfits can be mixed and matched to make a variety of outfits. Purchasing outfits with interchangeable components expands your possibilities and maximizes your wardrobe budget.

- Select a neutral tone such as black, dark gray, or navy around which to build your wardrobe. You can also choose contemporary colors such as pearl gray, steel blue, camel, and celery. When selecting colors, pay attention to those that best suit your skin tone.

- Do not overlook the important purchases of appropriate accessories and shoes. Budget these items into your overall plan.

- Purchase items that are washable to avoid dry cleaning expenses.

- If travel may be required for the interview and/or job, select clothing that is less likely to wrinkle.

- Although you are on a budget, do not cut corners when it comes to quality. Invest in clothing that is well made, of durable fabric, and of a classic design that is less likely to go out of style with the next clothing trend.

- Consider thrift shops when necessary. Often, thrift stores have merchandise that was worn minimally by executives and business people. Look for good name brands that offer quality. Inspect pieces for tears, frayed areas, and other signs of wear before purchasing. Check fabric for resistance to wrinkling by squeezing it in your hand.

- Finally, when in doubt, ask for help. Take someone shopping with you. This individual should be someone who has demonstrated the ability to dress professionally and whom you trust to help select the best items for your professional wardrobe.

success steps

PROFESSIONAL DRESSING ON A BUDGET

1. Begin budgeting early for your professional wardrobe.

2. Use the mix-and-match approach to stretch your wardrobe dollar.

3. Build your wardrobe around a neutral color base and add stylish, yet professional colors to your base.

4. Shop for quality rather than quantity.

5. Buy washable fabrics to minimize dry cleaning expenses.

6. Look for good-quality clothes in second-hand stores.

7. Seek the advice of an experienced and successful professional dresser.

REFLECTION QUESTION

- What concerns might you have about affording new outfits? What can you do to alleviate these concerns?

CRITICAL THINKING QUESTION

9–3. How can you learn to better appreciate the effects of dressing relative to your body type and skin tone?

CHAPTER SUMMARY

This chapter examined the elements of dressing for success in your job search. You considered the roles of elements such as body type and skin tone in the selection of clothing and how to select clothes based on these factors. Generally accepted standards of professional dress for interviews were also provided, as well as guidelines for accessorizing and attending to personal care issues. You also received suggestions for developing a professional wardrobe on a budget.

POINTS TO KEEP IN MIND

In this chapter, several main points were discussed in detail:

 Your dress and grooming is important and is a critical factor to getting hired.

Accepting that your personal appearance does make a difference and working on doing what is necessary to make a good impression will be what differentiates a successful individual from a less successful one.

By paying attention to clothing and color selections, individuals can enhance their outward appearance and in turn feel more confident.

▶ The presentation of your skills and abilities is the focus of the interview and is what needs to be heard. Don't let your clothes be the focus of the conversation.

▶ Being neat and clean is just as important as wearing the appropriate interview clothing,

▶ Establish a budget while still in college in order to be prepared to purchase the wardrobe items needed to dress for success.

LEARNING OBJECTIVES REVISITED

Review the learning objectives for this chapter and rate your level of achievement for each objective using the rating scale provided. For each objective on which you do not rate yourself as a 3, outline a plan of action that you will take to fully achieve the objective. Include a time frame for this plan.

1 = did not successfully achieve objective

2 = understand what is needed, but need more study or practice

3 = achieved learning objective thoroughly

	1	2	3
List appropriate clothing items that should be worn to an interview.	☐	☐	☐
Understand how first impressions can affect opinions of others.	☐	☐	☐
Explain how one's appearance can be improved by paying attention to dressing for one's body type and skin tone.	☐	☐	☐
Explain how one's outward appearance can affect one's internal confidence.	☐	☐	☐
Discuss considerations that should be given to one's interviewing attire.	☐	☐	☐
Discuss grooming tips that are important for professionals.	☐	☐	☐

Steps to Achieve Unmet Objectives

Steps   Due Date

1. ____   __________

2. ____   __________

3. ____   __________

4. ____

SUGGESTED ITEMS FOR LEARNING PORTFOLIO

▶ Dressing for Success Research: This activity will develop your understanding of dress that is appropriate in your field.

▶ Body Type and Skin Tone Appreciation: Completing this activity will increase your awareness of your body type and skin tone and help you choose styles and colors that complement both.

▶ Interview a Professional: Interviewing a professional will increase your awareness of dress expectations in your field.

REFERENCES

Brookhaven College, Career Development Center. (2004). Dressing for the interview. Retrieved March 19, 2005, from http://www .brookhavencollege.edu/pdf/careerctr/interviewattire.pdf

Career Clinic. (n.d.). Dressing for the interview. Retrieved March 19, 2005, from http://www.careerclinic.com/pages/ dressingfortheinterview.asp

King's College, Career Planning and Placement Office. (n.d.). Tips on interviewing. Retrieved May 26, 2006, from http://www.kings.edu/ Academics/CareerPlanning/interv2.htm

Larson, B. (2000, Summer). Dressing for the interview at a business casual environment [Electronic version]. Republished from the New Jersey Staffing Alliance's *Staffing News*. Retrieved March 19, 2005, from the Top Echelon Web site: http://www.topechelon.com/jobseekers/ larson.htm

Pages, M. (2005). No body's perfect. Retrieved March 22, 2005, from http://www.geocities.com/bluegumtrees/image.html?200522

Newberger, N. (n.d.). Dress for success. Retrieved May 26, 2006, from http://www.worktree.com/tb/IN_dress.cfm

Washington State University, Department of Apparel, Merchandising, Design and Textiles. (n.d.). Dressing on a tight budget. Retrieved March 19, 2005, from http://amdt.wsu.edu/research/dti/Budget.html

Wisconsin Department of Workforce Development. (n.d.). Grooming for employment. Retrieved March 19, 2005, from http://danenet.wicip .org/jets/jet-4814-p.html

10 Successful Interviewing

LEARNING OBJECTIVES

By the end of this chapter, you will achieve the following objectives:

- Explain the two types of questions that can be asked in a job interview.
- Discuss what makes an interview question illegal and explain appropriate responses to these types of questions.
- Understand accepted standards of interviewing.
- Discuss methods used to calm nerves before and during an interview.
- Define *nonverbal behavior* and provide examples of positive and negative nonverbal behavior in an interview.
- Discuss how to address your weaknesses or negatives in the interview.
- Discuss the purpose and methods of follow-up to an interview.
- Demonstrate the ability to find sample interview questions and create acceptable answers to each.
- Practice interviewing skills by participating in a mock interview.

 TOPIC SCENARIO

As the company's Director of Human Resources, Julie spends much of her time interviewing applicants for various job openings. Julie's secretary just called her to tell her that the next applicant, Susan Edge, had arrived. Upon arriving in the lobby to meet Susan, Julie began her assessment of the applicant. Sitting in the lobby was a woman with a navy suit, pale pink blouse, and matching navy blue shoes. Beside her was an attractive leather briefcase. As Julie approached, the woman rose and introduced herself as Susan Edge. Julie noticed that Susan waited until Julie extended her hand in order to receive a handshake. After the introductions, Julie escorted Susan back to her office. Upon entering the office, Susan waited to be offered a chair and then both Julie and Susan sat for the interview. Prior to the first question, Susan asked Julie if it would be acceptable for her to take notes during the interview. The interview then began.

Based on this brief scenario answer the following questions:

- What did Susan do to help Julie begin to form opinions about her professionalism and abilities?

- How in this brief scenario did Susan demonstrate her abilities as a detail-oriented individual?

- What kind of impression did Susan make by waiting to accept Julie's handshake and waiting to be asked to sit?

- If Susan had extended her hand first or had sat before being offered a chair, what impressions, if any, might have been made? Should these actions affect Julie's overall opinion of Susan?

 PREPARING FOR THE INTERVIEW

It is important to begin preparing for the interview as soon as it has been scheduled. Areas that require consideration when preparing for an interview include the following:

- Update your resume and reference list as needed and make copies to take to the interview.

- Prepare and organize your portfolio with anything that is related to the job.

- Make sure what you will wear has been purchased and is clean and ready.

- Purchase any necessary pens, paper, or other materials that may be needed for the interview.

▶ Consult a map or map Web site to determine the best way to get to the interview location.

Another aspect of preparing for the interview includes conducting research on the company. Employers expect applicants for a position have taken the time to research the company and what the job entails. The Internet can usually provide useful information. Locate the company's Web site and familiarize yourself with the company's current projects, events, and issues. A company's annual report can also provide significant information. Other sources of information for research include the business section of the newspaper, trade associations and journals, directories found at local libraries such as Dun & Bradstreet's *Business Information Reports*, the manuals of Moody's Investor's Services, and Standard & Poor's guides, as well as company literature, newsletters, and business magazines (University of Dayton Career Services, n.d.(a)).

©Digital Vision

The Internet is an effective resource for conducting industry research related to your job search.

apply it

Researching Companies

GOAL: To develop more information regarding companies of interest.

STEP 1: Research three companies for which you might like to work.

STEP 2: From the information that you find, prepare a brief report of your findings. Are you still interested now that you know more about the company? Why or why not? What Web sites were used?

STEP 3: Share your information with the class.

STEP 4: Consider placing this company information in your Learning Portfolio.

In addition to conducting research, applicants need to fully understand what skills and abilities they are bringing to the employer. They also need to be able to specifically relate their skills to the requirements of the job. Employers want to know that the applicant they choose is the best fit for the required tasks of the job.

The best way to prepare for an interview is to

▶ Obtain and review the job description of the position for which you are applying. If possible, obtain a copy of the job description prior to the interview. If this is not possible, you may be able to obtain a description of a job that is similar enough to provide you information about the tasks and responsibilities that are desired for the job. See Figure 10–1 for an example of a job description.

Job Description

Position: Medical Assistant

Reports to: Physician/Nurses/Office Manager

Responsibilities:

The MA is responsible for the flow of patients through the office. Serves as a liaison between the patient and the physician and assists in ensuring quality patient care. Works directly with the physician and nurses in providing care to patients. Works with other ancillary departments such as radiology and lab in arranging testing and procedures for patients.

Duties include:

1. Obtains information regarding the patient's past history and current illness.
2. Takes and records vital signs of the patient including weight, temperature, pulse rate, respiration, and blood pressure.
3. Escorts patients to exam rooms and prepares patients for exams.
4. Assists physician with the treatment of the patient.
5. Assists the physicians in procuring lab samples and requisitions.
6. Schedules appointments for all referred cases.
7. Assists other office staff, when necessary, in making appointments, calling patients, locating charts, and filing reports in the medical chart.
8. Manages medical and drug supply inventory. Originates orders as needed.
9. Maintains sample supply closet.
10. Keeps examining rooms clean and stocked.
11. Properly disposes of contaminated and disposable items.
12. Assists in retrieving past medical records for patients as required for the patient's office visit.
13. Retrieves labs, x-rays, and other test results. Pulls appropriate patient chart and attaches report(s) to the file for physician viewing.
14. Conducts routine lab work and EKG's as ordered by the physician.
15. Performs other duties as assigned by the physician/office manager.

Job requirements:

Graduation from an accredited MA program and current certification.
Enjoy working with people in a positive productive environment.
Possess the verbal ability to understand patient medical records, physician orders and medication orders, to be communicative with the patient and hospital staff.
Possess the ability to deal tactfully and effectively with patients, parents, and other employees, hospital staff, and the physician.

FIGURE 10–1. A job description outlines the responsibilities and expectations associated with a position. Doing an excellent job and advancing in your field often requires going above and beyond the expectations listed on the job description.

▶ Be clear on the knowledge that is necessary to do the job. Note the other skills and personal qualities that may be required or desired.

▶ If possible, discover what type of interview will be conducted. For instance, will it be a group interview, phone interview, online interview, or behavioral interview? Is the interview to take place over lunch or dinner?

▶ Anticipate the questions that may be asked and prepare answers in advance.

▶ Prepare questions that should be asked of the employer.

success steps

PREPARING FOR AN INTERVIEW

1. Review a job description, if possible. If a job description is not available, find out as much as you can about the position on the company's Web site or from Human Resources.

2. Be familiar with the knowledge you will need to do the job.

3. Find out what kind of interview will be conducted, if possible.

4. Anticipate questions that might be asked and how you would answer them.

5. Prepare questions to ask the employer.

INTERVIEWING QUESTIONS

An applicant will generally be asked two types of questions during an interview. Traditional questions seek factual information about an applicant, such as educational background and work experience. Situational questions ask the applicant to describe various situations and circumstances he or she has encountered. The purpose of situational questions is to assess more complex skills such as decision-making skills, use of ethical reasoning, and problem-solving strategies (University Career Services, n.d.). Being fully prepared for an interview requires the applicant to answer both the traditional and situational questions effectively and efficiently.

Depending on the company, more than one interviewer may attend the interview session. The purpose of a team interview is often to save both the employer's and the applicant's time. Although team interviews can be more challenging than the traditional one-on-one approach, it is important to mentally prepare for the possibility of a team interview. Caroselli (n.d.) suggests recognizing that team interviews are more stressful than traditional interviews and recommends making a connection with each interviewer and using various examples from your experience rather than repeating the same example. Be prepared for the chance of a team interview, as you may not be informed in advance that a team approach will be taken. As with traditional interview formats, practicing, researching the company, preparing intelligent questions, and listening effectively contribute to a less stressful and more successful team interview. In addition, seek the assistance of your career placement personnel and conduct research to familiarize yourself with team interviewing.

Preparing for questions that may be asked during the interview takes time and thoughtful reflection. One way to anticipate questions that might be asked is to seek advice from an expert, such as career placement personnel at your school. Or, research commonly asked interview questions on the Internet, using "interview questions" as your search term. Once you have examples of questions, consider recording well-thought-out answers. Use the questions and answers to conduct the mock interview activity introduced later in this chapter with a friend, family member, or a professional in your chosen career. Have the "employer" ask questions to which you must appropriately respond. After the mock interview, ask the "employer" to evaluate how you conducted yourself and the answers that you provided. Be open to constructive criticism and repeat the mock interview as many times as necessary to improve in areas that are weak.

Common interviewing questions include the following (University of Dayton Career Services, n.d.(b)):

▶ Why should we hire you?

▶ What is your biggest strength/weakness?

▶ Why did you choose your major?

▶ Where do you see yourself in five years?

▶ What specific skills do you bring to this position?

The following list includes questions that may be more challenging to answer. Take time to write your answers down as you consider each question (Mulligan, n.d.):

1. What do you see yourself doing five years from now?

2. How do you make yourself indispensable to a company?

3. Tell me about a time when your course load was heavy. How did you complete all your work?

4. Tell me about a time when you had to accomplish a task with someone who was particularly difficult to get along with.

5. How do you accept direction and, at the same time, maintain a critical stance regarding your ideas and values?

6. What are some examples of activities and surroundings that motivate you?

▶ **REFLECTION QUESTION**

• What types of questions do you think you might find most challenging in an interview? What steps do you need to take to become more comfortable with these questions?

7. Tell me how you handled an ethical dilemma.

8. Tell me about a time when you had to resolve a problem with no rules or guidelines in place.

apply it

Writing Interview Questions and Answers

GOAL: To demonstrate the ability to write interview questions and provide appropriate answers.

STEP 1: Write at least 30 questions that you think may be asked in an interview. For each question, provide a response.

STEP 2: Ask your instructor to review the questions and answers and make suggestions for improvements.

STEP 3: Consider the career placement personnel at your school as an additional resource for this exercise.

STEP 4: Consider putting your questions and answers in your Learning Portfolio.

There are some questions that employers cannot legally ask due to the nature of the questions. It is important for applicants to be aware of what these questions are and how to respond professionally to any such question that might be asked. Questions asked during an interview must pertain to the position and your ability to effectively perform tasks associated with it. The following are areas about which employers are prohibited from asking questions (University Career Services, n.d.; University of Dayton, n.d.(c)):

- birthplace, nationality, ancestry or descent of applicant, applicant's spouse, or parents

- marital or family status

- gender, race, color

- religion or religious days observed

- membership in organizations associated with a particular race, religion, or ethic group

- information about arrests, disabilities, or health conditions unrelated to job performance. Employers *are* permitted to ask questions about an applicant's ability to perform a specific task that is related to the job. For example, an employer can ask you if you can lift 30 pounds if that is a requirement of the job. The employer is prohibited from asking you if you have any disabilities.

If an illegal question is asked, it is probably unintentional. As a job applicant, it is important to respond professionally to any question that appears to be illegal. If handled correctly, the interviewer will not be made to feel uncomfortable as the question is left unanswered. Here are a few options for responding to illegal questions as recommended by the University Career Services of George Mason University (n.d., "Responding to Challenging Questions").

Option 1. Explore the meaning behind the question or its intent and respond to that meaning.

▶ For example, your response to "where were you born?" might be, *"If you are wondering about my status, I am authorized to work in the United States."*

▶ Your response to a question about marital status or young children might be, *"If you are concerned about my ability to travel, let me assure you that I am prepared to make all the necessary arrangements so that I can travel the amount of time you indicated is likely in this job."*

Option 2. Ask about the relationship of the information to the job.

▶ For example, if asked about your place of birth: *"I'm not sure what my place of birth has to do with my qualifications for this position."* Wait for a response from the interviewer and see if he or she can explain how this question connects to the job requirements. You can at this point choose to either answer the question or decline.

Option 3. Tactfully remind the interviewer that if not related to the job, such questions are illegal or inappropriate. However, with this approach you run the risk of coming across as uncooperative or confrontational. Avoid taking this tactic if at all possible. Keep in mind that illegal questions posed by the employer are typically not asked with any malicious intent (University of Dayton, n.d.(c)).

Option 4. Answer the question to avoid confronting the interviewer and possibly hurting your chances of being hired.

SUCCESSFUL INTERVIEWING TACTICS

Preparing for the interview will significantly help in the overall success of the experience. In addition to considering questions and your answers, what you will wear, and the materials you need for the interview, a few other simple rules should be followed for a successful interviewing experience. The

10

? CRITICAL THINKING QUESTION

10–1. What is your reaction to the following statement? "If an employer asks me a question that I do not want to answer, I will just tell the interviewer I am unable to answer the question."

following suggestions for a successful interview can help reduce stress and increase confidence (Hansen, n.d.):

▶ Make sure you know how to get to the interview. If necessary, do a dry run a day or two before the interview to make sure you know how long it will take to get there. Arriving at least 10 to 15 minutes ahead of the scheduled interview is suggested; arriving late to an interview is unacceptable. If a late arrival is unavoidable due to an emergency, call the company to alert the employer to the situation. Remember that a late arrival for any reason will make a poor impression. Always call as far in advance as possible if you must cancel the appointment. Do not simply fail to show up for the interview. If this occurs you not only ruin your chances for getting the job, but your actions show disrespect for the employer's time, as the time could have been used for interviewing someone else. Remember, too, that the professional world is a small one and word does travel. Your actions toward one employer may influence your chances with another.

▶ On the day of the interview, allow extra time for preparing and driving to the interview site. Allow for traffic and other possible delays.

▶ The night before the interview, prepare your briefcase with all the necessary items, such as copies of your resume, reference list, and portfolio. Take two or three pens and some paper. Consider all necessary items/information you may be required to supply the employer. For example, having the names and addresses of references might be beneficial should the interviewer request them.

▶ Take your cell phone for any last-minute calls you might need to make or to use in the event of an emergency. However, be sure to turn it off when you arrive at the interview.

▶ If you are not going directly to the interview from home, Pillsbury (n.d.) suggests that an "emergency kit" may be useful. Include items such as "an umbrella, an extra tie/pair of stockings, breath mints, a comb, an extra pair of glasses or contacts, tissues or a handkerchief, and few safety pins."

▶ As you arrive for your interview, present a calm and organized demeanor. If you have prepared effectively and allowed ample time, you will avoid arriving breathless and harried. Arrive with a pleasant friendly smile, greet the receptionist with professionalism, and offer your first and last name. Establish good eye contact as you speak. Remember that first impressions can make a difference.

▶ If a job application is presented to you, fill it out neatly and provide correct and accurate details as required.

success steps

EFFECTIVE PARTICIPATION IN AN INTERVIEW

1. Familiarize yourself with the location of the interview before the actual date.

2. On the day of the interview, allow extra time for preparing and arriving at the site.

3. Prepare your briefcase with necessary items ahead of time.

4. Take your cell phone. Be sure to turn it off when you arrive.

5. If you are not going to the interview from home, take an emergency kit of items that you can use to freshen up if necessary before the interview.

6. Enter the interview setting with a calm and organized demeanor.

7. Complete any paperwork that is requested.

DEALING WITH FEELINGS OF NERVOUSNESS

Most individuals feel nervous at interviews. The following are a few suggestions to help you calm feelings of apprehension, based on Bowman (n.d.).

- **Have realistic expectations.** Avoid elevating the position to your "dream job" or, conversely, telling yourself that you will never land the job. Keep the job prospect in perspective and focus on preparing for and doing your best in the interview.

- **Know what you bring to the job.** Establish a clear relationship between your experience and skills and the requirements of the job. Be able to articulate this relationship clearly and directly.

- **Prepare.** Research the company, update your resume and portfolio, and ready your wardrobe, all of which has been emphasized in this chapter. Thorough preparation and a working knowledge of your resume, the company, and the position can increase your confidence and reduce anxiety.

- **Take care of yourself.** Pay attention to your physical well-being. Get ample rest the night before your interview, eat a healthy and well-balanced meal beforehand, and avoid foods that don't agree with you.

- **Familiarize yourself with the interview site.** In addition to ensuring that you will be on time for the interview, arriving early provides you with an opportunity to focus and center your energy. Getting a brief overview of your surroundings can reduce nervousness. A stop in the restroom to ensure that you look your best will also help you relax.

> ### *success steps*
>
> **DEALING WITH FEELINGS OF NERVOUSNESS**
>
> 1. Have realistic expectations.
> 2. Know what you bring to the job.
> 3. Prepare.
> 4. Take care of yourself.
> 5. Familiarize yourself with the interview site.

Some individuals perspire more when anxious. If this is the case for you, make sure you have put on fresh deodorant and powder. Wear clothing that allows your body to breathe. If the interview room is warm, ask if it is acceptable to take off your jacket. It is better to be comfortable than dripping wet during the interview. Prior to shaking the interviewer's hands, wash your hands with hot water. This will eliminate or minimize sweaty and clammy palms.

The Santa Clara University Career Center (n.d., p. 1) suggests asking yourself the following questions to alleviate some of your anxieties by addressing fears objectively:

- What do I fear most about the interview situation?
- What is the worst thing that can happen?
- If I were giving advice to someone else in this situation, what would I tell him/her?

Nonverbal behaviors, such as eye contact and shaking hands, communicate as much about you as (perhaps more than) what you say.

THE IMPORTANCE OF NONVERBAL BEHAVIORS

An applicant's nonverbal behavior is just as important as the responses he or she gives to the interviewer's questions. During the interview, applicants need to be aware of what they might be communicating through their nonverbal behaviors. Nonverbal behaviors include your facial expressions, posture, and hand gestures. Examining and adjusting body language and appearance is critical to interview success and making a positive impression on the employer. The following examples illustrate how positive body language can make a difference (University of Dayton Career Services, n.d.(d)):

- Smile as you enter the office. A sincere smile indicates an approachable individual. Avoid a forced smile, but do appear friendly and pleasant.
- Convey confidence. Approach the interviewer and office staff with a self-assured manner. An erect posture and direct eye contact communicate assurance and poise.

The purpose of the interview is to provide both the applicant and potential employer the opportunity to exchange information and determine whether the position and applicant are a good fit.

10

> Offer a firm handshake. A firm handshake also communicates confidence and sincerity. Ensure that your handshake is neither too weak nor too strong and that the length of the handshake is appropriate. A weak handshake can indicate a lack of assertiveness, low self-confidence, and a lack of investment in the interview. Conversely, a handshake that is too strong can convey aggressiveness. A handshake that lasts too long can indicate nervousness and a lack of ability to modulate emotions such as excitement (University of Dayton Career Center, n.d.(e)).

> Carry your briefcase and coat in your left hand so that your right is free during introductions to shake hands.

> Make it a point to remember the interviewer's name and its correct pronunciation.

> Use a posture that conveys interest and attentiveness. Straight posture and leaning forward slightly with appropriate eye contact is recommended.

> Rest your hands in your lap or on the arms of the chair. If you are sitting at a table, you may rest your arms on the table with your hands folded loosely. It is acceptable to use hand gestures to emphasize your points, although not excessively. Folding your arms across the body is not recommended, as it may communicate nervousness or defensiveness.

> Pay attention to your mannerisms. Be aware of and avoid mannerisms that might be perceived as negative and annoying, such as playing with your hair.

success steps

NONVERBAL COMMUNICATION DURING THE INTERVIEW

1. Smile. Do not force a smile, but do appear approachable and friendly.
2. Convey confidence with your erect posture and direct eye contact.
3. Use a firm handshake.
4. Carry your briefcase in your left hand so that your right is free to shake hands.
5. Make it a point to remember the interviewer's name.
6. Demonstrate attentiveness by sitting straight and leaning forward slightly toward the interviewer.

7. Rest your hands in your lap, on the arms of the chair, or folded loosely on the table in front of you.

8. Use hand gestures in moderation.

9. Pay attention to your mannerisms and avoid those that are distracting or annoying.

HANDLING THE INTERVIEW

The purpose of an interview is not necessarily to get a job. Most of the time the purpose of the interview is to provide more information to the applicant and employer to determine if the fit is right. Often, an applicant really does not know if the job is right for him or her until the interview has taken place. Sometimes during the interview, either one or both of the parties may conclude that the job is not a good fit. This does not mean that the interview was a failure. The interview is only a failure if the applicant neither presented him- or herself professionally nor expressed his or her skills and abilities clearly enough for the employer to choose the right candidate for the job.

Once the interview begins, it is important to remain calm and confident. The preparation that has been done prior to the interview supports a relaxed and effective presentation. The following are some suggestions to help make the interviewing experience more positive (Bellevue University Career Services, n.d.; Hansen, n.d.):

▶ Not all individuals are perfect at the job of interviewing. If your interviewer is less than effective, it is your job as the applicant to remain courteous and answer the questions as asked. Provide thorough and effective information. Having difficulty with an individual interviewer does not necessarily mean you will not get the job. Remain professional and do not run the risk of ruining your chances due to an interviewer's inadequacies.

▶ Turn off all cell phones and pagers prior to entering the interview.

▶ Do not allow family members, children, friends, or other individuals to accompany you to an interview.

▶ Request a cup of water prior to the beginning of the interview. Nerves often create dry mouth. Do not chew gum or suck on a breath mint during the interview. Avoid yawning as it can indicate boredom.

▶ Answer each question with consideration and care. Some questions may not seem as important as others, but the interviewer probably has good reason for asking each one.

- Prior to answering a question, it is acceptable to pause and make sure your answer is well thought out. Moments of silence are reasonable in order to prepare a thoughtful response. Demonstrating the ability to reflect on and think through an answer reflects the ability to consider relevant issues and attend to details.
- Avoid making jokes and being overly friendly with the interviewer. You want to appear professional.
- Use good grammar. Avoid pausing words such as *um* or *uh*. Taking a moment to reflect and plan what to say is preferable.
- Speak up. Soft-spoken individuals may be seen as lacking confidence.
- Demonstrate effective listening skills. Never interrupt the interviewer. Effective listening will communicate a desirable workplace skill and enable you to answer the question more appropriately.
- Clarify questions as needed. It is appropriate to ask questions if you do not understand something. Clarifying questions will allow you to provide more effective and appropriate answers.
- Be positive about your experiences and achievements, but avoid exaggerating or embellishing the truth. Doing so will catch up with you later.
- When responding to questions, be as clear and succinct as possible. Whenever possible, answer questions with more than just a "yes" or "no." Provide examples when possible to further explain answers, but avoid rambling.
- Avoid topics such as religion and politics. If the interviewer brings up any controversial topics, remain vague and noncommittal. It is inappropriate to share your opinion.
- When answering questions, do not hesitate to demonstrate the knowledge you have gained about the company through your research. Employers will appreciate your efforts. Avoid being cocky about your knowledge, which may be perceived as showing off.
- Avoid discussion of your personal life.
- Avoid criticizing a former employer or colleague. If you experienced difficulties or are asked about a difficult time, describe the situation as a positive learning experience. Accept responsibility that is yours and describe how you would change for the better.
- Avoid overuse of hand gestures. If this is a natural inclination, then try folding your hands together on your lap. This will also help those who have a tendency to chew their nails (Dress for Success, n.d.).
- If you trip or accidentally knock something over, do not panic. Showing you can handle these types of incidents demonstrates that you handle pressure well (Dress for Success, n.d.).

- Always have some questions written down that you want to ask the employer. By asking questions you demonstrate your interest and intelligence.

- Focus on what you offer the company and how your abilities meet company needs. "Always keep the focus on what you can do for the company; the interviewer is most concerned with your ability to do the job and benefit the company, not with the company's ability to meet your expectations" (Bellevue University Career Services, n.d., "Selling Yourself during the Interview").

- Avoid appearing desperate for the job. The employer may begin to wonder why you have not been hired anywhere.

- Do not bring up salary and benefits. Bellevue University Career Services (n.d.) makes the following suggestions regarding salary and benefit discussions:

  - Salary is typically discussed in later interviews. Wait for the employer to raise the issue of salary and benefits. After the issue is mentioned, it is appropriate to ask questions.

  - Wait until the interviewer offers a salary figure before stating your expectations. If you are asked to identify an amount, ask what the salary range is for the position. If you have a minimum acceptable salary figure, it is acceptable to state it, but realize that doing so may eliminate you from consideration if the amount is not acceptable to the employer.

  - Keep in mind that benefits also contribute to the total package. Benefit packages that include health and life insurance, retirement plans, and other features are costly and can add significant value to your salary.

- If you are interested in the job at the end of the interview, tell the interviewer. Ask about the next step in the hiring process, to demonstrate interest. Find out when you should expect to hear from the employer.

- Obtain the name and title of the interviewer at the end of the interview. Get a business card if possible. It is appropriate to send the interviewer a thank-you note as follow-up to the interview.

- After you have left the company, spend a few minutes in your car or at a quiet place taking notes on your experience. Jot down your thoughts and further questions that may need researching.

It is difficult to totally fail in an interview. Employers typically are understanding about the stress that applicants are experiencing, and many employers do their best to alleviate applicants' anxieties.

INTERVIEWING SUCCESSFULLY

1. Remain courteous under all circumstances and answer the questions as asked.

2. Turn off all cell phones and pagers prior to the interview.

3. Do not allow family members, children, or friends to attend the interview.

4. Request a cup of water prior to the beginning of the interview in the event your mouth becomes dry.

5. Answer each question with consideration and care.

6. Prior to answering a question, it is acceptable to pause.

7. Avoid making jokes and being overly friendly with the interviewer.

8. Use good grammar. Avoid pausing words such as *um* or *uh*.

9. Speak up to avoid being seen as lacking confidence.

10. Demonstrate effective listening skills. Never interrupt the interviewer.

11. Clarify questions as needed.

12. Be positive about your experiences and achievements, but avoid exaggerating.

13. When responding to questions, be as clear and succinct as possible.

14. Avoid topics such as religion and politics.

15. When answering questions, do not hesitate to demonstrate the knowledge you have gained about the company through research.

16. Avoid discussion of your personal life.

17. Avoid criticizing a former employer or colleague.

18. Avoid overuse of hand gestures.

19. If you trip or accidentally knock something over, handle the situation with grace and poise.

20. Always have some questions written down to ask the employer.

21. Focus on what you offer the company and how your abilities meet company needs.

22. Avoid appearing desperate for the job.

23. Do not bring up salary and benefits.

24. If you are interested in the job at the end of the interview, tell the interviewer.

25. Obtain the name and title of the interviewer at the end of the interview so that you can send a thank-you note.

26. After you have left the company, spend a few minutes in your car or at a quiet place to record notes about your experience.

Addressing Your Weaknesses

Addressing your weaknesses can be one of the most challenging aspects of the interview. Knowing that honesty is essential, many struggle with how to present weaknesses in the most positive light. University Career Services (n.d.) lists the following common shortcomings that become apparent during an interview and suggests the following guidelines for addressing them.

▶ **Lack of related experience.** Draw on experience other than work such as that gained in school, through hobbies, or in volunteer experience. Consider skills that you have that are similar and can be applied to the experience you lack.

▶ **Lack of education or degree.** Emphasize skills you have developed through on-the-job training or other experiences, as well as self-taught knowledge and skills.

▶ **Poor academic performance.** Present examples of learning activities in which you have performed well. Point out other accomplishments and emphasize how they relate to the position you are seeking.

▶ **Frequent job changes.** Emphasize what you learned from your various jobs, especially as it might pertain to the job for which you are interviewing. Show how your job changes illustrate a pattern of professional growth. Explain how this job fits with your interests and goals.

▶ **Gap in employment.** Describe what you did during the gap in your employment history and what you did and learned during this period of time. If you were fired or quit a job, share what you learned from the experience.

Poor performance in an interview can be attributed to a variety of reasons. In addition to failing to address perceived negatives, other reasons for presenting poorly in interviews include doing too much talking and not enough listening, being arrogant, not communicating well, devaluing or overvaluing one's abilities and worth, and failing to clarify the responsibilities of the job

▶ REFLECTION QUESTION

• What scares you or makes you nervous about interviewing? How can you overcome these fears?

? CRITICAL THINKING QUESTIONS

10–2. If you lack experience in the job you are applying for, how can you address this weakness in a positive light?

10–3. How can you address other weaknesses, such as a poor academic record, frequent job changes, or others?

by asking appropriate questions (Weinstein, 2001). By practicing interviewing skills and gaining confidence in your abilities, you will become more successful in the interviewing process.

apply it

Mock Interviews

GOAL: *To demonstrate the ability to perform in a mock interview.*

STEP 1: Select a partner with whom you will complete this activity,

STEP 2: For the first round, one of you will act as the employer and the other as the job applicant. Using the questions developed in the Writing Interview Questions and Answers activity, ask and answer questions. Understand the importance of treating this exercise with as much sincerity and seriousness as you would an employment interview. After one of you has played the role of the employer and the other the applicant, switch roles and repeat the exercise.

STEP 3: After the exercise, reconvene as a class and discuss what was learned in the mock interviews, what areas were difficult, and how you might continue to improve.

10

INTERVIEW FOLLOW-UP

Following up after the interview is essential and can be done in a variety of ways. The first important step is to write a thank-you letter to the interviewer(s). If the interview was a team effort, send individual notes to each member. Thank-you letters can be handwritten only if your handwriting is neat. If not, type the letter and personally sign it. Ensure that the spelling of names and titles is correct. Send your thank-you note(s) as soon as the interview is over. The employer will appreciate your quick response. E-mails are acceptable but should still be followed with a traditional written thank-you note. This will make the thank-you more personal. Figure 10–2 provides an example of a thank-you letter.

At the end of the interview it is important to ask the employer when further contact from the company should be expected. If you have not received word within the designated time frame, it is acceptable to contact the employer to ask about the status of the hiring process (Santa Clara University Career Center, n.d.). If it is necessary to leave a message, provide your

- How well do you think you will do in your interviews?
- What are your plans to minimize the concerns that you still have about interviewing?

William Running Deer
432 East Brooks Avenue
Denver, CO 80000

November 20, 2005

Ms. Christina Chung
Human Resources Director
Everett Technologies
10067 Mountain View Road
Broomfield, CO 82222

Dear Ms. Chung:

Thank you for taking the time yesterday to meet with me regarding the office manager position at Everett Technologies. The programs we discussed seem to be leading the company in exciting new directions. I believe that my experience with and knowledge of streamlining systems and tracking data would greatly facilitate your implementation of these new programs. In addition, the positive relationships I have developed with office staff in the past have provided me with a foundation for working effectively with diverse individuals in the office setting.

Everett Technologies' innovative and forward thinking perspective is impressive and I believe I could contribute significantly to your growth. I would appreciate your serious consideration of my candidacy for the office manager position.

Thank you again for the opportunity to meet with you and learn about your company. I look forward to hearing from you.

Sincerely,

William Running Deer

FIGURE 10–2. An effective thank-you letter acknowledges the employer's time spent and the information provided as well as highlights your skills and positive perceptions of the position and organization.

correct phone number(s) and the best time to reach you. If you have not received a return call within 24 hours, follow up with another call. Unfortunately, some employers are not considerate in following up with job applicants. If you have had no return calls after leaving two or three messages in a week's time, then it may be necessary to assume that the job has been filled. It may be helpful to contact an individual other than the interviewer at the company, such as the director of human resources, to determine the status of the position. Make sure throughout the process that your efforts do not become bothersome to individuals at the company. Maintain a positive professional demeanor at all times.

? CRITICAL THINKING QUESTION

10–4. What is your reaction to the following statement? "It feels awkward to do mock interviews. They don't feel real and I just don't think the practice makes a difference."

CHAPTER SUMMARY

This chapter provided you with the foundation for preparing for and participating effectively in a job interview. Suggestions for preparing included updating your resume and reference list, organizing your portfolio, and preparing responses to potential interview questions. You reviewed strategies for successful interviewing as well as methods for minimizing nervousness before and during the interview. The impact of nonverbal behaviors on the interview was emphasized. You learned ways to address your weaker areas during the interview and reviewed general behaviors that are likely to contribute to a less stressful and more successful interview. Finally, you learned appropriate interview follow-up techniques, such as sending thank-you notes to the interviewer(s) and appropriately maintaining contact with the employer to track the outcome of the interview.

POINTS TO KEEP IN MIND

In this chapter, several main points were discussed in detail:

- Conducting research about the company where one will be interviewing is an important step to successful interviewing.
- Job applicants must be able to clearly and succinctly explain their strengths and abilities during the interview.
- Interviewing questions can be divided into two main categories: traditional and situational questions. To fully be prepared for an interview, an applicant must be able to answer both types of questions effectively and efficiently.
- Conducting mock interviews as practice can substantially increase success in employment interviews.
- It is illegal to ask certain types of questions during an interview. The job applicant must be familiar with what constitutes illegal questions and how to professionally respond if such questions are asked.
- An applicant's nonverbal behavior is just as important as the responses given to the interviewer's questions.
- An interview is only a failure if the applicant fails to present himself or herself professionally and fails to express his or her skills and abilities clearly enough for the employer to choose the right candidate for the job.
- Various types of interviews can occur, including one-on-one interviews, phone interviews, online interviews, and group

interviews. Applicants need to be prepared for any interview type they encounter.

▶ Follow-up after the interview is essential and can be done in a variety of ways, including sending an e-mail, writing a letter, and calling. Calls and e-mails should *always* be followed with written correspondence.

LEARNING OBJECTIVES REVISITED

Review the learning objectives for this chapter and rate your level of achievement for each objective using the rating scale provided. For each objective on which you do not rate yourself as a 3, outline a plan of action that you will take to fully achieve the objective. Include a time frame for this plan.

1 = did not successfully achieve objective

2 = understand what is needed, but need more study or practice

3 = achieved learning objective thoroughly

	1	2	3
Explain the two types of questions that can be asked in a job interview.	☐	☐	☐
Discuss what makes an interview question illegal and explain appropriate responses to these types of questions.	☐	☐	☐
Understand accepted standards of interviewing.	☐	☐	☐
Discuss methods used to calm nerves before and during an interview.	☐	☐	☐
Define *nonverbal behavior* and provide examples of positive and negative nonverbal behavior in an interview.	☐	☐	☐
Discuss the purpose and methods of follow-up to an interview. Discuss how to address your weaknesses or negatives in the interview.	☐	☐	☐
Demonstrate the ability to find sample interview questions and create acceptable answers to each.	☐	☐	☐
Practice interviewing skills by participating in a mock interview.	☐	☐	☐

Steps to Achieve Unmet Objectives

Steps   Due Date

1. ____   ___________

2. ____   ___________

3. ____   ___________

4. ____   ___________

SUGGESTED ITEMS FOR LEARNING PORTFOLIO

- Researching Companies: This activity will increase your awareness of important issues at companies of interest and contribute to effective interviews skills.
- Writing Interview Questions and Answers: Writing interview questions and answers will prepare you to answer actual interview questions more effectively.
- Mock Interviews: Practicing interviewing skills in mock interviews will give you practice for an authentic interview.

REFERENCES

Bellevue University Career Services. (n.d.). Strategies for effective interviewing. Retrieved March 19, 2005, from http://career.bellevue.edu/~career/intervue.htm#TOP

Bowman, C. B. (n.d.). Keeping a lid on interview anxiety. Retrieved November 6, 2005, from the Dow Jones Career Journal Web site: http://www.careerjournal.com/jobhunting/interviewing/19980812-bowman.html

Caroselli, M. (n.d.). How to survive a team interview. Retrieved November 5, 2005, from the Dow Jones Career Journal Web site: http://www.careerjournal.com/jobhunting/interviewing/19990630-caroselli.html

Dress for Success. (n.d.). Interview tips: Do's and don'ts. Retrieved March 19, 2005, from http://www.dressforsuccess.org/interview_tips/dosanddonts.asp

Hansen, R. S. (n.d.). Job interviewing do's and don'ts. Quintessential Careers. Retrieved March 19, 2005, from http://www.quintcareers.com/interviewing-dos-donts.html

Mulligan, B. (n.d.). Interviewers' favorite questions . . . and answers. Retrieved March 28, 2005, from http://www.jobweb.com/Resources/Library/Interviews/Interviewers_92_01.htm

Pillsbury, Ceil. (n.d.). Dress for success. University of Wisconsin-Milwaukee. Retrieved March 19, 2005 from the Career and Life Help Page: http://www.uwm.edu/~ceil/career/jobs/index.html

Santa Clara University Career Center. (n.d.). Interviewing & dressing for success. Retrieved March 19, 2005, from http://www.scu.edu/careercenter/resources/publications/interviewing.pdf

University Career Services. (n.d.). Interview questions . George Mason University. Retrieved March 28, 2005, from http://careers.gmu.edu/students/jobhunt/huntref/questions.htm

University of Dayton Career Services. (n.d.(a)). How and why to research a company. Retrieved March 19, 2005, from http://careers.udayton.edu/articles/articles.asp?research.txt

University of Dayton Career Services. (n.d.(b)). How to prepare for an interview. Retrieved March 19, 2005, from http://careers.udayton.edu/articles/articles.asp?intviewtips.txt

University of Dayton Career Services (n.d.(c)). Questions employers should NOT ask during an interview. Retrieved March 19, 2005, from http://careers.udayton.edu/articles/articles.asp?cannotask.txt

University of Dayton Career Services. (n.d.(d)). First impressions DO count!. Retrieved March 19, 2005, from http://careers.udayton.edu/articles/articles.asp?firstimpress.txt

University of Dayton Career Services. (n.d.(e)). The importance of a good handshake. Retrieved March 19, 2005, from http://careers.udayton.edu/articles/articles.asp?handshake.txt

Weinstein, B. (2001). Five biggest interview blunders. ITworld.com. Retrieved March 19, 2005, from http://www.itworld.com/Career/1834/ITW010426interview2/

10

CHAPTER OUTLINE

The Office of the Twenty-First Century

Making a Positive First Impression

Dealing with Difficult People in the Workplace

Performance Appraisals, Raises, and Promotions

Workplace Etiquette Do's and Don'ts

11 Professionalism in the Workplace

TOPIC SCENARIO

Susan started work at her current employment a little over a year ago. During this time, she has received a lot of praise regarding her work from both her coworkers and her supervisor. Her performance appraisal, which occurred three months ago, confirmed that her work is outstanding. Two months ago, a new supervisor took over Susan's department and recently announced that all employees would receive new performance evaluations based on his observations of the last two months. Susan just walked out of her meeting with her supervisor and is astounded by what he has told her. Rather than receiving high marks, Susan has now been rated as a marginal employee.

Based on this short description of Susan's situation, answer the following questions:

- What should Susan's reaction be?
- Regardless of Susan's reaction, must she deal constructively and professionally with the situation?
- What wrong conclusions might Susan be making about the new supervisor?

THE OFFICE OF THE TWENTY-FIRST CENTURY

How and where work is accomplished has changed dramatically as technology has advanced. Some of the options available to employees include flex time, compressed work schedules, job sharing, and telecommuting.

Each of these situations has its own issues, but there is general agreement in the business world that employers benefit by offering these options, because doing so boosts loyalty, strengthens morale, minimizes turnover, and reduces recruitment and training expenses, as well as costs due to low productivity (Hansen, n.d.[a]).

Telecommuting in particular has become a more viable and popular option for employment. The number of employees working at home grew from 41.3 million in 2003 to 44.4 million in 2004, indicating an increase of 7.5% (Hansen, n.d.[d]).

Some employers resist instituting telecommuting for a variety of reasons, including being unable to meet with individuals as needed and the traditional perception that employees must be on site to function productively. However, with further development of technologies that make telecommuting more efficient and effective, more companies are finding this to be a viable work option for their employees (Greenspan, 2002). Greenspan cites technology such as broadband connections, more powerful computers, Web-conferencing capabilities, and Internet-based tools as devices that contribute to effective telecommuting.

Successful telecommuting depends on a variety of factors. Employees who do well in a telecommuting circumstance are those who are self-disciplined, self-motivated, well-organized, and proficient at time management. Evaluating your organizational skills and work style is important before you propose telecommuting to an employer (Hansen, n.d.[b]). In addition, prior to beginning employment with a company, it is important that you and your prospective employer address how and where work will be performed. Even if telecommuting is not presently an option, proposing it at a later time may be appropriate.

apply it

Telecommuting Opportunities

GOAL: To develop understanding about what is involved in telecommuting and whether it is feasible in your profession.

STEP 1: Conduct research on the Internet and/or at the library to find out more about telecommuting in your chosen profession.

STEP 2: Write a brief report of your findings and be prepared to present it to the class.

STEP 3: Consider placing the report on telecommuting opportunities in your Learning Portfolio.

MAKING A POSITIVE FIRST IMPRESSION

Whether you are telecommuting or working on site, making a good first impression is important for overall job success and for establishing positive relationships with both your supervisor and coworkers. Consider the following qualities and skills as those most highly valued by employers when hiring a new employee (Marquette University Career Services Center, 2003–2004):

▸ Communication skills (verbal, written, and presentation)

▸ Honesty and integrity

▸ The ability to relate well to others

▸ Showing motivation, initiative, and self-direction

▸ A strong work ethic

The professional image you project, including your appearance, contributes significantly to the impressions you make at your interview and in the first days of your job.

©2005 Jupiterimages Corporation

- Teamwork skills and the ability to work collaboratively
- Analytical and critical thinking skills
- Flexibility and adaptability to change
- Ability to attend to details
- Organization skills
- Self-confidence
- An appropriately friendly and outgoing personality
- The ability to communicate with tact and respect
- Good manners and courtesy
- Creativity
- A sense of humor

In the early days of your employment at a new job, it is important to demonstrate these qualities and abilities in order to make positive first impressions. Coworkers and supervisors want to know that the individual they have hired and are working with has the skills and qualities needed to get along with others and accomplish the required tasks.

When first starting a job, the following behaviors are significant in making a good first impression (Hansen & Hansen, n.d.):

- Having a positive attitude and demonstrating enthusiasm about the job
- Dressing professionally
- Showing team spirit by demonstrating a willingness to cooperate and collaborate with coworkers
- Giving credit to team members as appropriate
- Learning the names of coworkers as quickly as possible
- Asking questions to clarify information and asking for help as needed
- Taking notes to show interest and to assure that you recall critical information
- Taking initiative and being proactive
- Arriving on time, if not early; leaving on time or later than required; demonstrating time flexibility when possible
- Demonstrating responsibility by being at scheduled activities and following through on assignments
- Avoiding involvement in office politics and gossip
- Conducting a minimal amount of personal business on company time

- Getting involved with after work functions
- Demonstrating good manners by saying "thank you," "please," and so forth as appropriate
- Remaining organized by utilizing instruments such as daily and weekly planners

success steps

MAKING A POSITIVE IMPRESSION

1. Have a positive attitude.
2. Dress professionally.
3. Show team spirit.
4. Giving credit to team members.
5. Learn the names of coworkers.
6. Ask questions to clarify information.
7. Take notes to show interest.
8. Take initiative.
9. Arrive and leave on time.
10. Demonstrate responsibility.
11. Avoid involvement in office politics.
12. Conduct a minimal amount of personal business at work.
13. Demonstrate good manners.
14. Remain organized.

ATTITUDE COUNTS

Having a positive attitude can make a difference in your pursuit of professional success by contributing to the overall atmosphere on the job. A positive work environment:

- makes the work environment more pleasant
- allows for more creativity
- promotes a teamwork environment
- creates a more productive environment

It can be difficult to maintain a positive outlook, however, in the workplace, where not everything goes right all the time. Negativity in the workplace is a reality. Although employers can influence employee attitudes, it is the responsibility of every employee to respond positively to less-than-ideal situations. The following are some suggestions on how this can be accomplished:

▶ **Learn from challenges.** When a problem occurs, consider it as a challenge that can be effectively dealt with. Use the challenge as a learning opportunity to develop methods for addressing this type of issue.

▶ **Offer solutions.** If you believe that improvements can be made, offer them in the interest of improving the situation and with a constructive and positive attitude.

▶ **Remind yourself of positive accomplishments.** If you are feeling overwhelmed, take a piece of paper and draw a line down the middle. On one side, write what needs to be accomplished. On the other side, begin a list of what has been accomplished. Seeing the "accomplished" list grow can help you feel a positive sense of satisfaction.

▶ **Monitor your "inner voice."** Realize the importance of what you tell yourself. Brandi (n.d., p. 2) tells us to "recognize the power of positive self-talk. Often our internal chatter is negative." Reprogram your own chatter to be more positive.

▶ **Do not wallow in negativity.** Focus on being creative to solve the issues rather than spending time in exuding negative energy or wallowing in that of others.

▶ **Keep situations in perspective.** Avoid overdramatizing situations and excessive worrying. These feelings are rarely (if ever) helpful. Many times, situations are not as bad as they seem, and solutions are attainable. Recognize needs for improvement, but view these situations as opportunities for growth—this is one way to remain positive.

▶ **Avoid joining in on the office gossip.** Gossip is destructive and can negatively impact attitudes and create an untrusting environment. Gossip "creates animosity, tension, and ill will" (Norris, 2000–2001, p. 2). Instead of gossiping, rechannel your energy into something positive. Remember, also, that gossip can backfire—it may haunt you in negative ways in the future.

---

success steps

MAINTAINING A POSITIVE ATTITUDE

1. Learn from challenges.

2. Offer solutions.

3. Remind yourself of positive accomplishments.

4. Monitor your "inner voice."

5. Do not wallow in negativity.

6. Keep situations in perspective.

7. Avoid joining in on the office gossip.

DEALING WITH DIFFICULT PEOPLE IN THE WORKPLACE

As in your personal life, you will also encounter difficult people at work. The difference with difficult coworkers, supervisors, or clients is that typically, you cannot simply ignore or dismiss them. Successful professionals have learned the skills required to work productively with various personalities and behaviors, including those that are sometimes difficult.

DEALING WITH DIFFICULT PEERS

Some individuals are simply irritating. Given this, there will be any number of times throughout your life when you will encounter such folks, including in your work environment. Dealing effectively with difficult people requires accepting the reality of their personalities and/or behaviors. But it is important to realize that not all annoying behavior needs attention or should be responded to. As long as someone's behavior does not disrupt the quality and quantity of work, the issue probably can be left alone. Examples of behaviors that may be annoying, but not necessarily disruptive, include poor hygiene, poor manners, and similar conduct that has little impact on productivity.

Some personality types and behaviors, however, do require attention and should not be accepted in the workplace. Examples of these include excessive socializing, emotional outbursts, engaging in inappropriate soliciting (such as for political or religious causes), plagiarism, and taking credit for another person's work.

Addressing these issues can be difficult, but ignoring them may be detrimental to overall job satisfaction and to company productivity. Consider the following suggestions for dealing with difficult people in the workplace (Heathfield, n.d.):

▶ **Assess your own behavior.** Make sure that you are not the problem—examine yourself. Your personality and/or behaviors may be contributing to the situation.

Be aware of behavior in the workplace that might be annoying or distracting to others.

▸ **Get an outside perspective.** Talk to a friend or trusted coworker to get his or her perspective of the situation. Another individual's opinion may not only provide useful information but also help determine a solution. Be careful, however, that seeking an outside perspective is not misconstrued as gossip.

▸ **Address the issue with the individual.** Have a private conversation with the person you are having difficulties with. Use "I" messages: "An 'I' message uses the template 'I *feel* [name the feeling] *when you* [describe the behavior] *because* [state the consequences or reasons for your feelings]' and is clear and direct. The sequence is critical: state your feeling first, then their part described in behavior terms, then what it means to you. If you begin with 'You . . .,' everything after that will be deflected and they'll probably say 'You . . .' also" (Robin, 1997–2004, p. 2).

▸ **Follow up as appropriate.** Conduct a follow-up if necessary. If the person's behavior has improved, no follow-up may be required. If change has not occurred, ask yourself how badly you want the change to take place. Will follow-up help the situation or escalate it unnecessarily?

▸ **Seek assistance if necessary.** Involve others if it is necessary to readdress the issue. You may want to include your supervisor or the individual's supervisor. Involving coworkers who have been affected by the behavior(s) at issue may also be helpful. A group approach may be more successful in convincing the individual that his or her behavior is not appropriate and that it is affecting many people. Whenever it is necessary to address problem behavior, first speak to the individual directly and be sure to follow the company's chain of command in the event you need to address the situation further.

▸ **Take additional action if necessary.** If all efforts have failed, the following are your remaining options:

   ▸ Limit the person's access to you. This is only possible if your work productivity is not affected by limited contact with the individual.

   ▸ Request a transfer to another division or department within the organization.

   ▸ Seek employment elsewhere.

Most importantly, you must consider the effects the situation may have on your stress level and your work. Based on this assessment, you can make wise choices.

success steps

DEALING WITH DIFFICULT PEERS

1. Assess your own behavior.
2. Get an outside perspective.
3. Address the issue with the individual.
4. Follow up as appropriate.
5. Seek assistance if necessary.
6. Take additional action if necessary.

REFLECTION QUESTIONS

- What person in your personal or professional life do you have difficulty with?
- Is there anything you can do to deal more effectively with the situation?

DEALING WITH A DIFFICULT SUPERVISOR

Your options for dealing with a difficult supervisor are different from those of dealing with a difficult peer. Handling a difficult supervisor is one of the most challenging, if not the most challenging, situations an employee can face. Difficult supervisors may demonstrate such behaviors as micromanaging, being overly controlling, rudeness, exhibiting sexist or racist attitudes, or being incompetent (Hansen, n.d.[c]). Although you may work under good supervisors during most of your career, you probably will encounter a bad one eventually. "One study found that almost 80 percent of the employees surveyed identified their supervisor as a lousy manager. And almost 70 percent in that 2001 study conducted by Delta Road stated that their immediate superior had 'no clue' what to do to become a good manager. Author Harvey Hornstein, Ph.D., estimates that 90 percent of the U.S. workforce has been subjected to abusive behavior at some time" (Hansen, n.d.[c], p. 1).

Consider the following guidelines for coping with a difficult or ineffective supervisor (Hansen, n.d.[c]):

▶ **Maintain your professionalism.** Act professionally in all situations. Demonstrate respect for your supervisor and behave as you would in any other professional encounter.

▶ **Speak assertively.** Do not confront your supervisor in an emotionally charged attack. Remain calm, state your position in a conversational tone, and use "I" statements to identify your feelings (as suggested for addressing a difficult peer) to avoid sounding accusatory.

▶ **Use a problem-solving approach.** Consider scheduling a meeting with your supervisor to discuss the elements of his or her behavior that you find difficult. Approach the issue with the attitude that you

11

are willing to do what is necessary to improve the situation. Avoid exhibiting an angry, blaming, or defensive attitude.

▶ **Go to your supervisor first.** Make every attempt to resolve the issue with your supervisor before going up the chain of command. Do not go to your supervisor's supervisor, unless as a last resort.

▶ **Vent frustrations outside of work.** It is normal to have frustrations and it is healthy to vent them. However, do so with a neutral and supportive third party. Do not express your frustrations and anger to coworkers.

▶ **Be patient.** Even if your supervisor has agreed that change is necessary and has promised to make changes, do not expect your supervisor to change immediately.

▶ **Be aware of other opportunities.** If your supervisor cannot or will not change, watch for opportunities to transfer to another department within the company. In some cases, you may also want to watch for opportunities outside the company.

▶ **Do not just ignore the situation.** It is important to address the situation in some manner. Simply ignoring problems with your supervisor can affect your performance at work as well as negatively affect both your physical and mental health.

▶ **Do a self-assessment.** Be aware of your own behaviors that you can change to improve your performance and relationships on the job. However, be objective in your evaluation and do not blame yourself for problems caused by an ineffective supervisor.

▶ **Document your observations.** Consider keeping a journal that documents your supervisor's inappropriate behavior.

▶ **Document your accomplishments.** Keep a record of your accomplishments as well as copies of work that you produce.

success steps

DEALING WITH DIFFICULT SUPERVISORS

1. Maintain your professionalism.
2. Speak assertively.
3. Use a problem-solving approach.
4. Go to your supervisor first.
5. Vent frustrations outside of work.
6. Be patient.

7. Be aware of other opportunities.

8. Do not just ignore the situation.

9. Do a self-assessment.

10. Document your observations.

11. Document your accomplishments.

Documenting your observations and your accomplishments will be useful in the event that such information is later required by upper management or—in extreme cases—for legal reasons.

RESOLVING CONFLICT

Interactions between disparate personalities and behaviors can lead to a variety of conflicts in the workplace. Conflict in the workplace can occur for a number of reasons, including employees feeling that they are being taken advantage of, unrealistic expectations, misunderstandings, and conflicting goals and values (Fiore, 1999–2004). Resolving conflicts effectively is important to maintaining a positive working environment.

Strong communication skills are critical in successful conflict resolution. By making "I" statements and actively listening, many potential conflicts can be avoided and actual conflicts can be minimized. The following are further suggestions on resolving workplace conflicts (Portland Community College, n.d.):

Addressing potential conflict in its early stages and defusing it by using effective communication techniques contributes to a pleasant work environment.

▶ **Clearly identify the problem.** Ensure that the problem has been identified correctly. Doing so ensures that efforts to resolve the issue will be appropriately directed, thus contributing to a more expeditious and effective solution. You do not want to address a problem only to find out that it is not actually the issue.

▶ **Determine whether it is worth addressing.** Determine how serious the problem is and how frequently it occurs. Making an accurate and fair assessment helps determine whether the problem is worth addressing.

▶ **Evaluate resolution methods.** Consider the simplest way to resolve the problem. Methods include sharing concerns during a conversation, apologizing, holding a meeting, or seeking mediation. Mediation, which involves a neutral third party who moderates discussion between the conflicted parties, is often an effective method for resolving disputes.

Exercising is a positive way to alleviate stress.

11

DEALING WITH STRESS EFFECTIVELY

Situations such as dealing with a difficult supervisor or coworker and resolving conflict can add to the more typical type of stress that is experienced on the job. Stress at work is a topic not to be underestimated (Reed Consulting, 2005). Research indicates that one in five employees suffers from stress at some stage in his or her working life and that stress contributes significantly to absence from work. In addition, stress on the job contributes to health issues such as heart disease and stroke.

Stress at work occurs for various reasons, including dealing with time pressures, work relationships, long work hours, and office politics (Reed Consulting, 2005). Recognizing work stressors and minimizing them when possible is important for your overall mental and physical health, which can significantly impact your ability to perform your job.

The following are general steps for being proactive in dealing with stress (McGarvey, 2001):

- **Say "no" when appropriate.** Be aware of your own time constraints and say "no" to deadlines and projects when necessary. It is important to have realistic expectations about work demands and about your abilities to meet them. Saying "no" is preferable to continuing to take on more work and risking possible failure and added stress.

- **Be organized.** Being organized allows your time to be used more effectively, providing for more to be accomplished in a shorter period. Disorganization can create added pressures and stress.

- **Use time wisely during the day.** Eliminate the need to rush. Arrive early when possible and set your schedule to eliminate rushing.

- **Develop sources of positive energy.** Reduce areas in your life and at work that drain your energy. Create positive energy in your life by making time for relaxation and hobbies and activities that generate positive energy.

- **Be healthy.** Exercise and establish healthy eating habits. Wholesome food gives you more energy, and exercise helps counteract stress. Get adequate rest each night.

- **Take care of yourself.** Find time in your day to relax. Pamper yourself each day in small ways. Get a massage or take a hot bath.

- **Look for learning opportunities.** Try to view issues at work as opportunities rather than as sources of stress. Your mind is a powerful tool. Thinking positively about an experience may make it less stressful. Do not see or expect problems or stresses where they may not exist.

- **Do not do it alone.** Ask for help and delegate tasks when possible. Surround yourself with individuals who are positive, have high energy, and are willing to take on challenges.

- **Create a peaceful office environment.** Surround yourself with items that center you and remind you of what is important.

- **Get physical.** At times of stress, do something physical. Take deep breaths, go for a quick walk, count to 10. Create calm within yourself.

- **Use energy wisely.** Focus on what is positive and good. Put the stress into perspective. Consider whether the issue is worth the negative energy that you are putting into it.

- **Find the humor.** Having a sense of humor in the workplace is critical to relieving everyday stress.

---

success steps

DEALING WITH STRESS

1. Say "no" when appropriate.
2. Be organized.
3. Use time in the day wisely.
4. Develop sources of positive energy.
5. Be healthy.
6. Take care of yourself.
7. Look for learning opportunities.
8. Do not do it alone.
9. Get physical.
10. Use energy wisely.
11. Find the humor.

REFLECTION QUESTIONS

- How effective are you at dealing with your daily personal and professional stressors?
- What can you do in your life to eliminate or diminish these stressors?

CRITICAL THINKING QUESTION

11–2. How critical are exercise and rest to one's overall pursuit of success?

PERFORMANCE APPRAISALS, RAISES, AND PROMOTIONS

Performance appraisal systems vary, depending upon the company, but their general purpose is to provide employees with written feedback regarding their work. In well-managed organizations, employees are never surprised by what is presented to them in the performance appraisal because they have received verbal feedback on an ongoing basis. In most organizations, appraisal results are used to determine pay increases and other rewards (Archer North & Associates, 2004).

Companies usually try to make their appraisal system successful, but not all systems work well. When complaints are lodged regarding performance appraisals, they often concern the type of assessment scale used and/or inconsistencies in what the employee has been told versus what is presented in writing. If inconsistency is an issue, employees should voice their concerns and address them in a professional manner. In some cases, it may be necessary to an employee to accept the appraisal results and improve areas in which his performance is weak. If this is the case, establishing weekly meetings with your supervisor to review your progress in these areas can improve future appraisals.

Often, raises are directly linked to performance appraisals. Consider the following suggestions when requesting a raise (Hansen, n.d.[d]):

- **Document your accomplishments.** Prove your value by providing examples of your work and showing what you have contributed to the company. Provide objective evidence supporting your request for a raise.

- **Ask for raises in a professional manner.** When asking for a raise, always maintain a professional attitude and demeanor. Remain objective and assertive.

- **Make sure your request is realistic.** Research what others in your field are being paid and make sure that your expectations fall within appropriate parameters.

- **Consider other compensation.** Be prepared to consider other options, such as benefits in exchange for monetary increases. Depending on the company's budget, benefits may be proposed as an option.

- **Use negotiation skills.** Practice your negotiation skills with a friend or family member. Know what you will and will not accept, as well as your reasons. Consider including a "bargaining chip" (something you are willing to give up) in your request.

- **Ask for raises in the right environment.** Request a raise in a scheduled meeting. Do not ask in the hallway or at another unscheduled event.

- **Make your wishes known.** If you believe you deserve a raise, ask for it. Don't hound your employer if it does not happen right away, but do stay consistent without being annoying.

- **Be proactive for the future.** If you do not get a raise, ask your employer what you can do to earn one.

REQUESTING A RAISE

1. Document your accomplishments.
2. Ask for raises in a professional manner.
3. Make sure your request is realistic.
4. Consider other compensation in lieu of a raise.
5. Use negotiation skills.
6. Ask in the right environment.
7. Make your wishes known.
8. Be proactive for the future.

Many employees begin in entry-level positions with the expectation and aspiration of moving up the ladder in the organization. A history of positive performance appraisals helps establish you as a strong choice for promotion. Other strategies to facilitate a promotion include the following (Hansen, n.d.[e]):

▶ **Establish relationships.** Establish relationships with individuals in the organization who can mentor you and promote you within the company.

▶ **Document your accomplishments and contributions.** Keep a record of your accomplishments that contribute to the company's bottom line.

▶ **Network within the organization.** Reach out to as many individuals in the company as possible. Demonstrate to them your accomplishments, strengths, and skills.

▶ **Demonstrate creativity.** Demonstrate your ability to be creative and innovative in your current position.

▶ **Demonstrate loyalty.** Show your loyalty and commitment to the organization through your actions and work.

▶ **Form positive relationships.** Establish a good working relationship with your current supervisor. Your supervisor should be your strongest supporter for further advancement.

▶ **Seek learning opportunities.** Find opportunities to expand your knowledge and skills. The more you can offer a company, the more valuable you become to it.

▶ **Take initiative.** Volunteer to take on more responsibility when possible.

11

> **Be responsible.** Earn a reputation for being a reliable employee.

> **Be professional.** Present yourself as a professional at all times. Actions and attire speak volumes.

> **Work collaboratively.** Build a reputation of being a team player.

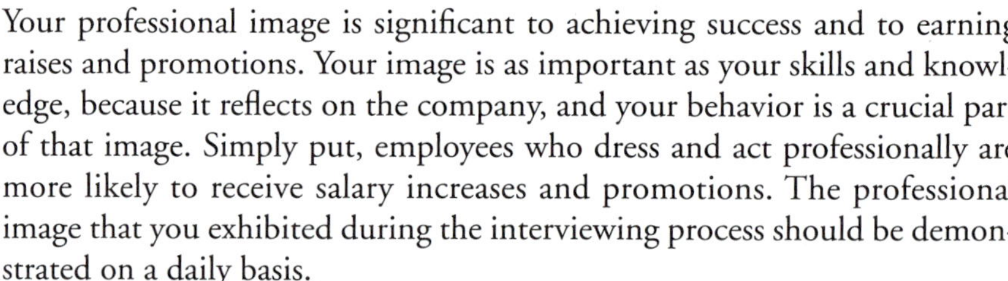

MOVING AHEAD IN AN ORGANIZATION

1. Establish relationships within the company.
2. Document your accomplishments and contributions.
3. Network within the organization.
4. Demonstrate creativity.
5. Demonstrate loyalty.
6. Form positive relationships.
7. Seek learning opportunities.
8. Take initiative.
9. Be responsible.
10. Be professional.
11. Work collaboratively.

REFLECTION QUESTIONS

- What are your professional goals and aspirations?
- What steps will you take to reach these goals?

CRITICAL THINKING QUESTION

11–3. What would you say to the following statement: "Performance appraisals should be taken with a grain of salt"?

WORKPLACE ETIQUETTE DO'S AND DON'TS

Your professional image is significant to achieving success and to earning raises and promotions. Your image is as important as your skills and knowledge, because it reflects on the company, and your behavior is a crucial part of that image. Simply put, employees who dress and act professionally are more likely to receive salary increases and promotions. The professional image that you exhibited during the interviewing process should be demonstrated on a daily basis.

"Successful impressions also require successful behavior" (Ritter, 2002, p. 2). The following behavior is important to creating the impression that you deserve raises and promotions (Bayer & Mallett, 2005):

> **Be approachable.** Say "hello" to coworkers you pass in the hallway and acknowledge their presence whenever possible and appropriate.

> **Avoid gossip.** Do not get involved in office gossip. Doing so is unproductive and promotes a distrusting relationship with others.

◗ **Follow the company's rules.** Those who break the rules are not only being rude but are demonstrating unprofessional behavior.

◗ **Use recommended telephone etiquette.** Follow guidelines regarding proper telephone etiquette that demonstrate professionalism.

◗ **Be aware of time.** Be prompt, but not so early that you appear to be wasting time or have nothing else to do. Do not keep others waiting, as it can send the message that you do not understand the value of their time.

◗ **Demonstrate manners during interactions.** Avoid interrupting others unless the interruption is valid and important to the discussion. Choose your words carefully and be tactful.

◗ **Make appointments.** Never walk into an office and sit down without asking permission or being invited to do so.

◗ **Return borrowed items.** Keep a record of items you have borrowed and return them to the correct owner in a timely manner. Consider a small token of appreciation, such as a thank-you note or tag attached to the item.

◗ **Keep a professional environment.** Treat your office space as an area that promotes professionalism. Avoid displaying personal items that make political or religious statements.

success steps

BEHAVIORS FOR SUCCESS

1. Be approachable.
2. Avoid gossip.
3. Follow the company's rules.
4. Use recommended telephone etiquette.
5. Be aware of time.
6. Demonstrate manners during interactions.
7. Make appointments.
8. Return borrowed items.
9. Keep a professional environment.

BUSINESS LUNCH MEETINGS

Business lunches offer another opportunity to demonstrate your professionalism. Depending on your position, business lunches may be commonplace or rare. Regardless of how frequently you attend such events, you must be prepared to present a positive image during them. Consider the following tips for business lunch etiquette (Franz, n.d., & Turner, 2004):

- **Turn off your cell phone.** Ensure that your cell phone is off or in vibrate mode prior to entering the meeting place. If you must receive a call during the lunch meeting, inform the attendees that this is the case and apologize in advance. If the call occurs, excuse yourself from the table to answer it. Only urgent business calls or emergency calls should be received. Make the call as short as possible.

- **Always be on time.** Arrive punctually, and when you arrive, offer firm handshakes and professional greetings to individuals at the table. If introductions have not occurred, introduce yourself and other attendees as needed.

- **Use appropriate table manners.** Sit down and immediately place your napkin in your lap. If you excuse yourself during the meeting, place your napkin on the left side of your plate, as this indicates to the server that you are not finished. When you are done, signal that you are finished by placing your napkin on the right side of the plate and your fork and knife across the plate at "4 o'clock." Avoid placing your elbows on the table. Never talk with your mouth full. Give less attention to your food and more attention to the individuals at the meeting.

- **Order modestly and wisely.** If you are not paying for the bill, do not order the most expensive item on the menu. Avoid ordering items that are messy to eat, such as ribs, wings, or spaghetti.

- **Avoid alcoholic beverages.** It is a good rule of thumb to avoid alcoholic beverages during a business lunch. Never order alcohol if your host has not done so. If you do have a glass of wine, have only one.

- **Be courteous to the wait staff.** Act professionally toward the wait staff. Remember that the image you convey represents that of your organization.

- **Appear confident.** Help yourself feel confident by dressing professionally. If you are nervous during the meeting, do not overcompensate by talking too much or too little. Listen to others at the table and join the conversation when appropriate. Small talk is appropriate at a business lunch, and you must be prepared to participate. If this is a skill that is difficult for you, practice! Never gossip during a business lunch.

- **Follow others' cues.** Do not rush the meeting if you are not in charge. It is not up to you to conclude when the meeting should end.

- **Work out the finances ahead of time.** If you called the meeting, you are responsible for the bill. If the meeting is a joint meeting, then determine ahead of time whether the bill will be split. Never work out the financial issues at the table. If you do not pay for the lunch, thank the person who does.

▸ **Know the appropriate use of table settings.** Bread and salad plates are to the left of your place setting, and your drinking glass is to the right. Use utensils from the outside in. The dessert fork is by the dessert plate or at the top of the place setting.

Proper etiquette is critical during business lunch meetings. For example, taking a cell phone call is not appropriate unless it is related to the meeting or a significant emergency.

success steps

ETIQUETTE FOR BUSINESS MEALS

1. Turn off your cell phone.
2. Always be on time.
3. Use appropriate table manners.
4. Order modestly and wisely.
5. Avoid alcoholic beverages.
6. Be courteous to the wait staff.
7. Appear confident.
8. Follow others' cues.
9. Work out the finances ahead of time.
10. Know the appropriate use of table settings.

apply it

Role-Playing a Lunch Meeting

GOAL: To simulate and experience a lunch meeting.

STEP 1: Set up a lunch meeting scenario in the classroom. Provide a table set with the appropriate utensils, napkins, plates, and so on. Have menus available for making selections. Serve food if possible. Select eight students in the class to play the role of the lunch attendees. Select one student to be the server. The other students will be silent observers. Select one student to play the supervisor who has called the luncheon, and give this student the purpose for the meeting and the topics to be discussed. In addition to business conversation, play out issues regarding cell phones, leaving the table, introductions, napkin placement, fork use, and so forth.

continued

continued

STEP 2: Role-play the lunch meeting from start to finish. Have the lunch go for about 15 to 30 minutes, with each participant playing the role provided to him or her.

STEP 3: At the end of the lunch meeting, have all students evaluate the situation and discuss what was learned.

COMPANY PARTIES

Most company parties offer an excellent opportunity to get to know and network with colleagues. During these events, individuals can promote themselves and their abilities as well as enjoy their coworkers' company. Following are some basic rules for making the best of a company party (Hansen, n.d.[f]):

- **Exhibit professional behavior.** Although the party is a social event, never forget who the attendees are or that your behavior will make either a negative or a positive impression on your colleagues.

- **Attend company events whenever possible.** Your presence makes a statement regarding your desire to be involved with the company, and if you don't attend, you are losing networking opportunities.

- **Enjoy yourself, but remain professional.** Drinking too much and/or making a fool of yourself will not present the image you want your employers to see.

- **Dress appropriately.** Find out what attire is appropriate for the event, and then choose an outfit that is fitting to the occasion, yet is fairly conservative. Avoid overly revealing or otherwise inappropriate attire.

- **Learn how to engage in small talk.** This is an essential skill at a company function. Avoid talking only about business. As always, avoid gossip. Avoid topics that stir peoples' emotions, such as politics and religion.

- **Be a good listener.** Allow others to talk about themselves. Learn as much as you can about your employers and other coworkers. Demonstrate interest by asking questions.

- **Greet people appropriately.** Keep your right hand free throughout the event so that you can shake hands during introductions. Introduce yourself to people you do not know.

- **Drink and eat in moderation.** Avoid becoming intoxicated if alcoholic beverages are served. Eat politely and in conservative amounts.

- **Make a professional exit.** Do not be the last person to leave the party. When you do leave, always thank your host.

success steps

ETIQUETTE FOR COMPANY PARTIES

1. Exhibit professional behavior.
2. Attend company events whenever possible.
3. Enjoy yourself, but remain professional.
4. Dress appropriately.
5. Learn how to engage in small talk.
6. Be a good listener.
7. Greet people appropriately.
8. Drink and eat in moderation.
9. Make a professional exit.

REFLECTION QUESTIONS

- What issue(s) about lunch meetings and company parties concern you?
- How can you be proactive in dealing with these concerns?

? CRITICAL THINKING QUESTION

11–4. Is it ever appropriate to let your guard down at a company lunch meeting or party? Explain your answer.

apply it

Research and Presentation

GOAL: To increase your understanding of the various topics discussed in this chapter.

STEP 1: Select one or two topics from the chapter that you want to research. Other class members should select other topics.

STEP 2: Research your topic(s) using the articles referenced in this chapter and other resources available on the Internet and/or at the library.

STEP 3: Write a brief report on what you learned from this activity and be prepared to make a presentation to the class.

STEP 4: Consider placing this report in your Learning Portfolio.

11

CHAPTER SUMMARY

This chapter addressed aspects of professionalism in the workplace, many of which go beyond the office setting. Professional behaviors that promote a positive impression in the workplace were summarized, and you learned effective methods for requesting raises and moving ahead in an organization. You also learned strategies for addressing coworkers' and supervisors' inappropriate behavior and steps for resolving conflict. In addition, this chapter addressed etiquette for work-related activities in which you may become involved, such as business meals and company parties. Overall, professionalism, a positive attitude, and being proactive were emphasized as key elements for success.

POINTS TO KEEP IN MIND

In this chapter, several main points were discussed in detail:

- Technological advancements offer options to employers and employees regarding where and how work will be performed. These options include flex time, compressed work schedules, job sharing, and telecommuting.

- Making a good first impression is important for overall job success and for establishing positive relationships with supervisor and coworkers.

- Although employers can influence employee attitudes, it is the responsibility of every employee to try and overcome negativity and remain positive.

- Successful professionals have learned the skills required to work productively with various personalities and behaviors.

- Dealing with difficult people is a challenge, but utilizing some basic communication tools can make your approach more effective.

- Resolving conflict effectively is important to achieving a positive work environment.

- Recognizing work stresses and minimizing them when possible is important for your overall mental and physical health, both of which significantly impact your ability to perform your job.

- A history of positive performance appraisals can help establish you as a strong candidate for promotion.

- Demonstrating professionalism through your attire and behavior—that is, maintaining a professional image—significantly impacts management decisions regarding raises and promotions.

LEARNING OBJECTIVES REVISITED

Review the learning objectives for this chapter and rate your level of achievement for each objective using the rating scale provided. For each objective on which you do not rate yourself as a 3, outline a plan of action that you will take to fully achieve the objective. Include a time frame for this plan.

1 = did not successfully achieve objective

2 = understand what is needed, but need more study or practice

3 = achieved learning objective thoroughly

	1	2	3
List areas that should be evaluated when assessing a job offer.	☐	☐	☐
List qualities that employers seek when hiring new employees.	☐	☐	☐
List problem personality types and behaviors that can be encountered in the workplace.	☐	☐	☐
List and explain the steps involved when dealing with difficult people.	☐	☐	☐
Discuss the pros and cons of telecommuting.	☐	☐	☐
Explain how good first impressions can be achieved at a new job.	☐	☐	☐
Understand methods for overcoming negativity and remaining positive.	☐	☐	☐
Explain methods for coping with a bad or ineffective supervisor.	☐	☐	☐
Discuss how to resolve workplace conflict.	☐	☐	☐
Understand the effects of stress and discuss how stress can be dealt with proactively.	☐	☐	☐
Describe the purpose of performance appraisals.	☐	☐	☐
Explain the do's and don'ts to requesting a raise and obtaining a promotion.	☐	☐	☐
Discuss positive and negative office behaviors.	☐	☐	☐
Discuss the issues that should be considered when attending a business lunch meeting and a company party.	☐	☐	☐

Steps to Achieve Unmet Objectives

Steps   Due Date

1. ____   __________

2. ____   __________

3. ____   __________

4. ____   __________

SUGGESTED ITEMS FOR LEARNING PORTFOLIO

Refer to the "Developing Portfolios" section at the front of this textbook for more information on learning portfolios.

▶ Telecommuting Opportunities: This activity will help you explore telecommuting opportunities in your field.

▶ Research and Presentation: The goal of this activity is to provide an opportunity to investigate a topic of your choice related to professionalism in the workplace.

▶ Role-Playing a Lunch Meeting: This activity will provide an opportunity to practice lunch meeting etiquette.

REFERENCES

Archer North & Associates. (2004). Introduction performance appraisal [electronic version]. Archer North Performance Appraisal System. Retrieved April 14, 2005, from http://www.performance-appraisal .com/intro.htm

Bayer, L., & Mallett, K. (2005). The etiquette ladies: Top ten "unquestionably rude" office behaviors [electronic version]. Retrieved April 13, 2005, from http://www.canoe.ca/LifewiseWorkEtiquette/ eti_work.html

Brandi, J. (n.d.). Creating a positive employee attitude in the workplace [electronic version]. Retrieved April 13, 2005, from http://www .sideroad.com/Management/employee_attitude.html

Fiore, T. (1999–2004). Resolving workplace conflict: 4 ways to a win-win solution [electronic version]. Retrieved April 19, 2005, from http:// www.businesssknowhow.com/manage/resolve.htm

Franz, C. (n.d.). Business lunch etiquette [electronic version]. Retrieved April 14, 2005, from http://www.sideroad.com/Business_etiquette/ busines-lunch-etiquette.html

Greenspan, R. (2002). Telecommuting gains ground [electronic version]. Retrieved April 14, 2005, from http://www.clickz.com/stats/sectors/ professional/article.php/1429771

Hansen, K. (n.d.[a]). Making your case for telecommuting: How to convince the boss [electronic version]. Retrieved April 14, 2005, from http://www.quintcareers.com/telecommuting_options.html

Hansen, R. S. (n.d.[b]). Is job flexibility right for you? A quintessential careers quiz [electronic version]. Retrieved April 14, 2005, from http://www.quintcareers.com/job_flexibility_quiz.html

Hansen, R. S. (n.d.[c]). Your first days working at a new job: 20 tips to help you make a great impression [electronic version]. Retrieved April 14, 2005, from http://www.quintcareers.com/first_days_working.html

Hansen, R. S. (n.d.[c]). Do's and don'ts of dealing with a bad boss [electronic version]. Retrieved April 14, 2005, from http://www .quintcareers.com/bad_boss-dos-donts.html

Hansen, R. S. (n.d.[d]). Do's and don'ts of requesting a raise [electronic version]. Retrieved April 14, 2005, from http://www.quintcareers .com/requesting_raise-dos-donts.html

Hansen, R. S. (n.d.[e]). Moving up the ladder: 10 strategies for getting yourself promoted [electronic version]. Retrieved April 14, 2005, from http://www.quintcareers.com/getting_promoted_strategies.html

Hansen, R. S., & Hansen, K. (n.d.[f]). Your first days working at a new job: 20 tips to help you make a great impression. Retrieved June 22, 2006, from http://www.quintcareers.com/first_days_working.html

Heathfield, S. M. (n.d.). Rise above the fray: Options for dealing with difficult people at work. Five tips for dealing with difficult people [electronic version]. Retrieved April 19, 2005, from http:// humanresources .about.com/od/workrelationships/a/ difficultpeople_2.htm

Marquette University Career Services Center. (2003–2004). Top qualities & skills employers seek [electronic version]. Retrieved April 14, 2005, from http://www.marquettte.edu/csc/students/documents/ Topskillsemployersseek.pdf

McGarvey, J. (2000). The top 10 ways to eliminate stress [electronic version]. CoachVille Resource Center. Retrieved April 20, 2005, from http://topten.org/public/FB/BF123.html

Norris, B. (2000–2001). Overcoming negativity in the workplace [electronic version]. Retrieved April 13, 2005, from http://www .briannorris.com/artilces/overcomenegativity.html

Portland Community College. (n.d.). Resolving workplace problems [electronic version]. Retrieved April 19, 2005, from http://spot.pcc.edu/ ~rjacobs/career/resolving_workplace_problems.htm

Reed Consulting. (2005). Stress at work [electronic version]. Retrieved April 13, 2005, from http://reed.businesshr.net/docs/guides/ stress.html

Ritter, J. (2002). Impress for success: A professional approach to your professional image [electronic version]. *The Galt Global Review*. Retrieved April 13, 2005, from http://www.galtglobalreview.com/careers/ dress_to_impress.html

Robin, D. (1997–2004). The gentle art of confrontation [electronic version]. Retrieved April 19, 2005, from http://www.abetterworkplace .com/084.html

Turner, T. (2004). Business lunch etiquette 101 [electronic version]. Retrieved April 14, 2005, from http://www.marketingpower.com/ content20039C5627.php

CHAPTER OUTLINE

Staying at the Forefront of Your Profession

Lifelong Learning Strategies and Professional Development

Lifelong Career Learning and Staying Current

Professional Certifications and Licensure

Documenting Professional Development

The Professional Supervision Process

Promotions and Career Advancement

12 Career Advancement Strategies

LEARNING OBJECTIVES

By the end of this chapter, you will achieve the following objectives:

- Explain the importance of continued professional learning and development and its relationship to career advancement.
- Identify and locate resources for continued learning.
- Apply information about individual learning style to the professional development and career advancement strategies.
- Describe the professional supervision process and explain how supervision processes can be used to pursue professional development goals.
- Describe the skills, functions, and roles of management.
- Describe the skills of leadership.
- Compare and contrast management and leadership.

 ## TOPIC SCENARIO

After graduating from school, Janna obtained an entry-level job with a local company and has been working in that position for several years. Janna likes her job and wants to remain with the company, but she feels it is time to advance to a management position. She has discussed her goals with her supervisor, who told Janna that she should develop her management and leadership skills. Janna set goals with her supervisor to pursue these suggestions.

Based on this scenario, answer the following questions:

- Where should Janna look for learning opportunities?
- How can Janna document her learning?
- How can Janna use the professional supervision process to support her efforts?
- What skills will Janna need to enhance her management skills?
- How do leadership skills differ from management skills?
- What will Janna need to do to develop her leadership skills?

STAYING AT THE FOREFRONT OF YOUR PROFESSION

Major factors in career advancement are being aware of current issues in your field, being able to apply new ideas to your work, and adapting to change in your profession. These abilities are achieved and demonstrated in several ways, which are discussed here.

 ## LIFELONG LEARNING STRATEGIES AND PROFESSIONAL DEVELOPMENT

You have probably heard the saying that learning does not end at graduation. Your ability to continue learning contributes to your effectiveness in daily activities as well as to your career advancement in the form of promotions and the assumption of leadership roles. Both of these aspects of career advancement will be discussed in this chapter.

LIFELONG CAREER LEARNING AND STAYING CURRENT

There are many sources to tap to help you remain current in your field. Recall information literacy, and the methods previously discussed, which can be used to support your continuing professional development.

PROFESSIONAL ORGANIZATIONS

Professional organizations are often an excellent source of information that will keep you current in your field. Membership in a professional organization offers the following benefits, all of which provide opportunity for continued learning.

- **Broad-based information.** A professional organization's primary task is to serve the profession it represents and keep its membership informed. Consequently, up-to-date information from all areas of the profession is typically available from such groups. For example, The American Occupational Therapy Association has specialized groups focused on education, practice issues, and political events that affect the field. A broad base of information allows members to access information in a variety of areas.

- **In-depth information.** In addition to a wide range of information, professional organizations can also supply in-depth information on a particular topic. Individuals whose job it is to monitor specific areas of a field can offer detailed and comprehensive information on that area.

- **Publications.** Most professional organizations produce a professional journal or other publication containing current information and updates about their fields. Some organizations offer specialty publications in specific areas of interest.

- **Conferences and seminars.** Professional organizations usually offer some form of annual conference and may sponsor additional seminars throughout the year. Conferences typically offer a choice of workshops and presentations on a variety of topics.

- **Expert contacts.** Many professional organizations offer members access to experts in a variety of areas within the field. These individuals are available to share their expertise and may be consulted via telephone, e-mail, or standard mail.

- **Electronic resources.** Online articles, libraries, and communication tools are frequently maintained by professional organizations. Some may be available to members at no charge or for a reasonable fee.

12

▶ **Networking opportunities.** Attending conferences, participating in electronic discussion groups, and becoming involved in other ways with your professional organization can provide numerous networking opportunities. Take advantage of these to become acquainted with other members of your profession.

Professional organizations offer many opportunities for professional development, including seminars, focus groups, and networking with professional peers.

apply it

Your Professional Organization

GOAL: To learn more about your field's primary professional organization.

STEP 1: Research your field's primary professional organization. Obtain information regarding membership and its benefits. Often, professional organizations offer reduced membership fees to students.

STEP 2: Consider how you might use some of the member benefits in your professional development and to support your professional interests. Seriously consider becoming a member of the organization to take advantage of these support systems.

STEP 3: Create a section in your Learning Portfolio for professional development documentation and information.

ONLINE RESOURCES

In addition to the common search engines and other tools, the Internet provides opportunities for you to be automatically updated about a variety of subjects. The following tools are especially useful in maintaining contact with colleagues and staying informed regarding professional developments.

Listservs

A listserv is a tool that allows participants to post questions and comments to a group of individuals who, in turn, have the opportunity to respond with answers, comments, and solutions. Most listservs have guidelines for etiquette and rules for participation. Some may have a moderator whose job is to ensure that guidelines and rules are followed. You can often locate listservs in your field through your professional organization or based on suggestions from colleagues.

apply it

Professional Listservs

GOAL: To gain experience using a professional listserv.

STEP 1: Contact your professional organization and whether it monitors any member listservs. Or, conduct an Internet search using "________ listserv" (insert your field in the blank) and explore your search results. If you select the latter option, you may want to check the listserv's reputation with your professional organization or another reliable source.

STEP 2: Select an appropriate listserv and sign up as a member. Participate in discussions and post questions.

STEP 3: Consider placing the information you receive from the listserv in your Learning Portfolio.

Databases and Online Libraries

Recall obtaining resources via the deep Web, which can provide access to databases and other more obscure documents. Search databases and online specialty libraries for current articles and other literature related to you field.

Simulations

Several fields have online simulations available that provide virtual experiences of real-life professional situations.

APPLYING YOUR LEARNING PREFERENCES TO CAREER DEVELOPMENT

Taking advantage of the way in which you learn most effectively can greatly enhance your career advancement, because if you seek educational opportunities that are suited to your learning style, you will enjoy the process more and thus retain the information better. For example, if you know that you are a hands-on learner, seeking simulations or seminars with an activity component will suit you better than simply listening to a lecture. If, however, you are an auditory learner, a lecture probably will meet your needs well.

success steps

USING OPPORTUNITIES FOR PROFESSIONAL DEVELOPMENT

1. Seek resources from professional organizations:
   - broad-based information
   - in-depth information
   - publications
   - conferences and seminars
   - expert contacts
   - electronic resources
   - networking opportunities
2. Use online resources:
   - listservs
   - databases and online libraries
   - simulations
3. Understand your learning style.
4. Learn from your supervisor, a mentor, or a coach.

apply it

Identifying Your Learning Style

GOAL: To gain insight into your learning style and how it can support your professional development.

STEP 1: Conduct an Internet search using "learning style inventory" as your search term. Locate an inventory you want to take and complete it. If you have previously completed a learning inventory, consider repeating the process, this time keeping career advancement and professional development in mind. Learning preferences can change over time and depending on what you are learning.

STEP 2: Review the results of the inventory. Add or modify information according to your experience and what you know about your learning patterns.

STEP 3: Make a list of professional education activities that are appropriate to your learning style. Consider using the Internet or professional organization resources to explore your choices.

STEP 4: Consider maintaining a list of professional learning activity ideas in your Learning Portfolio.

PROFESSIONAL CERTIFICATIONS AND LICENSURE

Professional development and continued learning is often linked with certifications and licenses that you must keep current in order to practice in your field. Examples of professionals who are required to maintain current certifications are teachers and nurses. Requirements to maintain current credentials typically include a specific number of continuing education hours that must be completed within a certain period. Each profession has its own requirements; review your field's guidelines. Regardless of the field, continuing education can support credentialing requirements and advance your career. Choose education opportunities that support your goals.

DOCUMENTING PROFESSIONAL DEVELOPMENT

It is critical to keep records of your professional development, including documentation of continuing education for licensure and certification purposes. Ensure that you receive course-completion documentation for each continuing education activity that you finish. This documentation should be on official stationery, such as letterhead, and include the number of hours completed and the signature of an authorized person.

THE PROFESSIONAL SUPERVISION PROCESS

Professional supervision involves numerous techniques, including teaching, directing, mentoring, and coaching. A common perception of supervision is that a supervisor "watches over" employees, but true professional supervision is a complex process directed at developing employees' professional skills that facilitate their career advancement. As such, professional supervision is another tool for professional development.

DIRECTING

Directing is the process of leading someone through a task or activity, and there are times when direction is appropriate and necessary. Recent graduates, for example, who are new to the field often benefit from direct guidance. In addition, more experienced employees who are learning a new or advanced skill may also find direction through their learning process helpful. Although you should increase your ability to be independent whenever possible, asking for direction in certain situations demonstrates a realistic understanding of your skills and your job as well as your willingness to learn.

Direction may take the form of corrective feedback, or constructive criticism, which may be necessary when issues of safety, compliance with ethics and regulations, and similar concerns are at stake. Used appropriately, corrective feedback can be used to facilitate learning.

TEACHING

Teaching differs from directing in that teaching provides learners with information and skills that they will apply independently. Teaching can be, and usually is, a part of directing. As you assimilate the teaching of your supervisor, you will become more independent, decreasing your need for direction.

COACHING

Coaching is a technique in which someone (in this case, your supervisor) encourages, challenges, and supports the person being coached (you, in this scenario). The coaching approach is less like the teaching approach and more like the process that sports coaches use with their teams. The employee takes the lead in learning and applying the information while the supervisor guides by encouraging or challenging as appropriate.

MENTORING

Mentoring is a process that goes beyond technical aspects of the job and includes considerations of the employee's growth and development as a person as well as a professional. A mentor may engage in activities such as

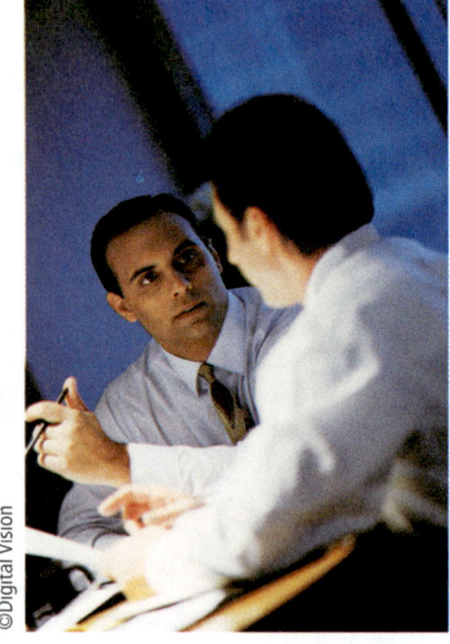

Professional supervision offers a one-on-one opportunity for exploring areas for professional development. Working closely with your supervisor gives you the chance to set and pursue professional goals.

helping the mentee understand how to navigate corporate culture, determine which skills to develop to advance professionally, and expand the personal skills needed for success.

In the real world, supervisors are likely to use each of these methods on occasion, depending on the situation and the needs of the employee.

Your supervisor does not do all the work, however—you have responsibilities as a learner in this situation. Consider these actions you can take to make the most of your supervision experience (Berger, 2003):

- **Know yourself.** Acknowledge your strengths and weaknesses. Capitalize on your strengths and improve your weak areas through professional development.

- **Clearly state your needs and goals.** Let your supervisor know what motivates you, the type of direction you need, how you learn most effectively, and what your professional goals include.

- **Be open to learning.** Approach being supervised as an opportunity to learn and use your supervisor as a source of professional information. Actively involve yourself in the supervision process by asking questions and participating in discussion. Accept corrective feedback (constructive criticism) as helpful information intended to support your professional growth. Incorporate corrective feedback into your professional development goals.

- **Set goals.** Set goals based on what you wish to accomplish in your career. Identify areas of professional interest and seek the resources to pursue them. Discuss your career advancement plans with your supervisor so that he or she can assist you in this process.

- **Keep written records.** Keep written records of your supervision sessions, your goals, and your progress toward reaching them. Use your documentation to guide your supervision and career advancement.

12

success steps

GETTING THE MOST FROM SUPERVISION

1. Know yourself.
2. Clearly state your needs and goals.
3. Be open to learning.
4. Set goals.
5. Keep written records.

REFLECTION QUESTION

- What are your professional goals?

? CRITICAL THINKING QUESTION

12–1. How could you best use supervision to reach your professional goals?

apply it

Supervision Goals

GOAL: *To set goals for enhancing your professional development and career advancement.*

Note: *This activity is intended for use in the workplace. It may be adapted for academic advising or used in the student's current employment.*

STEP 1: In an electronic or print document (select whichever is easier for you to use), create a table with five columns. From left to right, label the columns "Goal," "Steps/Time Frames," "Methods," "Revisions," and "Outcomes."

STEP 2: In the "Goals" column, write your long-term goal. In the "Steps/Time Frames" column, break your long-term goal into smaller steps. Assign a completion date to each step. In the "Methods" column, note resources and techniques you can use to achieve these steps and, ultimately, your goal.

STEP 3: Note any necessary revisions in the "Revisions" column. For example, if you need to adjust time frames or methods, record that information in this column. In the "Outcomes" column, keep a record of your results as you work toward your goal. You may find it more convenient to record certain pieces of information in a journal-style document.

STEP 4: Share your goal document(s) with your supervisor for input and support. Be sure to let your supervisor know how he or she can help you achieve your goal.

STEP 5: Consider placing your goals and related documentation in your Learning Portfolio.

PROMOTIONS AND CAREER ADVANCEMENT

Professional development activities are frequently directed at helping you move ahead in your field. Advancement into management and leadership positions requires the possession of specific skills in addition to technical expertise.

INTERPERSONAL SKILLS

The ability to relate effectively to colleagues at every level of an organization is critical to job success. Interpersonal skills become increasingly critical, however, with advancement to more senior levels of an organization, because management and leadership roles are typically more people oriented than strictly technical positions. Recall the in-depth discussion of communication skills. Be aware that communication is a complex topic and that there are many additional resources you can tap to develop strong management and leadership skills. Elements such as emotional intelligence, team building, group dynamics, and others are subjects that are worth investigating.

©Digital Vision

Being able to work effectively with individuals at all levels of an organization requires interpersonal skills and is important to your career advancement.

apply it

Communication Techniques

GOAL: To become familiar with advanced communication techniques.

STEP 1: Create a list of communication skills and topics that you want to develop or about which you want to learn. Which might you wish to expand on to build your management and leadership skills? Consider exploring such topics as emotional

continued

continued

intelligence, group dynamics, assertiveness, effective questioning, and conflict resolution.

STEP 2: Conduct an Internet search using the skill(s) or topic(s) that you select. Create an electronic or print resource file of articles and other information from your search results.

STEP 3: Set goals and identify methods for applying the information you obtain and for practicing the skills that you learn. Keep a record of your progress.

STEP 4: Consider placing the resources, your goals, and progress notes in your Learning Portfolio.

MANAGEMENT

Management skills are a subset of interpersonal skills. They relate to the mission and purpose of an organization and help ensure that daily tasks are executed in a manner that contributes to organizational goals. Becoming a successful manager requires possessing these specific skills and being able to carry out certain functions. Managerial tasks include staffing, budgeting, ensuring adequate productivity, writing and implementing policy and procedure, and ensuring appropriate communication within a work unit and with other work units in the organization.

Management Skills

There are three major areas in which managers must be skilled to perform their duties effectively. Each of these areas can be elaborated upon, and much has been written on management skills. The following, however, is a summary of these skill sets (Allen, 1998a).

- **Technical skill.** Technical skill includes the ability to perform the job for which you were trained. For example, a computer programmer must be able to program a computer, and a medical assistant must know how to take an accurate medical history.

- **Human skill.** This is the ability to work effectively with people. Managers must be able to work successfully with the individuals they supervise as well as with an organization's upper management. Examples of human skills include communication and negotiation skills as well as the ability to work collaboratively.

- **Conceptual skill.** Conceptual skills are the ability to generate, apply, and carry out ideas. Examples include implementing new programs and interpreting policy and procedure.

Management Functions

The duties of a manager are directed at ensuring that the work unit functions efficiently and in keeping with organizational goals. Managers use their skills to carry out the following interrelated functions (Allen, 1998b).

- **Planning.** Planning is the process of determining how the work unit will contribute to organizational goals in the future. The manager's planning function includes developing processes and strategies.

- **Organizing.** The manager's organizational role is related to the tasks of preparing and allotting resources for the most efficient completion of tasks. Organizing involves setting up resources and systematizing processes to complete work requirements.

- **Directing.** As managers guide and supervise employees, they are engaging in the function of directing their work unit to contribute to organizational goals. The function of directing is likely to be related to the supervision processes that were discussed previously.

- **Controlling.** The function of controlling is important to maintaining the quality of work performed by a work unit. Outcomes are compared to the plan, and if they fall below expectations, the manager must identify shortcomings and implement improvements. Managerial functions can be seen as a cycle, beginning with the planning function and moving through organizing, directing, and controlling (Allen, 1998b). When needed, corrections are identified, and the planning stage is revisited so that strategies can be revised.

Managerial Roles

There are three major roles that managers must assume according to the demands of various situations (Allen, 1998c). Each role has subroles specific to the particular level of management. The primary roles are as follows:

- **Interpersonal role.** The manager must interact with numerous individuals and other organizations. In assuming the interpersonal role and depending on the situation, a manager may represent an organization in the community, his or her work unit to upper management, or upper management to the employees in his or her work unit.

- **Informational role.** The manager is responsible for collecting, monitoring, and disseminating information. The manager may receive and transmit information to and from a variety of sources, including outside the organization and both vertically and laterally within the organization.

▶ **Decisional role.** The decisional role requires the manager to determine how information is best used to meet organizational goals. The manager must make judgments regarding how information is to be disseminated and applied to goals, as well as how it will be used to meet changing demands and to allocate resources.

Managers assume multiple roles and exercise numerous skills.

LEADERSHIP SKILLS

Leaders are those who "challenge, inspire, enable, model, and encourage" (Kouzes & Posner, 1987, p. 1). Consider leadership as an attitude and a way of viewing events rather than as a position. Leadership skills are typically viewed as constructive and positive within an organization, and while it is beneficial for managers to possess leadership qualities, these characteristics can be developed by anyone to enhance his or her opportunities for career advancement. Consider developing the following attributes of a leader (Solomon, 2003).

▶ **Look to the future.** Leaders function in the present and attend to tasks at hand, yet at the same time are oriented to the future. A quality of leadership is being able to look ahead, see the future as a chance for growth and development, and communicate this vision to others.

▶ **View change as opportunity.** Leaders look for the positive elements of change. As part of looking to the future, leaders view change as a chance to make improvements.

▶ **Do your job ethically.** A quality of leadership is the ability to incorporate ethics into decisions and actions. Leaders demonstrate integrity by honoring regulatory guidelines and codes of ethics. Leaders strive for fairness and have a sense of justice.

▶ **Be oriented to people.** Leaders are aware of the needs of the people around them and honor their personal and professional needs, within reasonable limits. Leaders are able to direct, encourage, teach, mentor, or coach as the situation requires and do so in a manner that facilitates the development of those with whom they work.

▶ **Be open to learning.** Leaders make mistakes, and when they do, they approach mistakes as learning opportunities. Leaders admit to errors and strive to remedy them and to change their behavior based on what they have learned.

▶ **Think proactively.** Being proactive means looking ahead and anticipating needs. A leader communicates perceived future needs and supports efforts to respond to change constructively.

▶ **Take initiative.** Part of responding proactively is taking initiative. Taking initiative means being able to recognize a need and taking the responsibility to find a method of meeting it. At times, this may mean taking on responsibilities above and beyond those defined in one's job description. A leader sees what needs to be done and takes appropriate steps to initiate actions that are within ethical, professional, and legal boundaries. Taking initiative can be a significant factor in career advancement.

▶ **Be a problem solver.** Leaders do not see everything through "rose-colored glasses." Leaders approach issues with a problem-solving attitude by acknowledging problems and areas that, if improved, would contribute to a more effective organization. Far from being negative, leaders identify problems objectively, set emotional reactions aside, and offer feasible suggestions for improvement.

Comparison of Management and Leadership

Management Skills	Leadership Skills
Task oriented	People oriented
Concerned with the present	Concerned with building for the future
Practical	Visionary
More directive	More inspiring
Controls and manages others	Inspires and empowers others
Focuses on status quo	Focuses on innovation

FIGURE 12–1. Management skills and leadership skills are distinct, although they overlap in some ways. Most successful individuals possess both types of skills and apply each at appropriate times.

- What individual(s) have you perceived as a leader?
- What were the characteristics of the individual(s) that qualified him or her as a leader?

12–2. Besides those mentioned, what other leadership characteristics can you identify?

12–3. How do leadership qualities contribute to an individual's professional advancement?

12–4. How do leaders and their attributes contribute to the growth of the organization?

---

success steps

TIPS FOR LEADERSHIP SKILL DEVELOPMENT

1. Look to the future.
2. View change as opportunity.
3. Do your job ethically.
4. Maintain an orientation to people.
5. Be open to learning.
6. Think proactively.
7. Take initiative.
8. Be a problem solver.

CHANGE MANAGEMENT

Change is inevitable in today's rapidly moving world. Thus, advancing your career depends significantly on your ability to respond to change (Pritchett, 1994). Consider the following suggestions for adjusting to change (Solomon & Jacobs, 2003):

- **Look for the opportunities in change.** Frequently, change opens new niches and creates advantages. A positive response to change involves identifying these opportunities and applying your skills and abilities to take advantage of them.

- **Recognize common emotional responses to change.** Individuals demonstrate a variety of responses to change, from strong resistance to excessive optimism. It is important to moderate responses to change by maintaining an objective outlook and approach. Leaders recognize their emotional responses and keep them in perspective, and help others do the same.

- **Be a creative problem solver.** Use creative thinking techniques to approach change and address the issues associated with it. Incorporate leadership skills by developing creative responses that reflect ethics and regulatory guidelines.

- What strengths do you possess as a manager? Which management skills do you need to develop?
- What strengths do you possess as a leader? Which leadership skills do you need to develop?

---

success steps

RESPONDING POSITIVELY TO CHANGE

1. Look for the opportunities in change.
2. Recognize common emotional responses to change.
3. Be a creative problem solver.

apply it

Management and Leadership

GOAL: *To become familiar with the differences and similarities between management and leadership.*

STEP 1: Conduct an Internet search for articles on management and leadership using "management" and "leadership" as your search terms. Consider having classmates complete the same search. Compare results and expand on each other's information as much as possible.

STEP 2: Write a compare-and-contrast paper exploring the similarities and differences between management and leadership. Ask any classmates who have completed the search activity to do the same.

STEP 3: Ask class members to present (anonymously, if they prefer) situations from their work experience that required supervisors' involvement. The situations should be presented in a manner that preserves the confidentiality of businesses and individuals. Review the scenarios as a class and discuss whether management or leadership techniques or a combination of both would have effectively addressed the situation.

STEP 4: Consider placing your research materials, your compare-and-contrast paper, and any insights you gain through this activity in your Learning Portfolio.

CHAPTER SUMMARY

Professional advancement depends on your ability to remain current and knowledgeable about developments in your field. This chapter outlined numerous sources for obtaining professional information and knowledge, including professional organizations, professional publications, electronic sources, and supervisors and mentors. Management and leadership skills were compared and were discussed in terms of how both can be developed to advance your career.

POINTS TO KEEP IN MIND

Several main points were discussed in detail in this chapter:

- Major factors in career advancement are being aware of current issues in your field, being able to apply new ideas to your work, and being able to adapt to change in your profession.

 **12**

▶ Professional supervision involves numerous techniques, including teaching, directing, mentoring, and coaching.

▶ It is critical to keep records of your professional development, including documentation of continuing education for licensure and certification purposes.

▶ Your ability to continue learning contributes to your effectiveness in daily activities as well as to your career advancement in the form of promotions and the assumption of professional leadership roles.

▶ Professional development and continued learning are often linked with certifications and licenses that you must keep current in order to practice in your field.

▶ Taking advantage of the way in which you learn most effectively can greatly enhance your career advancement, because if you seek educational opportunities that are suited to your learning style, you will enjoy the process more and thus retain the information better.

▶ Professional organizations may be the most effective source of information for remaining current in your field.

▶ Professional organizations usually offer some form of annual conference and may sponsor seminars throughout the year.

▶ A professional organization's primary task is to serve the profession it represents and keep its membership informed. Consequently, up-to-date information from all areas of the profession is typically available.

▶ Most professional organizations produce a professional journal or other publication.

▶ In addition to the common search engines and other tools, the Internet provides opportunities for you to be automatically updated about a variety of subjects.

▶ Professional supervision is another tool for professional development.

▶ Interpersonal skills become increasingly critical with advancement to more senior levels of an organization, because management and leadership roles are typically more people oriented than strictly technical positions.

▶ Management skills relate to the mission and purpose of an organization and ensure that daily tasks are executed in a manner that contributes to organizational goals.

▶ Consider leadership as an attitude and a way of viewing events rather than as being a position.

▶ Developing leadership capabilities is possible regardless of your "official" position with your organization.

▶ Leadership skills include being oriented to the future; seeing the future as a chance for growth; being able to communicate that vision to others; and functioning with integrity, fairness, and a sense of justice.

▶ Taking initiative means anticipating people's needs and approaching mistakes with a problem-solving attitude.

▶ Advancing your career depends significantly on your ability to respond positively to change.

▶ A constructive approach to change include welcoming change as an opportunity for growth, understanding emotional responses to change, and approaching change with a spirit of creative problem-solving.

LEARNING OBJECTIVES REVISITED

Review the learning objectives for this chapter and rate your level of achievement for each objective using the rating scale provided. For each objective on which you do not rate yourself as a 3, outline a plan of action that you will take to fully achieve the objective. Include a time frame for this plan.

1 = did not successfully achieve objective

2 = understand what is needed, but need more study or practice

3 = achieved learning objective thoroughly

	1	2	3
Explain the importance of continued professional learning and development and its relationship to career advancement.	☐	☐	☐
Identify and locate resources for continued learning.	☐	☐	☐
Apply information about individual learning style to the professional development and career advancement strategies.	☐	☐	☐
Describe the professional supervision process and explain how supervision processes can be used to accomplish various professional development goals.	☐	☐	☐
Describe the skills, functions, and roles of management.	☐	☐	☐
Describe the skills of leadership.	☐	☐	☐
Compare and contrast management and leadership.	☐	☐	☐

Steps to Achieve Unmet Objectives

Steps	Due Date
1. _______________________________________	__________
2. _______________________________________	__________
3. _______________________________________	__________
4. _______________________________________	__________

SUGGESTED ITEMS FOR LEARNING PORTFOLIO

Refer to the "Developing Portfolios" section at the front of this textbook for more information on learning portfolios.

- Your Professional Organization: This activity is designed to familiarize you with your professional organization.

- Professional Listservs: The goal of this activity is to provide you with experience using a professional listserv.

- Identifying Your Learning Style: Complete this activity to understand how your learning style affects your professional development.

- Supervision Goals Management and Leadership: This activity will help you set supervision goals for your professional development.

- Communication Techniques: Complete this activity to develop your advanced communication skills.

- Management and Leadership: The goal of this activity is to familiarize you with management and leadership skills.

REFERENCES

Allen, G. (1998a). Management skills [electronic version]. Retrieved May 19, 2005, from http://ollie.dcccd.edu/mgmt1374/book_contents/1overview/management_skills/mgmt_skills.htm

Allen, G. (1998b). Managerial functions [electronic version]. Retrieved May 19, 2005, from http://ollie.dcccd.edu/mgmt1374/book_contents/1overview/managerial_functions/mgrl_functions.htm

Allen, G. (1998c). Managerial roles [electronic version]. Retrieved May 19, 2005, from http://ollie.dcccd.edu/mgmt1374/book_contents/1overview/managerial_roles/mgrl_roles.htm

Berger, S. (2003). Personnel considerations and supervision. In A. Solomon & K. Jacobs (Eds.), *Management Skills for the Occupational Therapy Assistant* (pp. 85–100). Thorofare, NJ: Slack, Inc.

Kouzes, J. M., & Posner, B. Z. (1987). *The Leadership Challenge.* San Francisco: Jossey-Bass.

Pritchett, P. (1994). *New Work Habits for a Radically Changing World: 13 Ground Rules for Job Success in the Information Age.* Dallas: Pritchett & Associates.

Solomon, A. (2003). The roles and responsibilities of the occupational therapy assistant in management. In A. Solomon & K. Jacobs (Eds.), *Management Skills for the Occupational Therapy Assistant* (pp. 1–21). Thorofare, NJ: Slack, Inc.

Solomon, A., & Jacobs, K. (2003). Change management. In A. Solomon & K. Jacobs (Eds.), *Management Skills for the Occupational Therapy Assistant* (pp. 23–28). Thorofare, NJ: Slack, Inc.

12